D1380251

NEIL RAFFERTY and PAUL STOKES are two of Britain's least respected journalists. Stokes has written for the *Scotsman* and the *Daily Record*. He lives in Glasgow's fashionable West End, where he prances between trendy cafés. Rafferty covered politics for the Press Association and the *Sunday Times*. He lives in unfashionable Berwickshire with four chickens and a dirty hoe.

To Amy and Debby

All the material in this book is entirely fictional and should not in any way be regarded as factual. Apart from the article by Oscar the Dog. That's real. And so are the opinion polls.

1: bl © Kurhan | Dreamstime.com; br © Ffotograff65 | Dreamstime.com. 2: t © Sipa Press / Rex Features. 3: t © Pictureone.net | Dreamstime.com; b © Webking | Dreamstime.com. 4: t © Paulcowan | Dreamstime.com; b Zts | Dreamstime.com. 5: © Dave Allocca / Rex Features; © Sutton-Hibbert / Rex Features; © iStockphoto / zdenkam. 7: © James Fraser / Rex Features. 9: Isselee | Dreamstime.com; bl © iStockphoto / Sportlibrary; br © Anatoly Tiplyashin | Dreamstime.com. 10: t © Norbert Kesten / Rex Features; b Marion Curtis / Rex Features. 11: t © Paha_l | Dreamstime.com; b © Lindsey Parnaby / Rex Features. 12: t Maceofoto | Dreamstime.com; b © Cbeckwith | Dreamstime.com. 13: © Paulprescott | Dreamstime.com. 14: b © Velefante | Dreamstime.com. 17: t © Nasser Bu-hamad | Dreamstime.com. 18: l © Ljupco | Dreamstime.com; r Mason's News Service / Rex Features. 19: © Kelpfish | Dreamstime.com. 20: t © iStockphoto.com / MilosJokic; b © Lars Christensen | Dreamstime.com. 21: t © Niderlander | Dreamstime.com; bl © Christophriddle | Dreamstime.com; br © Davidmartyn | Dreamstime.com. 22: t © Moodville | Dreamstime.com; b © Macdsean | Dreamstime.com. 23: t © iStockphoto.com / spxChrome; b © Moemrik | Dreamstime.com. 25: t © Rex Features; b © Armonn | Dreamstime.com. 26: © Richard Young / Rex Features; b Chandru_ganeson | Dreamstime.com. 27: © Alisdair Macdonald / Rex Features. 29: t © iStockphoto.com / jgroup; bl © iStockphoto.com / jacomstephens. 30: t © Rex Features; b © Sipa Press / Rex Features. 31: t © Sophielouise | Dreamstime.com; b © James Fraser / Rex Features. 32: © Paczani | Dreamstime.com. 33: © NASA. 34: t © Niderlander | Dreamstime.com; b © Mikeledray | Dreamstime.com. 35: t © iStockphoto.com / WinterWitch; b © David Hartley / Rex Features. 38: br © Sipa Press / Rex Features. 40: b © Cbeckwith | Dreamstime.com. 41: t © Pmtavares | Dreamstime.com; bl © iStockphoto.com / aguirre_mar. 42: b © E Goodenough / Rex Features. 43: t © Kayella | Dreamstime.com; b © KPA / Zuma / Rex Features. 44: © Tim Rooke / Rex Features. 45: © iStockphoto.com / sandramo. 47: b © iStockphoto.com / lisegagne. 49: t © iStockphoto.com / mseidelch; br © iStockphoto.com / wragg; br © iStockphoto.com / webphotographeer. 50: t © KPA / Zuma/ Rex Features; b © Griffin024 | Dreamstime.com. 51: t © iStockphoto.com / njw1224; b © Akarelias | Dreamstime.com. 53: t © Ian Dickson / Rex Features; b © Andre Csillag / Rex Features. 57: t © iStockphoto.com / jsmith; bl © Diademimages | Dreamstime.com; br © iStockphoto.com / MHjerpe. 58: t © Alexkalina | Dreamstime.com; b © Pryzmat | Dreamstime.com. 59: t © David Hartley / Rex Features; b © Starblue | Dreamstime.com. 60: b © KPA / Zuma / Rex Features. 61: l © Most Wanted / Rex Features; c © ITV / Rex Features; r © Henry Lamb / BEI / Rex Features. 62: t © iStockphoto.com / killerb10; b © DBvirago | Dreamstime.com. 63: l © Adrianhillman | Dreamstime.com; r © Rupert Hartley / David Hartley / Rex Features. 65: © Ankevanwyk | Dreamstime.com. 66: t © Webking | Dreamstime.com; b: l © creativepictures.com. 67: © Prahakid | Dreamstime.com. 68: t © Lars Christensen | Dreamstime.com; b © Sofiaworld | Dreamstime.com. 69: t © Adrianhillman | Dreamstime.com; br © Dobri | Dreamstime.com. 70: t © iStockphoto.com / HenkBentlage; b © Bacek | Dreamstime.com. 71: © iStockphoto.com / Birkholz. 72: b © Robynmac | Dreamstime.com. 73: © iStockphoto.com / Kativ. 74: b © iStockphoto.com / Chris3fer. 75: © David Hartley / Rex Features. 77: t © iStockphoto.com / Liliboas; br © iStockphoto.com / Kurhan. 78: t © Maco0708 | Dreamstime.com. 80: t © Pressmaster | Dreamstime.com; b © Tomd | Dreamstime.com. 81: © Stevies | Dreamstime.com. 82: t © Robert Hallam / Rex Features; b © ITV / Rex Features. 83: t © iStockphoto.com / blackred. 85: © Stefano Carofei / Rex Features. 86: t © iStockphoto.com / Obak; b Warner Br / Everett / Rex Features. 87: b © Cbeckwith | Dreamstime.com. 88: l © Diademimages | Dreamstime.com; r © Stefano Carofei / Rex Features. 89: t © iStockphoto.com / nostroom; bl © Yellow_ | Dreamstime.com; br © iStockphoto.com / AK2. 90: t © iStockphoto.com / stray_cat; b © iStockphoto.com / terex. 91: t © iStockphoto.com / creacart; b l–r © iStockphoto.com / MarkFGD; © iStockphoto.com / GlobalP; © Johan63; r © ITV / Rex Features. 92: © iStockphoto.com / Rockfinder. 94: t © Anatoly Tiplyashin | Dreamstime.com; b © Jocic | Dreamstime.com. 97: © Joseasreyes | Dreamstime.com; br © Kuzma | Dreamstime.com. 98: b © Hermes-sicily | Dreamstime.com. 100: t © Michael Ward / Rex Features; b © Francesco Giudicini / Rex Features. 102: t © iStockphoto.com / CherylCasey; b © iStockphoto.com / markgoddard. 105: ITV / Rex Features. 106: t © Chris Ratcliffe / Rex Features; b © Aidaricci | Dreamstime.com. 107: t © iStockphoto.com / Sally Carns; c © Irochka | Dreamstime.com. 108: t © Forca | Dreamstime.com; b © Thewebco | Dreamstime.com. 109: t © akg-images / ullstein bild; bl © Sebcz | Dreamstime.com; br © Cbeckwith | Dreamstime.com. 110: t © Rex Features; b © iStockphoto.com / Whiteway. 111: t © Johnbell | Dreamstime.com; r © Stockstudios | Dreamstime.com; bl © Gimbat | Dreamstime.com. 112: t © Albln | Dreamstime.com. 113: © iStockphoto.com / EricHood. 114: t © Perkmeup | Dreamstime.com; b © Olgabesnard | Dreamstime.com. 115: © Bacek | Dreamstime.com. 117: © Fotosmurf02 | Dreamstime.com; bl © Andresr | Dreamstime.com. 118: t © iStockphoto.com / dcdebs; b © iStockphoto.com / Soubrette. 119: © Looby | Dreamstime.com. 120: t © iStockphoto.com / actual-_size; b © Emicristea | Dreamstime.com. 121: © Shaoweiwei | Dreamstime.com. 122: t © Tritooth; b © iStockphoto.com / jane. 123: t © Bacek | Dreamstime.com; b © Burovnikov | Dreamstime.com. 125: t © Goodynewshoes | Dreamstime.com; bl © Lucasarts | Dreamstime.com; br © Pimages | Dreamstime.com. 126: t © Baronoskie | Dreamstime.com; b © Kurhan | Dreamstime.com. 127: © Warner Br / Everett / Rex Features. 128: t © Pawelpaciorek | Dreamstime.com; b © Webking | Dreamstime.com. 129: © iStockphoto.com / RoyKonitzer. 130: t © Rex Features; b © Taily_sindariel | Dreamstime.com. 131: © Christiaan Briggs. 133: t © iStockphoto.com / Henrik5000; b © Photoeuphoria | Dreamstime.com. 134: background © iStockphoto.com / Zastavkin; t © Zanskar | Dreamstime.com. © The Travel Library / Rex Features. 135: © Peter Brooker / Rex Features. 136: bl © Clockey | Dreamstime.com. 137: tr © Icholakov | Dreamstime.com; bl © iStockphoto.com / theboone; br © iStockphoto.com / Antrey. 138: t © Rex Features; b © Athenanova | Dreamstime.com. 139: © iStockphoto.com / THEPALMER. 140: t © Colour59 | Dreamstime.com; b © Dejan83 | Dreamstime.com. 141: top row, l–r © iStockphoto.com / Yuri_Acurs; © iStockphoto.com / Juanmonino; b © Isselee | Dreamstime.com; middle row, l–r © iStockphoto.com / barsik; © iStockphoto.com / MoniqueRodriguez; © iStockphoto.com / Juanmonino; bottom row, l–r © iStockphoto.com / GreenStockCreative; © wellesenterprises; © iStockphoto.com / EricGerrard. 143: © iStockphoto.com / rfwil. 145: t © David Hartley / Rex Features; b © Dedivan1923 | Dreamstime.com. 146: b © Zamonzie | Dreamstime.com. 147: © iStockphoto.com / Stockphoto4u. 148: t © Htjostheim; b © Rex Features. 149: © iStockphoto.com / MichaelBlackburn. 150: t © Shariffc | Dreamstime.com. 151: b © Winjohn | Dreamstime.com. 154: © iStockphoto.com / elenaray. 155: t © Boyfriend | Dreamstime.com; © Cristi-_m | Dreamstime.com. 156: t © iStockphoto.com / duncan1890; b © Wildcat78 | Dreamstime.com. 157: bl © James Fraser / Rex Features. 158: b © iStockphoto.com / Malikith. 159: t © Millerimages | Dreamstime.com. 160: t © Blakely | Dreamstime.com. 161: bl © iStockphoto.com / nico-_blue. 162: t © Sipa Press / Rex Features. b © Nikitu | Dreamstime.com. 163: t © Alisdair Macdonald / Rex Features. b © Joegough | Dreamstime.com. 165: t © Millan | Dreamstime.com; bl © Milosluz | Dreamstime.com. 166: t © iStockphoto.com / Yuri _Acurs; Rmackay | Dreamstime.com. 167: b © Michaeljung | Dreamstime.com. 168: t © Brailean | Dreamstime.com; b © Eaniton | Dreamstime.com. 169: tl Vladimirdreams | Dreamstime.com; tr © iStockphoto.com / mrbfaust; bl © jeannehatch; bc © iStockphoto.com / WinterWitch; b © Millan | Dreamstime.com; b © dlewis33. 170: t © Adkok | Dreamstime.com; b © Andi Southam / BSB / Rex Features. 171: © Chriskruger | Dreamstime.com. 173: background © iStockphoto.com / AK2; © Millan | Dreamstime.com. 174: © Elwoodchu | Dreamstime.com. 175: t © ITV / Rex Features; b © Haveseen | Dreamstime.com. 176: background © Carbi | Dreamstime.com. 177: © Zimmytws | Dreamstime.com; bl © Photomo | Dreamstime.com; br © Koco77 | Dreamstime.com. 178: © iStockphoto.com / LICreate. 179: t © iStockphoto.com / Gelpi. 180: t © Rex Features; b © Cbeckwith | Dreamstime.com. 181: t © iStockphoto.com / FotoAta; b © iStockphoto.com / shatteredlens. 182: © Gibsonff | Dreamstime.com; © Homeriscool | Dreamstime.com. 183: ITV / Rex Features. 185: © Markfgd | Dreamstime.com.

HALFWIT NATION

by

the daily mash

Neil Rafferty and Paul Stokes

Additional material by Jennifer McKenzie and Matt Owen

Thanks to: Anne and Lew Stokes, John and Pat Rafferty, Uncle Hugh, the Ravens, Chris Horkan, Campbell Deane, Euan McColm, James Wills, Duncan Proudfoot and Hugh Barker, Craig Williams, Christopher Hope, Matt Bendoris, Rob Lyons, Simon Scott, w00tmedia, Design is Central, Rupert Vereker and all those who stopped looking at internet pornography for five minutes to laugh at our jokes.

CONSTABLE

Constable & Robinson Ltd
3 The Lanchesters
162 Fulham Palace Road
London W6 9ER
www.constablerobinson.com

Copyright © Neil Rafferty and Paul Stokes, 2008

First published in the UK by Constable,
an imprint of Constable & Robinson Ltd.

The right of Neil Rafferty and Paul Stokes to be identified as the authors of
this work has been asserted by them in accordance with the
Copyright, Designs and Patents Act 1988.

All rights reserved. This book is sold subject to the condition that
it shall not, by way of trade or otherwise, be lent, re-sold, hired out or
otherwise circulated in any form of binding or cover other than that
in which it is published and without a similar condition including
this condition being imposed on the subsequent purchaser.

A copy of the British Library Cataloguing in
Publication Data is available from the British Library

ISBN-13: 978-1-84529-912-5

Design and layout by e-Digital Design
www.e-digitaldesign.co.uk

Printed and bound in China

1 3 5 7 9 10 8 6 4 2

contents

the daily mash

it's news to us   www.thedailymash.co.uk   No. 1

PEOPLE WHO KNOW HOW TO FUCKING PARK ON BRINK OF EXTINCTION

DRIVERS who can position their car in the middle of a parking space at a supermarket are sliding closer to extinction, conservationists have warned.

Research teams have recorded a sharp decline in numbers over the last decade, despite efforts to educate the public about how easy it is to just put your fucking car in the middle of a parking space.

Dr Tom Logan, head of species protection at the WWF, said: 'There is a series of white lines separated by spaces roughly the same width as a car, plus a little bit more. Let's think of that as the first Great Big Clue shall we?

'As we approach, we then have to ask ourselves: "Do I park on the white line, do I straddle the white line or do I get my huge, chocolate-covered face out of my fat, unwashed arse and just put the *fucking car* in the middle of the *fucking space?*"'

Yet another symptom of climate change? Or just an unspeakable bastard who deserves to die?

Conservationists have blamed the crisis on a combination of poaching, loss of habitat and an unbelievable selfishness by a bunch of total bastards who deserve to die on a spike.

'There are now fewer than 50 people in the UK who are able to do this,' said Dr Logan. 'That's not just a tragedy for our planet, it's doing my head in every time I go to Homebase.'

WWF warned that drivers who can park in the middle of a space will soon share the fate of people who knew not to park four feet from the fucking kerb, extinct since 1993.

Dr Logan added: 'A mountain gorilla could do this with its fucking eyes shut, but for some reason the average British motorist seems to think every car park in the world was made just for them.

'Or maybe they think that if they park on the white line Graham-fucking-Norton is going to jump out from behind a bottle-bank and send them on holiday to Orlando.

'Anyway, the point is we need more money.'

---

news

POWER OF POSITIVE THINKING FAILS TO HALT CALIFORNIA WILDFIRES

news

BRITAIN ADVISED TO FILL UP ON BREAD

Carla Bruni to be the new face of Ginsters

Bring me a Steak & Mushroom Pie

12 songs by Carla Bruni

CARLA Bruni, the incredibly hot wife of French President Nicolas Sarkozy, is to be the new face of Ginsters savoury treats.

The Cornish firm said the former supermodel and singer would bring a touch of continental finesse to its irresistible range of bakes, pastries and spicy tortilla wraps.

The first television commercial will feature Bruni as a plumber, driving down the A34, when she is suddenly overwhelmed by an insatiable desire for a Ploughman's Roll and a Buffet Bar.

She pulls in at a petrol station near Didcot, runs into the shop, tears the wrapper from the Ginsters savouries and starts devouring them.

A member of staff approaches, but soon backs off when she snarls at him with the sound of an angry tiger. The commercial ends with the slogan, 'Imagine Smearing a Cheese and Onion Slice across Carla Bruni's Bum.'

Bruni said she first dreamed of working with Ginsters while writing her third album, *Bring Me a Steak and Mushroom Pie.*

The French first lady said last night: 'When I attended ze official banquet at Buckingham Palace I could not finish my dinner because I had spent all afternoon is ze bath with a copy of *TV Quick* and an enormous pile of scotch eggs.'

NEWS BRIEFLY

TOBACCO DISPLAYS TO BE REPLACED WITH 'ASIAN SUCKFEST MONTHLY'
'Mummy would be so angry if she caught me looking at cigarettes,' says 12-year-old porn fiend.

WOODY ALLEN GETS SCARLETT JOHANSSEN TO DO STUFF WITH BANANAS
'I know, we'll call it *Broadway Memories*,' says Oscar-winning director.

12-YEAR-OLD WINS ANNOYING, PRECOCIOUS BRAT OF THE YEAR
'Silence while I play my trombone!' says tiny git.

'I'LL TELL YOU WHAT'S A HATE CRIME – THAT OUTFIT'
Shadow home secretary dismissed as 'a pig in knickers'.

Housewives demand £20 an hour for eating Jaffa Cakes and watching Trisha

Busy, busy, busy.

BRITAIN'S housewives would earn the equivalent of £30,000 a year if someone paid them to eat Jaffa Cakes all day, according to new research.

The study found housewives work for nine hours a day, including an hour of *Trisha*, an hour of *Law and Order* and two *Will and Grace* double-bills.

Although Jaffa Cakes often overlap with other household tasks, including phone calls and magazines, an increasing number of women are now forced to set aside at least two hours a day as 'Jaffa Cake time'.

Dr Henry Brubaker, director of the Institute for Studies, said: 'A professional Jaffa Cake eater is £20 an hour, easy.

'Then there's the £30 an hour you'd have to pay a nutritionist to sit around all afternoon with her bloated friends, drinking tea and comparing live yoghurts.

'And I certainly would not want to have to pay a head chef to drive to the retail park three times a week and pick up a large cardboard bucket filled with deep-fried chicken parts.'

Tom Logan, a 42-year-old engineer from Bath, said: 'If you want to pay thirty grand a year for my wife's cooking, be my fucking guest.'

I'll do it if you land a helicopter on my parents' lawn, Kate told Wills

KATE Middleton agreed to do that thing Prince William has been asking her to do for months, but only if he landed a Chinook helicopter on her parents' lawn.

Friends of the couple said the £30,000 stunt was 'worth every penny' if you knew what the thing actually was.

A source close to the Prince said: 'It's game on. William has kept his end of the bargain. This is a big test for their relationship.'

William is now said to be looking to forward to doing the thing, which his grandfather assured him is, 'even better than you think it's going to be.'

It is understood the Prince first suggested doing the thing on his birthday last year, but was told there was absolutely no way.

One royal insider said: 'His pleading became very insistent. At one point he even claimed it was the "law of England" and if she didn't do it, she'd be thrown in a dungeon.

'But Kate stuck to her guns and said if he really wanted it he would have to get his RAF wings, land a helicopter on the lawn, wave to her parents and

Takes a lot of spunk.

then take off again.'

The insider added: 'I'm sure there are dozens of girls who would have been delighted to do this particular thing, but he's been determined to do it with Kate. It shows a lot of character.'

Worthless Opinion Poll	
Why are you driving on the hard shoulder?	
I'm 82-years young	10%
Chasing a deer	22%
Full of booze	31.8%
What is this 'hard shoulder'?	36.2%

Pensioner sex is dirty and wrong, say docs

DIRTY pensioners are having sex even though the thought of their naked bodies is so revolting it makes normal people sick, doctors warned last night.

GP Nikki Hollis said she had to hit one old man with a broom after he came to her surgery and demanded she look at his diseased genitals.

She said: 'Another woman came in and asked me to inspect her leathery parts, but as soon as she removed her huge knickers I threw up in my bin.'

Dr Hollis added: 'What pleasure can any man get from having sex with a woman who can tie her tits

Unspeakable depravity.

in a bow behind his head?'

Henry Brubaker, of the Institute for Studies, suggested that older people were carrying on with sex because they were not aware that it was comprehensively disgusting.

He said: 'We think it might be something to do with their lack of teeth.

'Unfortunately the team I assigned to measure them while they were at it were forced to claw their own eyes out.

'Conversely, when I recently spent an evening sitting on the end of a bed while a pair of gorgeous 20-year-old girls made love to each other for hours, I found it to be a joyous, life-enhancing experience.'

Andy Murray appoints excuses coach

BRITISH number one Andy Murray has completed his preparations for dropping out of Wimbledon with the appointment of a world-class excuses coach.

American Paul Bratter has been brought in to strengthen Murray's range of cop-outs after a difficult few weeks in which he was forced, once again, to complain about his fitness.

Bratter, who has worked with Sir Alex Ferguson and a series of England cricket captains, said: 'I knew Andy needed my help when he started complaining about having a sore wrist.

'It's amateur hour. Show me a teenage boy who doesn't have a sore wrist and I'll show you a goddamn liar.'

In recent weeks Murray has been reduced to random swearing and 'wrist problems'.

Murray is in dire need of a new range of excuses after missing the French Open, dropping out of the top 10 and readying himself to be sidelined during Wimbledon fortnight.

Bratter, who created Colin Montgomerie's classic 'American crowds' excuse, added: 'We need to generate a new platform of excuses for Andy. We need him to fall in love and then be rejected on the eve of key tournaments.

'We need to sign him up to Amnesty International. This boy needs to be distracted by a social conscience that's as big as his bank balance.

'When he loses a third-round match at Wimbledon next year I want him to be able to blame it on the Chinese government's oppression of Tibet. Now that's a goddamn excuse.'

Idiot stockbrokers continue to ruin your life

STOCKBROKERS are preparing for a third day of running around and waving their hands in the air, shouting, 'Noooooooooooooo!!!'

In London, the FTSE 100 ate all its clothes and crashed its Aston Martin into the Bank of England before running around the Monument shouting, 'Noooooooooooooo!!!'

In Frankfurt the Dax opened its bowels into the waste paper basket and then smeared, 'I hate shares' in excrement on the walls before running out into the street shouting, 'Neeeeeeeeeeeiiiiiiiin!!!'

The CAC in Paris had its worst

Look at this picture of a meadow for a while.

day since it threw up on its new suit after a bad snail, while in New York the Dow Jones took an assault rifle to work and posted a video on YouTube.

Evan Davis, the BBC's economics editor, said: 'The world's stock markets are like a finely tuned barrel of eels.

'As they plunge, sea levels rise, leading to a fall in the price of dogs. Even if cat prices remain stable a recession then occurs. No one knows why.'

Davis added: 'People often ask me why they have to lose their job and their home because a man in an expensive shirt made some terrible decisions. I tell them no one knows.'

ADVERTISING FEATURE

It's the faith-based toy that's taking America by storm!

Treat your children to our lifelike homosexual and then watch them 'stone it to death' in accordance with scripture. *

Combining playtime with biblical morality lessons the **CARNAL ABOMINATION ACTION FIGURE™** can be persecuted safely on the kitchen floor.

And if they like that then why not try the other figures from our exciting range, including Moses, Samson and even the Whore of Babylon.

Includes stones, bindings and execution post!

'These toys are not just about having fun, they can also be used to tell children about the warmth of God's love. Children can pose the action-figure Moses in so many ways. As long as they don't pose him masturbating or fellating a burly Egyptian soldier, that's okay with us.'

The Association for Christian Retail

*Always read instructions before ritual execution.

Do we really need ambulances?

by GEORGE MONBIOT

THEIR screaming sirens, their back-to-front writing and their writing and their dirty diesel engines have become a fixture in our modern lives, but does anyone ever stop to think if we actually need them?

Allow me spell it out for you. Ambulances are notoriously inefficient in terms of fuel consumption. They are either screaming along dual carriageways at more than 90 mph, on their way to some self-inflicted 'emergency'. Or they are plodding along carefully at 30 because they are carrying some fascist polluter with a fractured spine.

I performed a peer-reviewed calculation on my phone and discovered that British ambulances make up 0.00023% of our annual CO_2 emissions. Look at that figure again and tell me you don't feel an overwhelming sense of shame.

It is my belief that we must re-order Britain as an ambulance-free society. It won't be easy. De-ambulancification never is. But we must reach down to the very roots of our being and rip up everything that allows the ambulance to prosper.

Why do we need ambulances? Because people hurt themselves. Or get sick. Therefore our first step must be to stop using things.

Hoovers, Magimixes, television sets and Anglepoise lamps are not just power-sucking planet-killers, they are death traps. I use none of these things and yet I am still able to go about my day and make a comfortable living writing articles about ambulances. *Why can't you do the same?*

More than half of all British heart attacks are caused by budget airlines. *Peer-reviewed fact!* Every time you fly you are causing a heart attack which requires the dispatch of an ambulance to take the fat polluter to hospital where it is hooked up to electrical machines, only to recover and go on yet another holiday to one of 74 budget European destinations. And so your filthy, gassy circle keeps on turning.

Those of you who have ever been so complacent, so self-absorbed, so wilfully ignorant as to allow yourself to be carried in an ambulance should ask yourselves this question: Am I really good enough to go on living among people like George Monbiot and some of his friends from university?

If the answer is 'no' and you do decide to end yourself, please try to do it properly. The last thing we need is another ambulance hurtling down the M4 because you failed to take enough pills.

🔍 IN FOCUS: Who was right, Disney or Shakespeare?

The amazing chest of Pocahontas.

AS ANY historian will tell you, all the history we know is based on two key sources: William Henry Shakespeare of England, and Walter Ian Disney of Florida.

Historians are therefore split into two schools: 'Willies' maintain that all the world is a four-billion-year-old stage and that history is a series of tragedies, interspersed with jokes that everyone laughs at but no one understands.

Meanwhile Disneyists believe that Robin Hood was a very big fox, Moses looked like an Austrian ski instructor and that the Native American princess Pocahontas had absolutely magnificent tits.

Disneyists also blame war, famine and contagious diseases on something called the 'International Zionist Conspiracy'.

KEY FACT: *The Little Mermaid and the International Zionist Conspiracy is due for release in summer 2010.*

To the people, I present my vision
by Gordon Brown

WHEN I was a small boy somewhere in Scotland, I remember meeting a poverty-stricken old man who coughed phlegm and bits all over me. Even though I was just a child, I vowed to do whatever I could to cure that man of his illness, and then destroy him.

During my time as prime minister I have often reflected on my legendary Scottish childhood and the values I inherited from my local community in Fife, or possibly the Stirling area.

And those are the values I still cherish today: an unshakeable belief in the power of News International and an unquenchable thirst for revenge.

As we move into 2009 let me assure you that I am still bursting with good ideas. I'm not going to tell you all of them, otherwise you might get very excited and take the rest of the week off. That may feel good now, but it's not going to stop the Chinese building 5,000 new coal-fired power stations and invading the Moon.

This year we face many challenges, both as individuals and as unremarkable cogs in the Great Machinery of State. That is why the Labour government will move to end this historic injustice by abolishing individuals and the fear and confusion they provoke. My plan to number everyone may cost billions of pounds, and perhaps even a few lives, but at least everyone will know where they're supposed to sit.

As a young boy in Dunfermline, or possibly Bathgate, I would ask my father, 'Why are all of those people outside our house so disgusting?' My father

> 'During my time as Prime Minister I have often reflected on my legendary Scottish childhood'

would tell me that it was because they lacked health. Some were unhealthy because they lived in a hole and drank paraffin, but most were unhealthy because of capitalism. I never forgot part of that story and when I entered Parliament in 1983 I made a vow: 'No more holes, no more paraffin.' Thanks to record levels of investment many of those holes have now been filled and people are encouraged to enjoy paraffin responsibly.

But if Britain is to be a healthy society, it must, above all, be a healthy society. I have consulted with the country's leading experts and they have told me that the one thing this will require, above all else, is a good deal more health. That is why, from today, I am giving new powers to doctors so that they can tell people to stop being unhealthy. Over the next two years, the NHS will refuse to treat more than two million people and will instead send them home with a leaflet about fruit.

Not only do I think Britain is ready for fruit-based leaflets, but I believe that 2009 will be remembered as the year the great British people finally got over their petty obsession with house prices and paying bills and rediscovered the immense pride in having a prime minister who is now one of the best in Europe at dealing with chicken diseases.

But above all I believe, and strongly suspect, that 2009 will be remembered as the year David Cameron suffered a tragic and perfectly straightforward accident when he was alone in a field somewhere.

TOMORROW: Marks & Spencer? I shit 'em

In Agony with PETULA SOUL

Dear Petula,
I have just embarked on an affair with a colleague at work. We meet every day in the stationery cupboard for a Cup-a-Soup® and a quick knee-trembler. At first I though he was just using me for sex but now I am worried it is developing into more than just lust. Last time we met he threatened to tell my boyfriend that we were having an affair, unless I finished with the other man and spent more time with him. I am now worried that he might tell my husband about us too. To be honest I am not so bothered about that, but if I have to go through a very public divorce it's bound to upset my lesbian girlfriend. I picked up a bloke in a nightclub last night to discuss the whole thing with him but just ended up having it off by the dustbins behind the club as usual and then going home on the bus. Do you think I should finish with my work colleague? I would miss the sex during the day.

Ashlee,
Aylesbury

Petula says:

Dear Ashlee,
As a professional Agony Aunt I am often confronted with situations that would strike the normal person as bizarre, if not downright perverse. So it's always nice to get to a relatively straightforward letter from someone like yourself. Of course you should not finish with your colleague, or not until you have found someone else anyway. No married woman I know goes a whole work day without dropping them for some stray bloke or other, why should you be any different? One thing does concern me about your letter: you say you have sex at work every day, and you have a husband, a boyfriend, a lesbian lover and you pick up men on the way home at night – yet you have only a Cup-a-Soup® at lunchtimes. I would have thought a Pot Noodle™ the absolute minimum. You don't want to end up wearing yourself out!

NEWS BRIEFLY

HOMEOWNER LOAN ADS BANNED FROM KIDS' TV
Children pressuring parents into consolidating all their debts into one low monthly payment.

NEW BABY HAS 'ASBO WRITTEN ALL OVER IT'
'He's got his father's contempt for civilised society,' say friends.

CHURCHES 'FULL OF DRUNK PEOPLE'
'It's like a Saturday night in there on Sunday morning,' says organist.

SCOTLAND TO BUY SECOND-HAND CAR WITH OWN MONEY
Bold initiative will culminate in the purchase of a 1997 Vauxhall Corsa.

Psychic Bob's Week Ahead

Taurus (20 APR – 20 MAY)
Opportunities to widen your social circle with a broad-minded other are on offer when you meet a blind person with no sense of smell who already has genital herpes. Lucky.

Gemini (21 MAY – 20 JUN)
Family is more important than ever, especially your ancestors. Dig one up and take it into work. Or just make some soup.

Cancer (21 JUN – 22 JUL)
You'll see things in an usual way today after one of your eyes gets kicked out in a fight.

Leo (23 JUL – 22 AUG)
A shared interest draws you closer to someone at work. Now you can both dress up as women.

Virgo (23 AUG – 22 SEP)
Something small triggers a big emotional response inside. If only your husband's vibrated like that!

Libra (23 SEP – 23 OCT)
Mercury changes direction and suddenly missing folders reappear and the printer works. He really is an arse.

Scorpio (24 OCT – 21 NOV)
At work and home people are jockeying for position. Tell them to be patient: you've only got three holes!

Sagittarius (22 NOV – 21 DEC)
Try to spend more time on the road and less in a ditch with your head smashed through the windscreen.

Capricorn (22 DEC – 19 JAN)
Your love life gets a boost, and you get to give your wrist a day off. The size of your forearms!

Aquarius (20 JAN – 19 FEB)
If you're single, there is no better time to meet someone new. Same if you're married.

Pisces (20 FEB – 20 MAR)
A task you've done a thousand times suddenly seems much more difficult. You're sober.

Aries (21 MAR – 19 APR)
Neptune, planet of garibaldis and digestives, asks to see your jammie dodger.

the daily mash

it's news to us   www.thedailymash.co.uk   No. 2

FAT KIDS TO BE CHASED TO SCHOOL BY DOGS

CARS are to be banned from the school run and children chased to their classes by angry dogs under new Government plans to eliminate childhood obesity by 2010.

Children will initially be given a ten-minute start on the dogs, but this lead will be phased out over two years, after which the dogs will also be poked with sticks before being released.

The children will be given a pound of steak mince and a cat to throw on the ground to distract the dogs should they get too close, however once both have been used up 'they are on their own', the government said.

Ed Balls, the minister for school children, said drastic measures were needed because most kids were now so fat they had to lie down at all times or else their bones would crumble under their own weight.

He said: 'I personally have seen a six-year-old literally dissolve in his own fat before my eyes. We have to act now or else the whole country could soon be ankle-deep in wobbly child blubber.'

Mr Balls also warned that if the latest measures to halt the rise in obesity failed then the Government would not hesitate to ban children from school altogether.

He said: 'Our research shows a direct link between attendance at school and rising child weight.

'Before they all started full-time education British children were all so nice and thin they could fit up chimneys and crawl under fast-moving and dangerous machinery. Now look at them.'

Pick up the pace, fatty.

---

news

ENERGY COMPANIES ALL BACK SAME HORSE IN 3.50 AT LINGFIELD

news

WOMEN FIND IT HARDER TO QUIT SMOKING DURING PERIODS, SAYS INSENSITIVE PRICK

'Sex and the City' totally empowering, says manky slapper

They changed the world by talking about cocks.

SEX and the City is totally empowering and totally feminist – but in a good way, fans of the show said last night.

Sissy Palmer said she had secretly worried she might be an easily manipulated, man-obsessed skank who dressed like a transvestite prostitute until she saw the movie this week.

But the fashion PR said she now realised she was a strong, independent woman in touch with her sexuality who liked white wine and occasionally left her knickers in an alley.

She said: 'For too long we have allowed men to be at the centre of our lives, to dictate how we dress, and how we act. Well now it's our turn to get what we want.

'If I want to go out in crippling heels and a tiny skirt, and do it next to the bins with some guy I met in a bar, then no outmoded patriarchal view of society is going to stop me.

'I dress like this to please myself. Yeah, all the plain girls stare, the jealous hairy bitches, but only because I can have the men they can't. I can have any man I want. How feminist is that?'

Palmer added: 'So I sleep with a lot of guys, but I'm totally in control and it's all on my terms. I'm a suffragette in crotchless panties.

'When I'm lying on my back with my ankles round my ears, I'm thinking, "If only Emmeline Pankhurst could see me now."'

Tom Baldwin, a speed-dater from Dagenham said: 'Of course you're a feminist, love. Good for you. Now let's go outside and you can suck my ding-dong.'

Worthless Opinion Poll	
How are you dispersing teenagers?	
Ninja robot vampires	14.1%
The power of Jesus	15.7%
Jugs of horse urine	20.2%
Rubbing groin, smiling	50.1%

Brad and Angelina in bank charge refund victory

BRAD Pitt and Angelina Jolie have become the latest celebrities to reclaim excessive bank charges.

Hollywood's hottest couple announced they have successfully recouped almost £300 in unauthorised overdraft fees after a terse exchange of letters with Lloyds TSB.

Pitt said: 'We were having dinner with Susan Sarandon and Tim Robbins and they were raving about it.

'They showed us a website where we could download the template letters and read the success stories of other bank cus-

The Dixie Chicks have reclaimed more than £800 from NatWest.

tomers. It was really inspiring for us on a personal level.'

Pitt and Jolie, who met while filming *Mr and Mrs Smith*, said the bank initially refused their request but soon backed down after the threat of court action.

Pitt said he plans to spend the refund on a new set of golf clubs or 'maybe a small shed'.

OTHER CELEBRITIES TO RECLAIM BANK CHARGES THIS YEAR:

• Dame Judi Dench
• Billie Piper
• Phillip Schofield
• Johnny Depp
• James McAvoy
• Queen Latifa
• The Dixie Chicks

BBC GIVES UP

THE BBC will give up as of midnight tonight, the Director-General Mark Thompson has confirmed.

Unveiling the corporation's autumn and winter highlights, Mr Thompson said the return of Patsy and Ricky to *Eastenders* and the Christmas special edition of *To the Manor Born* showed a clear commitment to not caring in the slightest any more.

Mr Thompson said: 'When viewers hand over £150 a year they don't simply expect more of the same.

'They expect us to dig up more of the same from the 1980s and 90s.'

He added: 'Next year we're spending more than £100 million on a full-length film version of *Ever Decreasing Circles* and the much anticipated cartoon adaptation of *As Time Goes By* with Judi Dench and Geoffrey Palmer.

'What else have we got, let's see. Oh yes – Michael Palin will go somewhere foreign and be pointed at by people who've just seen *Monty Python and the Holy Grail* for the first time.

'David Attenborough will present the 26-part series *The Life of Pine Cones* and we'll have a big costume drama based on a

New 26-part series: *The Life of Pine Cones.*

thick, important book, starring that guy who used to be in *All Creatures Great and Small*. Not Robert Hardy or Dr Who. The other one.'

Mr Thompson said all other programmes will be presented by someone chosen from the BBC's Smart Arse Rotation, including Jonathan Ross, Clive Anderson and Ian Hislop.

Worthless Opinion Poll

How are you exploiting immigrants?

Backyard production of *Friday the 13th*	15%
Giant chess pieces	27%
Loft insulation	28%
Impersonating me at work	30%

IN FOCUS: So that nation shall broadcast 'Strictly Come Dancing' unto nation

IN 1921 the government launched the British Broadcasting Corporation with the aim of educating the public and bringing civilisation to every corner of the globe. Initially this involved six hours a day of light jazz, followed by a stern, but fascinating lecture from the Lord Chancellor about the importance of Britain's gas works. Little has changed over the decades and today the BBC educates and enlightens the nation with six hours a day of celebrities doing things you would not normally expect celebrities to be doing, and stern, but fascinating lectures from Kirsty Wark about the importance of sounding clever at dinner parties. The BBC receives generous public funding thanks to a series of short but terrifying films warning people that if they do not contribute towards Jonathan Ross's £3-million salary they will rot in jail.

Pay me or go to jail.

Sting's next album will be 'just awful' critics predict

STING'S next album has been panned by critics more than two years before he is due to start recording it.

Carl Shurz, chief reviewer of rock bible *Twang*, said the album would probably be called something stupid like *Comanche Scallops* and sound like 'a cow giving birth next to the M25'.

Einar Gilkyson, writing in the German jazz magazine *Fahrtz*, described it as 'an impending crime against humanity' and predicted the largest ensemble of badly tuned lutes in musical history.

Shurz said: 'At *Twang* we don't normally give an album a terrible review until it has at least been recorded.

'But as soon as I heard that Sting was even thinking of making another record, I felt compelled to review it as quickly and as badly as possible.'

Meanwhile Gilkyson, one of the most influential reviewers in jazz, said *Comanche Scallops* would be an 'unrelenting exercise in self-congratulatory masturbation by a musician who clearly has his fingers on the wrong way round'.

He said the opening track, probably called something vacuous like 'Love Mussel', would most likely be a disgust-

'Approximately 48 minutes of rancid pish.'

ing, free-jazz workout featuring Sting on the lyre and Winton Marsalis on the alto euphonium.

He added: 'Ostensibly an ode to the Belgian national dish of moules frites it will in fact be a 15-minute paean to the art of tantric cunnilingus.

'I expect to be physically sick.'

'Ich bin nicht ein Nazi,' says Philip

PRINCE Philip has denied claims he is a Nazi, insisting his passionate racism is merely a hobby.

He said that despite his large collection of flags and uniforms, there was no ideological basis to his bigotry and that it was just something he liked to dabble in at weekends.

The Prince said he was outraged by suggestions that he was a Nazi sympathiser, stressing it was not his fault that he and his family 'had spent so many happy holidays with the Führer, amidst the glorious mountain air of Berchtesgaden'.

Prince Philip, a member of the Argentinian wing of the Danish-German Royal House of Hammer-Cushing-Karloff, is

'Und vot do you do?'

related to most of the crowned heads of Europe, and at least four of their horses.

When they met during the war, the young Princess Elizabeth quickly fell in love with the tall, dashing Zeppelin pilot in his shiny, black boots.

The Countess of Barrhead, a contemporary of the couple, said: 'Philip was so handsome. In many ways he reminded me of Obergruppenführer Heydrich.

'She was completely smitten and would have done anything for him – even planting a bomb under the Lord Chancellor.'

The Prince said last night: 'Ich bin nicht ein Nazi. Ich liebe der Juden und der poofenshnabels.'

He added: 'Ich bin nicht liebe der Chinesenplafs, der Froggenheimers und der Dago-Woppenshnauzers, mit der greasenshlaft und garlickenpoop!'

India unveils world's shittest car

TATA, the Indian car giant, yesterday unveiled what it claims is the world's shittest mode of transport.

The company said the 'Nano' – Hindi for 'death turd' – is designed to be both affordable and a complete piece of shit.

The car, to be built initially for the Indian market, will cost around £1,200 – roughly 1,200 times the average weekly wage and three times the price of a house.

The manufacturers have warned that in certain parts of the country it will be advisable to maintain the top speed of 43 mph in a desperate attempt to avoid being chased down by hungry leopards.

The car has no air bags and no air conditioning, despite average Indian summertime temperatures of 150 degrees Fahrenheit.

The company has also cut costs and increased the danger by removing the hand brake and filling the glove compartment with killer wasps.

Tata expects to sell more than 400 million Nanos, despite the fact that most Indians have absolutely nowhere to go.

Motor industry analyst Tom Logan said: 'The Nano is likely to be the first in a range of incredibly dangerous pieces of shit and is confirmation that Indians remain the world's most expendable people.'

WHAT MAKES THE TATA NANO SO SHIT?

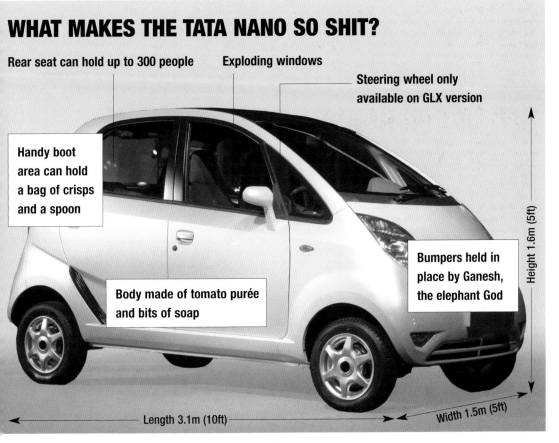

Rear seat can hold up to 300 people

Exploding windows

Steering wheel only available on GLX version

Handy boot area can hold a bag of crisps and a spoon

Body made of tomato purée and bits of soap

Bumpers held in place by Ganesh, the elephant God

Height 1.6m (5ft)

Length 3.1m (10ft)

Width 1.5m (5ft)

Leo conceived after I wore a bag on my head, reveals Cherie

CHERIE Blair has revealed how she conceived her fourth child after agreeing to wear a bag on her head.

Mrs Blair said her husband refused to have sex with her until the bag was safely in place and a photograph of Spice Girl Geri Halliwell had been stapled to the front of it.

In her memoirs, *Speaking for Money*, she writes: 'We were at Balmoral, having a lovely supper with the Queen, Kiefer Sutherland and Andre Agassi, when I announced to the entire table that I had forgotten my contraceptive coil and that perhaps Tony and I should use this opportunity to conceive another child.

'Tony turned to me and said "I love you, but there's just no way. Either we use a turkey baster or you stick a bag on your head."

'It was then that Prince Philip suggested we attach a photograph of someone famous to the bag as that "might help the prime minister to become fully engorged."

'There was general agreement around the table and people started pitching in with ideas about whose photograph we should use.

'Kiefer suggested Cameron Diaz, while Andre was adamant we should go with Catherine Zeta Jones. Then dear Prince Philip shouted, "I know, what about a Spice Girl!"

'Tony banged the table saying, "Yes, that's the one," and ordered Alistair to fetch a really good close-up of Geri Halliwell with her mouth open.

'Her Majesty then made the very wise observation that if we

Mrs Blair would sing the chorus of '2 Become 1' at the moment of climax

did it "doggy-style" Tony could just flip the bag around and have Geri staring back at him all the way through.

'Meanwhile Prince Philip was already clearing a space in the corner of the dining room, but I insisted we go upstairs. There are some things you should keep private.'

Wayne Rooney's wine cellar 'a poof', say City fans

THE wine cellar of Manchester United striker Wayne Rooney is such a total poof, according to rival supporters.

Manchester City fans have ridiculed the England superstar's collection saying it is bland, predictable and filled with 'New World rubbish'.

Bill Johnson, editor of manchestercitywinelovers.com, said: 'Can he tell the difference between a Shiraz and a Grenache? Would he prefer an '83 or an '85 Bordeaux? And why is he such an ugly Scouse twat?

'Darius Vassell has a shed full of ripe, meaty Burgundies and

robust whites from the Loire valley, while Dietmar Hamann is an expert in Riesling and Gewürztraminer. And anyone who says different will get kicked squarely in the nuts.'

Rooney began collecting wine after his fiancée Coleen McLoughlin returned from a very nice weekend at a Marriott Hotel in the Lake District.

According to friends, Rooney likes to unwind with a glass of Chilean Cabernet. He is also a fan of New Zealand whites and has been known to rub a bottle of Cloudy Bay into a recurring groin injury.

Filled with New-World rubbish.

Johnson added: 'Rolando Bianchi spent his childhood in the hills above Bergamo, helping out on his uncle's vineyard and acquiring a palate that makes Wayne Rooney look like a fat prick.'

ONE WOMAN'S WEEK: Prole Model

by KAREN FENESSEY

THIS week, I have gained a glimpse into the disturbing mess that fills up the minds of today's youth.

My investigative senses were pricked by a discovery in the school computer lab which thrust me into the distasteful world of eating disorders, such as bulimia. I can't even begin to imagine what kind of pointy, jabby little women with downy coats of body hair will grow out of the morons who make up the female contingent of our school's P7s.

On my way to lunch, I noticed that the door to the computer lab was ajar. Upon further investigation, I exposed a P7 girl, whose name is Courtney. My moves were stealthy like the leopard, and I'm not exaggerating when I say, 'That girl nearly shat herself.' She clumsily clicked away the page she'd been looking at and stuffed her things into her bag. With a red face of shame, she scuttled off as I yelled my authority at her for showing such lunchtime disobedience. It was only as I was chasing that coward out of the room that I stopped and thought, 'Hey! Wait a minute . . .' She had stuffed her camera into her bag – what had she been doing with it?

I went back to the computer to investigate. When I clicked back a page, I found some photographs of what I can only describe as 'Courtney's midriff' uploaded onto a site called 'Pro-Ana'. Courtney had accompanied her pictures with a little message which left me in no doubt that 'Pro Ana' is actually text-speak

for 'Eating disorder!' She had written about how she was so proud of her progress because she could see her ribs now and had only eaten half a rice cracker that day. This was pure lies – I couldn't see any of Courtney's ribs in that photo and she was obviously holding her stomach in (plus, the shot was totally amateurish). Some of the other members of the

> 'No number of rice crackers will change the low-calibre stock you're from'

site had already sent messages to her, like, 'Wow – you are inspirational' and, 'It's only a matter of time before you can see your chest bones too.'

I knew then that it was my duty to expose both this faddy nonsense and Courtney for what they truly are (she'll learn not to run off when Miss Fenessey is demoralising!). Posing as a 29-year-old called 'Carrie' I left the following message:

'As the only adult here, I feel it's appropriate to point out a few home truths to you gals. No number of rice crackers will change the low-calibre stock you're from. It's about time that you got over this stupid fad and admit that you are never going to be models. Not everyone has the model-gene which is so crucial if you want to be famous and universally adored. Sometimes I regret turning down a

career in modelling myself. I am one of these sickening people who can eat whatever they want and still look stunning, but I knew when it came down to it that I wanted to use my superior brain to get ahead in life and not my visible chest bones. Why can't you all look to women like Jordan and Britney Spears? They are not all stunted up like a fucking refugee, but curvy and successful women who are totally happy with their bodies. *Marie-Claire* magazine writes that you people are ill and deserve sympathy, but we both know that you are just a bunch of attention-seeking munters who will never get an honours degree from Strathclyde University. Well, I can't sit about wasting my day here – I have a date tonight with my boyfriend, Donny, where I will probably eat as much as I want and then have sex because I drive men wild! PS Courtney does not look like this picture in real life. She is actually quite chubby and yesterday I saw her eating an entire bag of Haribo Tangfastics in the playground.'

I can only pray that my words have hit home.

Worthless Opinion Poll What's wrong now?	
Weekend home too cottagey	15%
Caviar too lumpy	19.4%
Bentley too leathery	24.5%
Big fat man hands	40.9%

In Agony with PETULA SOUL

Dear Petula,
I go out drinking with my girl pals every night after work. We tend to get really hammered down the pub and afterwards pick up blokes in Pitta the Great before heading off for a quick knee-trembler in the nearest alleyway. Most times I get a bit of a seeing to from some bloke and a free kebab, which normally lasts longer than he does. I don't like to speak with my mouth full, as it is unladylike, so when they finish before I'm through with my doner I usually don't get their names. Do you have any tips on how to get chilli sauce stains out of your crop top?

Hot Stuff,
Haddington

Petula says:

Dear Hot Stuff,
Is that what modern womanhood has come to, meaningless sex with a different stranger every night in some filthy back alley? Sounds fantastic. Back in my day we had commitment and marriage, and quick sex with the same man every night in the same bloody position in the same boring old bedroom. So all that campaigning in the 1970s was not wasted after all. Vanish.

Do you have a problem you'd like Petula to help with?
e: petula@thedailymash.co.uk

NEWS BRIEFLY

EXTRA TAX ON POOR 'LABOUR'S FINEST HOUR', SAYS BROWN
'If Nye Bevan were alive he'd be blowing me right now,' insists prime minister.

BAFTA GLORY FOR 'ALLOTMENT'
'It's a great night for people who grow their own leeks,' says Keira Knightley.

HUGE, DISGUSTING INSECTS ON BRINK OF EXTINCTION
Endangered list finally includes huge, poisonous beetles and stick insect bigger than a cat.

Psychic Bob's Week Ahead What does the future hold for you?

Taurus (20 APR – 20 MAY)
Faced with a decision today you're unsure what to do. The left shoe is the one with the red sticker, remember?

Gemini (21 MAY – 20 JUN)
With your demanding job and your active social life, you are always on the go, and yet you always have energy. Everyone hates you.

Cancer (21 JUN – 22 JUL)
You had a great first date, you've emailed, so why haven't they agreed to a second date? Ask them to return the picture of your penis.

Leo (23 JUL – 22 AUG)
When it comes to attracting people, you're an unbeatable combination. You buy your own drinks and will sleep with anyone.

Virgo (23 AUG – 22 SEP)
There is a chance you'll get something you have been wanting for a long time. But there's a much bigger chance you won't.

Libra (23 SEP – 23 OCT)
Sure, you could send an email to a special someone, but why not wow them by writing it in your own blood. It's got to work eventually.

Scorpio (24 OCT – 21 NOV)
You're feeling pulled in opposite directions. Part of you wants to stay in and read and part of you wants to go to the vicar's sex party.

Sagittarius (22 NOV – 21 DEC)
You work hard, and it is easy to forget to take care of yourself. But you still stink.

Capricorn (22 DEC – 19 JAN)
Spend some time thinking about your perfect future. Then forget it. It's not going to happen.

Aquarius (20 JAN – 19 FEB)
One minute they are begging you to leave, the next they won't move, even though you have stopped strangling them. What can it mean?

Pisces (20 FEB – 20 MAR)
You are about to enter a period of rapid personal growth. Make sure your flies are done up.

Aries (21 MAR – 19 APR)
Try something different this weekend. Visit an art gallery, and *then* get drunk and give a stranger a blow-job in an alley while he eats his chips.

THE ANIMAL KINGDOM

HANDS UP WHO HASN'T SHAGGED THIS CAMEL

A BEAUTIFUL camel who also claims to be a part-time model is really just a dirty skank who is mad for cock, one of her ex-boyfriends revealed last night.

Osman Iqbal said he started dating Afia six weeks ago only to discover she was also sleeping with at least two of his close friends.

He accused his former lover of being a 'whore of the desert' who spreads her giant legs for a pint of water and a packet of medjool dates.

Iqbal said: 'When I first see Afia I captivated by her beautiful dark eyes, her lovely smile and the sexy way she move. She also fantastic kisser.

'I lie with her most every night, she warm and generous and sensitive lover. It not my first time with camel but I not so experienced. She very patient.

'I ask her pose for pictures. I take nice shots, not dirty ones. I get her enter in Miss Camel World beauty contest in Abu Dhabi.

'But when I show Afia pictures my friends they all go, 'Ha, ha, ha, ha, ha,' and say she dirty camel bitch who do it with anyone round back of mosque at weekend.'

He added: 'Azaad, he say to me, "I have her many time, one time Fatih and me spit-roast her while Hasan film it on mobile phone."

'If she win I put sex tape on the internet and tell *News of World*. There no way she get marry Bruce Forsyth then.'

Dirty bitch.

PETS Not for eating. Except maybe the cat.

17

'Fuck Broccoli.'

Massive conk

CANCER-PROOF MOUSE WON'T STOP SMOKING

A LABORATORY-bred mouse which is immune to cancer will not stop smoking and has become 'a nightmare to live with', researchers say.

The genetically modified 'supermouse' has trebled the number of cigarettes it smokes from 20 to 60 a day, and taken up cigars and a pipe.

It eats nothing but beef and has bought itself a motorcycle to drive to swingers' parties where it indulges in casual, unprotected sex. It has also started taunting cats.

Dr Roy Morton, head of cancer at the Institute of Mice, said the mouse had turned into 'a right bastard' since learning of its near immortality.

'The whole place just stinks of fags and mouse sick. Every time I turn on the light he is at it with one of the other mice, staring back at me with a big "fuck off" grin on his face.

'I asked him if he'd like to go on a little run in his wheel the other day and he told me he'd much rather have some skunk and a go on my assistant Rebecca. He's disgusting.'

Friends of the mouse say he was a happy family mouse with a good job and prospects before the doctors introduced him to cigarettes and alcohol as part of their experiment.

'I don't think I had ever seen him drunk before, and if he did smoke it was maybe the odd slim Panatella on his birthday or at Christmas. They've created a fearless monster,' said one.

Pest control expert Bill McKay said the scientists were 'foolish meddlers' who had obviously never suffered an infestation of mice.

He said: 'Why don't these tossers invent a mouse which drops dead when it shits on my kitchen floor?'

'What the fuck is wrong with that gerbil?' ask zoologists

A NEW species of mammal, described as a weird-looking gerbily thing with a massive honk', has been discovered in the mountains of Tanzania.

The team, from the Institute for Studies, photographed the shrew-like animal on the forested slopes of the Udzungwa Mountains, after getting lost on the way back to their hotel.

Team leader Professor Wayne Hayes said: 'I had just dug myself a nice neat hole, I had my copy of *What Car?* and I was getting ready to deposit yesterday's goat-based concoction, when all of a sudden this long, freaky nose pokes out of the undergrowth.

'I got a hell of a fright and shouted to my mate Dave, I said, "Dave, get the tennis racket! There's a huge nose coming straight at me and I can't move 'cause I'm having a shit!"

'Dave comes running with the tennis racket above his head, shouting, "Geroutofityadirtybastard!" but then I see that it's actually pretty harmless and just has this enormous fucking hooter.'

Dr David Hobbs added: 'It started to scamper away but I managed to jump on it and grab it by the nose. It squeaked for absolutely fucking ages.'

The team's mammal specialist Dr Steven McKay, said: 'For such a small thing, it's actually quite big. We called it an "elephant shrew", mainly because of the stupid nose and the big fat stomach.

'Dave wanted to call it the "Angela Shrew" after his fat, big-nosed wife.'

It's got a really big eye, so what?

Giant squid same as normal squid only bigger, say zoologists

A HUGE squid found off the coast of Antarctica is basically the same as a normal squid, only much, much bigger, a team of disappointed zoologists said last night.

Professor Wayne Hayes, of the Institute for Studies, said they first encountered the enormous specimen while watching the second round of the World Snooker Championships from Sheffield.

Professor Hayes added: 'When they brought it in I was like, "Jesus Christ, that's a right fucking stoater. Is it dead?"

'I says to Dave, "Dave, d'you wanna switch off the telly for five minutes and maybe give me a hand with the world's biggest squid that's just been dumped in my lap, as per usual?"

'Every time someone finds something huge and disgusting in the sea it somehow finds its way to my office with a post-it note on it.

'I'm like, "Excuse me, in case you hadn't noticed, I am trying to watch the fucking snooker!"'

Dr David Hobbs said: 'Anyway, I gets out me big squid book while Wayne gets stuck in with his Stanley knife and a pair of pliers.

'I was thinking, "I bet it's got green blood or its face is inside out. Or it's got eyes on the end of its tentacles. Or maybe it fell out of space ship!"

'But once we start delving around in there it's obvious it's just a really, really big squid.'

Dr Hobbs added: 'To be honest, I think we'll probably just eat it. Have you been watching the snooker?'

PUPPIES!

THESE puppies are absolutely adorable, it was confirmed last night.

As the UK and international news agendas reached new heights of misery, these little Labrador puppies remained so cute you could just eat them up.

It is understood one of the puppies likes to chase his tail while another is developing quite an appetite for old slippers.

The puppies, none of whom have been locked in a dungeon or fallen victim to a massive natural disaster, are currently sleeping all

curled up together in a big box lined with an old blanket.

Sources close to the puppies revealed that at this age they like to sleep a lot, which is just as well because when they are awake it is 'complete chaos around here'.

And although newspapers have been laid down in the kitchen and the hall, there remains much to be done in the control of pee-pees and poo-poos.

The puppies' official spokeswoman said: 'We vewwy sowwy we poo-pooed in your shoe again. We wuv you.'

'Can we come and live with you?'

MIRACLE CAT KNOWS WHEN OLD PEOPLE ARE ABOUT TO BE RACIST

MOLLY, a ginger cat at a Bournemouth nursing home, has displayed an uncanny ability for identifying elderly racists.

Staff at Bellingham Lodge say the four-year-old cat will jump into the lap of one of the elderly residents, usually during the six o'clock news.

Assistant manager Susan Carter said: 'Anything on the news about terrorism, asylum or immigration will have Molly pacing around the floor.

'As soon as one of the residents says, "It's because of all these . . ." she jumps into their lap. It's as if she can sense their racism.

Can Molly smell racism?

'If George Allagiah is presenting the news, then Molly can get quite agitated as the racist remark could come from anywhere in the room.'

She added: 'Last year we had one old gentleman who was Conservative candidate in the 198 general election. Molly would follow him everywhere he went.'

Staff say they are surprised the large number of women caught out by Molly's sixth sen for bigots.

'Our old ladies do love to have go at ethnic minorities and foreigners,' said Carter. 'I think it helps swelling go down in their legs.'

the daily mash

SYSTEM NO LONGER WORKS, CONFIRMS UN

THE socio-economic system which has governed much of the globe for over a century finally stopped working at around 9 p.m. last night, the United Nations has confirmed.

UN Secretary-General Ban Ki-moon made the announcement as retail giant Wal-Mart stopped Americans from buying rice and the cost of butter in British supermarkets reached 94p.

With poor people in fertile countries rioting because they could not afford to eat the food they had just grown, the UN chief said it was time for him to hide in a cupboard.

He added: 'As of this moment, free markets, capitalism and the rule of law are – oh, how should I put this? – fucked into a cocked hat.

'We're planting crops for fuel instead of food in order to make it cheaper to drive to the shops where we then buy food that is much more expensive because we've planted crops for fuel instead of food. You can see where I'm going with this, right?

'Meanwhile, the banks are borrowing money from taxpayers so that they can then lend the same money back to the taxpayers at a higher rate of interest than they borrowed it from them in the first place. Seriously, is it just me?

'Anyway, point is, we're a bit stumped. The communist one doesn't work either – in fact it's probably even worse, and you just end up queuing to buy matches and soap and huddling around oil drums, swigging home-made vodka and smoking pathetic, little fags made out of hedge clippings.

'So, if anyone does have any spare systems lying around that

Ninety-four fucking pence!

they're not using, please do email me at spankymoon69@unitedna-tions.com.'

Trevor Hart, a shopper from Gloucester, said: 'I don't know nothing about systems, all I know is I just paid 94p for some butter. What the fuck's that about?'

---

news

BRITAIN EXPLODES AT BOTH ENDS

news

SMELL OF PISS REMOVED FROM TRAINS BY 2014

'Genius' chimps spend all day throwing faeces

GENIUS chimps who out-performed students in an intelligence test still spend most of their day throwing excrement at each other, scientists confirmed last night.

Dr Wayne Hayes, director of chimps at the Monkey Institute, said he thought the memory challenge overstated the chimps' intelligence as none had showed any humility in victory.

He said: 'All they did was frantically scratch at each other's privates and bare their buttocks at their poor opponents. I don't call that clever.'

He added: 'The main thing they all seem to remember is what time I feed them, and where it was they left a really smelly, sticky piece of chimp dung.

'I just LOVE throwing faeces.'

'They are also very good at remembering that my assistant Rebecca does not like being chased around a cage by a gang of hairy backsides with bright pink erections.'

Dr Hayes cautioned against attributing too much significance to the chimps' success, pointing out they had only defeated a group of first-year university undergraduates.

'Out of that lot, I know who I'd choose to go to Starbucks for me,' he said.

One other key test of memory involved the offer of free tickets to see the Spice Girls on their reunion tour.

He added: 'The students accepted immediately, but every single chimp said 'no thanks' on the grounds that they remembered the video for 'Viva Forever'.

Society of the future may be forced to eat food

THE people of the future may be forced to eat real food instead of pills, scientists have claimed.

Experts have changed their predictions after new research showed that seeking essential nutrients from a little plastic bottle full of shiny capsules may not be entirely good for you.

Dr Cathy Smith of the Institute for Studies said: 'We always assumed the best way to absorb healthy vitamins and minerals was by guzzling little tablets, manufactured by the billion in Taiwan.

'They were made with succulent,

The Bananatron 6000.

natural ingredients such as polyethylene glycol, sodium lauryl sulfate and chlorophyll.

'Then the whole delicious concoction was given a special coating of something called "shellac". If you're the nautical type, you'll know this as "boat varnish".

'But, sure enough, you do a little bit of research and whaddya know? It kills you.'

Dr Smith said the jetpack-wearing consumers of the future will now be forced to find time in their superfast, digitally-enhanced schedules to eat cumbersome, gaspowered fruits and vegetables.

She added: 'We will now have to design food that looks adequately futuristic. Who's up for a chrome-plated tomato or a banana that plays films?'

Worthless Opinion Poll	
Why didn't you vote for Obama?	
You lookin' at me boy?	8.4%
Wha'd you say boy?	11.1%
You ain't from round here, are ya, boy?	35.5%
Yeeee haw!	45.1%

Most households now switching energy supplier every 20 minutes

MORE than 50 per cent of British households are switching energy supplier three times an hour, according to an industry survey.

Regulator Ofgem said Britain has embraced the switching culture thanks to a combination of rising energy costs, price comparison websites and an endless stream of confusing bullshit.

The most popular reasons for changing supplier include boredom, concerns over the use of hybrid embryos and 'that funky black gospel choir with the shiny jumpsuits'.

Nikki Hollis, from Watford, said: 'So far today we've been with Scottish Hydro, Southern Electric and nPower.

nPower say they no longer squash cats.

'But I've just been speaking to EDF who told me nPower make their electricity by squashing cats in a vice. I told them I'd have to think about it.'

Bill McKay, from Bristol, said: 'I signed up for Off-Peak Friendly Juice because it was three times cheaper than PeakLife EcoMeter, but it turned out that was just a lot of shite they told me over the phone.'

He added: 'I'm planning to make some lunch using EDF, listen to Leona Lewis with British Gas and then switch to Ecotricity so I can watch *Lark Rise to Candleford* with something approaching a clear conscience.'

Ofgem said there were now 8.6 million different tariffs available from more than 16,000 different suppliers, most of whom also provide high-speed broadband, basket-weaving lessons and a free pig.

Monocle grease and penny farthing oil removed from inflation basket

TYPICAL household goods including monocle grease and penny farthing oil have been removed from the basket of items used to measure inflation.

Officials say they want to bring the Consumer Price Index up to date without going so far as to include things that people actually buy.

A Treasury spokesman said: 'There are two kinds of inflation. There's the inflation we talk about on the news, which generally hovers around the 2% mark.

'Then there's the inflation that you pay in the shops, and God only knows what that is.'

He added: 'Have you seen the price of petrol? In the name of balls! Thank Christ I work for the government.'

Minsters are revamping a range of official indices, with the London Media Twat Index updated to include Inca hats and books about Afghanistan.

From April the Index for People with Constipation will

The new basket will include a range of modern, everyday purchases including spats, violin cases and sheet music for Dixieland jazz.

include muffins, fruit smoothies and the *Daily Express*.

Meanwhile the Index of Annoying Pricks has been expanded to include the word 'methinks'.

William enjoys another spiffing day out

HIS Royal Highness Prince William was in fine spirits last night after another absolutely spiffing day out.

The future king took off in a light aeroplane and flew it around until he felt like doing something else.

The Prince said it made a 'pleasant change' from the rigours of the Fulham Road or having his foreskin hoovered every morning by the Royal Company of Foreskin Hooverers.

His Royal Highness revealed: 'I was worried that flying around might prove to be ghastly and something of a bore. But actually, it was all rather jolly.

'I wonder why people don't

'I'm having a lovely time, thank you for asking.'

use their planes all the time. What is the point of owning one and then just leaving it in your field?'

In preparing for the role of monarch, the Prince will spend a year having really terrific days out with the armed services, before focusing on his main constitutional duty of not being a Catholic.

The Prince added: 'Next month they're going to give me a boat with helicopters on it that I get to drive around the sea for a couple of days. That's got "spiffing" written all over it.'

Prince William later spent the evening in Boujis nightclub, throwing bottles of champagne at the wall and urinating into the FA Cup.

He was then driven to Kate Middleton's apartment, where she danced seductively for him dressed as Jessica Rabbit.

Bag ban forces residents to throw their shopping home

SHOPPERS in the village of Minchinhamptonsteadbury have been forced to throw their goods home after a total ban on bags.

Residents are slowly coming to terms with the new method of transporting their weekly shop, after a successful campaign to collect all the bags in the village and throw them into Steadbury Reservoir.

Under the new regime, shoppers at the village co-op start throwing their goods as soon as they reach the end of the checkout. Each item is then picked up and tossed in the direction of the shopper's home.

Margaret Gerving, a retired deputy headmistress said: 'It's good exercise and it encourages you to buy round food like melons, oranges and turnips as there's a decent chance they'll roll for a few yards.

'Some members of the bowling club

Will roll for a few yards.

have become really quite proficient. Until they get to the bottom of Minchin Rise of course, at which point it turns into a total bloody nightmare.'

Mrs Gerving added: 'Bags of flour tend to just hit the ground with a dull thud. There's no bounce in them at all. And I have to wrap my bottle of sherry in a duffel coat.'

Councillor Brian Stotten said: 'Things are bit chaotic at the moment. You have to run past the Co-op as there's stuff flying out the whole time.

'A lot of people are getting their shopping mixed up and I've seen a few knives. We simply have to get this sorted before Christmas.'

Philip letters warned Diana about the Chinese

PRINCE Philip sent a series of crude death threats to Princess Diana which often included thinly veiled attacks on the Chinese, an inquest heard yesterday.

The unsigned letters, sent between 1992 and 1997, usually began with 'My dearest Diana' before predicting her death and alerting her to the dangers of the 'yellow peril'.

The inquest jury at the Royal Courts of Justice was shown more than 20 letters, some made from newspaper cuttings, others written in an untidy, child-like scrawl.

Martin Bishop QC told the court: 'At first, the source of these letters was a total mystery.

'Indeed, any normal reader would have been stumped but for the unprovoked racial slurs tagged on to the end.'

Mr Bishop added: 'I put it to you that there is only one man in this country who would have gone to such lengths to cast aspersions upon the Chinese.'

One letter reads: 'My dearest Diana, I am no marriage counsellor but that won't stop me from killing you.' He added: 'Never

leave the room when drinking with an Oriental.'

In another letter from the summer of 1997, Philip wrote: 'I see you have taken to consorting with a brown man. PS What are those Chinese devils plotting now? Any ideas?'

Denys Finch-Hatton, a Royal expert, said: 'The early- to mid-1990s was very much the high point in the Duke of Edinburgh's China-hating phase.

'He's getting on a bit now so these days he makes do with hating the Arabs and the French.'

Wenger refuses to brand referees a bunch of Man Utd-loving bastards

ARSENAL manager Arsène Wenger last night refused to condemn referees as a collection of bastards who would do anything to help Manchester United win the league.

As his team's title hopes came to an end, Wenger remained tight-lipped on the penalty and free-kick decisions made by a man who probably has Ronaldo posters on his wall and dreams of tender, post-coital snuggling with Ryan Giggs.

The Arsenal manager said: 'I do not want to say anything about what bastards they are.

'There is also no way I'm going to accuse them of giving away penalties like they were romantic gifts for their Old Trafford lover boys.'

Wenger asks the prime minister why he hasn't killed all the referees.

He added: 'I would never claim that referees hold secret meetings

to plot how they can thwart me, before praying to a giant, golden statue of that miserable, Glaswegian halfwit.

'Nor will I speculate that more than half of all premier league referees lie awake at night thinking about rubbing their excited hands all over Wayne Rooney's lightly oiled buttocks.'

A spokesman for the Referee's Association said: 'As Mr Wenger points out, all Premier League referees are completely impartial and would never favour one team of towering, Cheshire-based superheroes over another consisting largely of sweaty, mal-odourous Frenchmen.'

He added: 'Do you ever just lose yourself in Rio Ferdinand's eyes?'

Bank profits plunge from obscene to repulsive

RECORD bad debts in the US home loan market will see bank profits fall from eye-poppingly obscene to unspeakably repulsive, City analysts warned last night.

Early indications suggest bank earnings in the last quarter of 2007 were down to below 'what-a-bunch-of-fucking-thieves' compared to 'and-the-pricks-still-won't-extend-my-overdraft' for the same period in 2006.

David Chappell, chief econo-mist at Donnelly-McPartlin, said: 'Millions of buck-toothed rednecks with no credit history and a disturbing fondness for Jack Daniels were allowed to

How banks see you.

borrow 40 times their non-existent wages to buy a burnt-out toilet in a crack alley.

'Banks, being the cautious types they are, said, "No problemo, and while you're at it, get yourself a Chevy Trailblazer and a big-screen TV for watching *WrestleMania*,

you odious waste of semen.

'"And for goodness sake don't worry about proof of earnings – we'll roll it all up into one big loan at a fantastic rate of 69.9% APR, which, trust me, is incredi-bly low for your sort of person."'

He added: 'This strategic anomaly has led to a short-term dip in profitability and created the impression that banks are somehow ordinary, everyday businesses. Aha ha ha.

'The fact is, they control every aspect of your lives – often in ways you dare not imagine – and could, if the notion takes them, snap you in half like a dry twig.'

Marks & Spencer? I shit 'em

by Mervyn King, Governor of the Bank of England

SO there I am setting up the stall, right, early doors, when who should amble over all casual-like but my old pal, Mr Marks and Sparks himself, Sir Stuart knobbing Rose. The total cock-fucker. Still I was glad it was him. I thought at first it might have been the Excise. Tossing fuck-tits.

Anyway, he's all hand-made suit and silk tie. Very posh. None of that polyester shit like he knocks out himself up west. 'Nice schmutter,' I says. 'Autograph, is it?' all coy like, and he nods, looking sheepish. 'Autograph, my arse,' says I. 'You lying tit arse sock banger. What do you think I am? Some kind of swivel-eyed shitting jock felcher?'

'Look Merv,' he says. 'Me and the boys, the Selfridges, Peter Jones, even that demented Arab fuck at Harrods well, we've been talking and well . . . well, we think that interest rates are too high and all that, well, you know it's not good for any of us, is it? You neither, on the stall here, not good for business at all.'

'No fucking problemo, mate,' I says. 'I'll get on the dog now, chew up Charlie Bean at the Bank and have a few points shaved off before you can fiddle. How low you want to go?' And he says, all trusting like, 'Oh I don't know, I reckon fifty should do it for now.'

'Fifty,' I say, all slow and deliberate. 'Fifty. You seen the latest inflation report, you

'He's all hand-made suit and silk tie. Very posh. None of that polyester shit like he knocks out himself up west'

fucking cock holer? I'm up to my piss flaps in petrol prices and gas bills and you want fifty basis off? I've got the mad jocko on the phone every 15 minutes telling me to fucking uncrunch some credits or he's going to string me up by my knob from the Monument, and you want me to open my arse and let you pump it just because no tart in Britain wants to be seen dead in a pair of your minge-mufflers anymore? You fucking fuck-butter. Fuck right off.'

So then he's givin' it all,

'Merv, Merv, it's not just me, it's the whole market that's off, everyone's suffering, even that mad fucker Green at Bhs.' In fact the only ones coining any shilling at all, he says, is those ponces at Waitrose, and that's only because they don't mind selling to the gays.

'Pissing fuck,' I say. 'Look around you Rosey, my stall is totally knobbed, and I don't sell nothing to nonces, not even if I'm wearing gloves. Just while we've been talking I've knocked out ten hooky copies of *The Golden Compass* on disc and four of a porn DVD my mate Barry made with some drunken slut he picked up in a titty bar. I've sold four boxes of stolen Mars Bars, a Japanese steel, extending truncheon, a flick knife, two tasers and a Nazi helmet. Recession? You wanna get yourself down the fucking market. There's no recession here.'

Any road up, better get myself spruced. Speaking to a load of bankers at the Mansion House tonight. Cock-mingers.

Worthless Opinion Poll Why are you stealing body parts?	
Nibble trays	10%
Car-sharing	25.4%
Mad for cock	29.4%
Makin' soup	35.2%

In Agony with PETULA SOUL

Dear Petula,
I am a 16-year-old lad and I think I am becoming confused about my sexuality, although I can't say for sure. For some years now I have been binge-wanking over the lady's girdle section of my mum's Freeman's catalogue. However, while playing the fleshy clarinet with some gusto last week I turned the pages so quickly that, before I knew it, I had run out of ladies and so 'accidentally' loosed off my love porridge all over a man in some pale-blue Y-fronts, and I was not sick afterwards. I also read the other day that chafing causes gayness, although it could be the other way around. Anyway, I have a small red patch at the top of my right leg. Am I gay, or are my trousers too tight for cycling?

Confused,
Cumbernauld

Petula says:

Dear Confused,
It is often said that most young men of your age will go through a phase at which they are unsure of their sexuality and fear they might turn out to be demented perverts. Utter rubbish! Most lads of your age are perfectly normal and healthy and have no interest in fiddling with the parts of their fellow men. Yuk. Indeed, even by your tender age a huge number are experienced lovers capable of showing the divorced older woman what she was missing all those years she spent murmuring words of encouragement to the now, thankfully departed, Mr Floppy. It should not be too hard to work out if you are a sexual deviant or not. Have you ever been to see The Wizard of Oz *or* The Sound of Music *while wearing a dress? Do your hands flop forward at the wrist? Do you enjoy ball games? Do you like cock? If you answered 'yes' to any of the above you are definitely a degenerate sex fiend, although you might just be a member of the local rugby team.*

Do you have a problem you'd like Petula to help with?
e: petula@thedailymash.co.uk

Taurus (20 APR – 20 MAY)
You're not an artist, but you can still have fun doodling. Ask a cutie to sit for you. You might get to see pubes!

Gemini (21 MAY – 20 JUN)
Remember the number of that guy you slept with? Dig it out and call. He might know why it burns when you pee.

Cancer (21 JUN – 22 JUL)
Someone you've been secretly admiring is checking you out. That's them with the binoculars. Next to the policeman.

Leo (23 JUL – 22 AUG)
Pick up the phone and call a friend. Ask them what they are wearing.

Virgo (23 AUG – 22 SEP)
Now's the time to update your online dating profile. Craft some clever copy, and then add some recent photos of someone else.

Libra (23 SEP – 23 OCT)
People are hanging on your every word this week. Maybe it's because you have a gun.

Scorpio (24 OCT – 21 NOV)
Start the week by writing down all your social engagements. Next.

Sagittarius (22 NOV – 21 DEC)
You meet someone new who really likes you, but you're not so keen. Sleep with them until someone better comes along.

Capricorn (22 DEC – 19 JAN)
When you meet someone you like, don't just point at your crotch and make grunting noises. Point at theirs too!

Aquarius (20 JAN – 19 FEB)
Are you feeling uncertain about what the future holds? Me too. I'm shitting it.

Pisces (20 FEB – 20 MAR)
Maybe losing your partner is an improvement. Now you can masturbate whenever you like!

Aries (21 MAR – 19 APR)
Some little thing sets you off in a big way. Clean it off her shoes, it's the least you can do!

NEWS BRIEFLY

POLICE THREATEN TO STOP SHOOTING BRAZILIANS IN THE FACE
'Without the police this country would be swarming with Brazilian electricians, undermining our values and that,' says Scotland Yard.

PAISLEY QUITS TO SPEND MORE TIME HECKLING THE POPE
'While I have been glaring at terrorists across the Cabinet table, this silver-tongued witchdoctor has been spreading his voodoo message unmolested.'

the daily mash

it's news to us   www.thedailymash.co.uk   No. 4

BANKS FUCKED

BANKS in the UK were fucked yesterday, after a landmark court ruling.

A High Court judge said the Office of Fair Trading can now take a good, long run-up at the banks and fuck them into the middle of next week.

Coming hard on the heels of the sub-prime loan crisis, the industry is now bracing itself for a shafting of absolutely humongous proportions.

Mr Justice Smith stressed his judgement did not necessarily mean the banks deserved to be fucked, but warned that a comprehensive humping was all but inevitable.

Julian Cook, an analyst at Donnelly-McPartlin, said: 'Remember that bit in *Raiders of the Lost Ark* when the big, baldy German guy is punching Indiana Jones and then turns round to see the propellers coming straight towards him? That's how fucked they are.'

Meanwhile, millions of account-holders are looking forward to playing their part in fucking the banks.

Tom Logan, a sales executive

'Have you heard how fucked the banks are?'

from Lincoln, said: 'They've been charging me £35 every time I go 20p overdrawn and then using my money to buy piece-of-shit American mortgages.

'There are simply no words to describe how much I am going to enjoy fucking them.'

Bank chief executives last night demanded an urgent meeting with the chancellor to ask if there is anything he could do to prevent the imminent fuck-fest.

A Treasury spokesman said: 'Holy shit, they're even more fucked than us.'

---

news

RICH PEOPLE VERY HAPPY

news

FRUITY CHEWS COUNT TOWARDS FIVE-A-DAY, SAYS DOC

Forty-somethings a bunch of whining turds, says report

PEOPLE in their forties are a bunch of whingeing tits who should count their blessings, according to new research.

Henry Brubaker, of the Institute for Studies, said it was unclear why comfortably off forty-somethings should complain all the time, but he suspected it was because they were horribly self-absorbed.

He said: 'Your average 40-year-old should have a good job and a nice house, a family and will be looking forward to the death of his parents so he can pay off the rest of the mortgage.

'If you're a woman the worst that can happen is your husband runs off with a teenager even though she has to lift up his beer belly just to get it in, and will then leave him after a week for someone who's not suffering from stress-related impotence.

'Of course, he then ends up in a bedsit while you get the house and half his pension and you don't have to have sex with him every time you want new shoes.'

Katie Wilson, 22, said: 'I've just graduated from university with £30,000 of debt, I'm working in a call-centre, and if I'm lucky I might just have paid off three per cent of it by the time I'm 45. But I'm not depressed. I'm drunk.'

The Queen Mother didn't get depressed while she was kneeing Hitler in the face.

Roy Hobbs, 85, said: 'I didn't fight Hitler for six years so these bastards could take to their beds because they've got crow's feet and a bald patch.'

Syria outsources evil plotting to North Korea

SYRIA is to outsource its evil plotting to North Korea in a £3-billion deal to create the world's biggest terror brand.

The rogue state will employ 300 sinister-looking Asiatics at a nuclear facility near Damascus in a diabolical plan to wipe Israel from the face of the earth.

Meanwhile, 100 specially trained Syrians will travel to North Korea to train its population to look even more terrifyingly insane on television than they do already.

Bashar al-Assad, the president of Syria, said: 'Only North Korea offered the vertical synergies necessary to make the numbers stack up.

'The Koreans impressed us with their bottom-up approach and

Kim is focused on delivering sustained, long-term strategic growth and having *cra-zee* hair.

their lust for blood, while offering us a client-focused, holistic solution to all our terror needs.'

Kim Jong-il, Heavenly Supreme Commander of the Korean People's Army, said: 'This merger of two of the strongest names in world terror will create a results-driven, customer-facing force for evil without the need for major downsizing.

'While we are the global number one at looking stony-faced and menacing, they are world leaders in goggle-eyed public insanity and firing guns into the air.'

Bill McKay, a terror analyst at the Institute for Studies, said: 'Jesus H. Christ. Get me a spade, three tonnes of ready-made concrete and 6,000 cans of baked beans.'

England expects Scotland to put out

ENGLAND has now spent so much money on Scotland that it is expecting some 'fairly spectacular sex', it was claimed last night.

Despite recent gifts including free school meals and free prescriptions, Scotland has failed to express her gratitude in a physical way.

England said last night: 'My friends were always telling me that Scotland was a really beautiful country and that I was lucky just to be able to sit next to her.

'I didn't mind the little things like her own football team, her own BBC or even the odd parliament here and there. But now it's starting to cost me serious wedge and, at the end of the day, I've got needs.

'Just last week she was saying she doesn't want Trident. Well, she's getting Trident – she's getting lots of Trident or she can fuck right off.'

England said the relationship had been difficult for about 800

She would not have supported South Africa.

years but there was always the expectation of a 'big sexual payday'.

'A couple of years ago I turned up with an engraved, 18-carat free personal care for the elderly. It was a lovely thing and I reckoned I might at least get some tongue and a quick rub in the groin.

'Instead she stood there like I owed it to her and asked for a 75 per cent increase in health and education spending. It's not like she's got a job.'

England added: 'Now that I've coughed up for the school meals and the prescriptions I think it's only reasonable to expect a commitment to some fairly serious below-the-belt time. And maybe even the Big Slipper.'

🔍 IN FOCUS: The Repulsive Celts

BRITAIN is a diverse country made up of around 14 different nations, including England, Yorkshire, Alton Towers and Saab drivers. Despite their differences, most of these nations tolerate each other and rarely feel the need to declare total war. The only exception to this rule is a race known as the Repulsive Celts who inhabit the windy, bog-ridden extremities of the British Isles. The Welsh Celts are short, dark, angry people who enjoy inventing malicious gossip about their neighbours and then turning it into a beautiful song. The Irish are dark, angry, short people whose belief in Jesus is second only to their belief in ignoring everything Jesus ever said. Meanwhile the Scots are angry, short, dark people who eat deep-fried concrete and say 'hello' by hurling a bottle straight at your head. The Scots are also very good with money, especially yours.

Every four years the Scotsmen pick a new 'Chief'.

Google aims to capture market for bullshit

GOOGLE is to create its own internet encyclopaedia in a bid to corner the growing market for online bullshit.

The search engine giant said that 98 per cent of the internet is now unverifiable shit written by people who have no idea what they are talking about.

However, it said more effort was needed to bring this gibberish together to provide internet users with one fast and reliable source of self-regarding drivel.

Tom Logan, Google's head of knowledge, said the internet had revolutionised the way people formed worthless opinions about important subjects.

He said: 'A few years ago most people were still getting things wrong because of their own ignorance, superstition and prejudice, much as their ancestors would

Google plans an entire section on why *The Da Vinci Code* was only scratching the surface.

have done in medieval times.

'Thanks to the internet, stupid people all over the world can peddle their own shit while simultaneously imbibing the shit of millions of others leading to an exponential growth in shit, the full meaning of which we are still struggling to grasp. But it's bound to be shit.'

Many experts have described the Google project as a direct attack on Wikipedia, the online knowledge base that describes itself as a communal encyclopaedia and blancmange.

However, Wayne Hayes, one of Wikipedia's chief editors, dismissed the threat from Google saying his organisation had nothing to fear.

'We are an online knowledge company with many years of experience. According to Wikipedia, Google is either a movie actor from the 1920s or a homoeopathic remedy for piles.'

Flower was asking for it, says bee

A DAFFODIL who accused a Bumblebee of groping it in a public park was asking for it, the bee claimed last night.

According to the bee it was flying on its normal route collecting pollen when it suddenly caught sight of bright yellow shape waving at it in the breeze.

As it flew over to take a closer look, the bee said the daffodil started to sway sexily from side to side before it opened up its petals and flashed its stamen.

The bee said: 'I was just flying around minding my own business. Yes, I was looking for a bit of pollen if there was any on offer, but you tell me, what bee isn't?

Skank.

'I didn't make the first move, it wasn't me standing there with me bits flapping around in the air for everyone to see, filthy tart.

'If they aren't up for a bit of action they shouldn't flaunt themselves like that. I'm a normal red-blooded male. I was aroused. She led me on. I couldn't stop myself.'

Nikki Quinn, chair of the flower rights group Reclaim the Park, said bees had to recognise that when a daffodil said no, it meant no.

She said: 'Every flower has the right to flap where it pleases, when it pleases, with as many stamens showing as it wants, without being pestered and molested by these pervert bees.

'We just do not accept that a bee is incapable of a little self-control, whatever the temptation, and if it is, then it can always go and visit those dirty begonias by the boating pool.'

Suspended above the earth, the shuttle performs its elegant ballet once more. But only the best and the brightest are chosen for this celestial dance. The brave men and women of NASA reveal their hopes, their fears and why there's simply nothing better than being...

FUCKED-UP AND IN CHARGE OF A SPACESHIP

Ferguson apologises to premenstrual Reading fans

SIR ALEX Ferguson has apologised for upsetting Reading supporters at the weekend, saying he had not realised they were having their period.

The Manchester United manager admitted his offensive gesture at the Madejski Stadium was excessive given the delicate hormonal balance of the opposing fans.

'Football can be a tough old game,' said Ferguson. 'Especially if you're just some wee lassie with the painters in, who bursts into hysterics if you put sugar in her tea.'

Nick Oaks, spokesman for the Reading FC Supporters'

Association, said: 'We were all feeling very upset and vulnerable after Ronaldo's goal.

'To then make a rude sign and raise his voice like that was just horrid. He said he didn't raise his voice, but he did.'

Oaks added: 'My friend Wesley is facing a particularly difficult week at work and this was the last thing he needed.'

Ferguson admitted to being 'insensitive' adding: 'I didn't realise how emotionally fragile they would be, especially after

Reading fans like Galaxy when the painters are in.

the previous night's episode of *Grey's Anatomy*.

'The next time we play Reading I'll bring along plenty of chocolate and tampons for everybody.'

Biofuels taste awful, say Africans

BIOFUELS are incredibly salty and don't really go with anything, hungry people in the Third World said last night.

As food crops are ploughed up to make way for biodiesel plants, local people in Africa, Asia and South America said they would really prefer rice, corn or some form of wheat.

Western governments believe biofuels can deliver three key objectives, including: reducing CO_2 emissions; guaranteeing energy security; and plunging the developing world into an endless, downward spiral of food riots and civil war.

Professor Henry Brubaker, of the Institute for Studies said: 'At the

Needs a lot of brown sauce.

moment it does make it somewhat impractical for half the global population to have their dinner.

'But in 40 or 50 years biofuels will be so efficient that we will be able to grow the crops in Africa, ship the fuel to America, refine it and then use it to ship cheese-based food products back to whoever's still living in Africa.'

Charles Diogo, a farmer from Mozambique, said: 'I really did try to like it, but I'm sorry, it's just a bit too diesely for my palate.

'But it's okay, don't worry, I'm sure we'll find something else to eat, somewhere.

'It's very important to us that you are able to drive to Asda in a more environmentally friendly way.'

My wedding is going to be so much better than yours

Just three weeks to go and I'm so excited. The final preparations are being made and I can assure you it is going to be a magical day. So much better than yours.

The theme will be 'Lillies'. A spray in the church and delicate, oval arrangements on every table. You chose roses, did you not? Are you actually a member of the Cilla Black fan club?

My dress is being flown in from a workshop in the hills above Perugia. It is a dazzling combination of scrubbed taffeta and the most exquisite hand-ruffled lace. My friends cried when I showed them the sketches. My dressmaker, Allessandro, has given it the code name 'Project Angel'. I understand you bought your dress from a shop. Tell me, did your husband begin his affair that day?

Upon arrival each guest will be handed a flute of chilled vintage Taittinger with a fresh raspberry floating playfully on top. At your wedding you served Cava. Perhaps you meant to be fashionable. Or were you just being frugal? You may as well have passed round a lukewarm bottle of Tizer with bogies in it.

For the entrée we are serving roast veal fillet with a risotto of morels, crispy salsify and champagne velouté. Delicate, sophisticated, nuanced. At your wedding you served char-grilled chicken breast and baked salmon. There's a word for that isn't there? Oh yes, 'swill'.

Our honeymoon begins with scuba-diving in Zanzibar and then to a mountain retreat in Bhutan. No phones, no internet. Just two people, gloriously in love. Remind me, how many diseases did you bring back from Phuket?

All in all I think you will agree that it is shaping up to be an absolutely enchanting, unforgettable occasion. Unlike your wedding which was a load of shite.

✍ DIARY: Basil Brush

I say, do you know, I went into the local sweet shop to buy myself a quarter of everlasting gobstoppers the other day, only to discover it had been taken over by a bunch of foreigners!

'A quarter of your finest gobstoppers please, my good squire!' I said, but the fella behind the counter shook his head and pointed to a load of pongy old sausages hanging from the ceiling. I took one look at the ghastly things and told him: 'Pheeeww! If you think I'm eating any of your dirty, foreign muck you must be a Scotch egg short of a picnic.'

When I got home, I told Mr Nick I'd changed my mind and that I would be attending the BNP meeting that night, after all. The sooner we get rid of these lazy, stinking Polaks, the better.

The Blooming Nice People meeting was an absolute scream and afterwards Mr Nick and I went to an Indian restaurant and had chicken and chips and ice cream for afters. Both of us said 'no thank you' to the foreign menu. Who wants to end up smelling like Mr and Mrs Patel? Pooo! What a bloomin' awful whiff!

Mr Nick and I visited the council today to complain about some gypsies who've been camping on the round-about. The council man said that they were perfectly within their rights, and that we shouldn't call them pikeys, gippoes or any other 'racialist'

names. 'Ooooooh,' I said, and scrunched up my nose.

Well, I've never seen Mr Nick quite so angry – apart from that time he got jolly batey when those two queer fellows next door asked to borrow some butter. Anyway, he told me to jump in the car as we had a little job to do. Soon enough we were racing through the darkened streets towards the gypsy encampment, where we waited until midnight before torching the place. On the way home I turned to Mr Nick and said: 'How's that for a camp fire?' Boom! Boom!

In Agony with PETULA SOUL

Dear Petula,
I have been married for some years now and for a long time my husband and I had a very active sex life. In recent years things have cooled off a bit and now we make love around once a month, if I am lucky. However, on a bad month it can easily be double that. In the last few weeks my husband appears to have become totally disinterested in having sex with me at all. I am worried that he may be having an affair. What will happen if he's getting loads outside the home and then she chucks him? He'll be straight back here heaving away on top of me every night just like in the bad old days. What can I do?

Stressed,
Streatham

Petula says:

Dear Stressed,
This is a worrying development, and probably far worse than you realise. In my experience husbands who shag around tend to get a taste for it and will soon start humping anything that moves, and quite a lot that doesn't, including their wives. If that's the case you might well soon find yourself transfixed by the sight of his sweaty manboobs swaying from side to side as he heaves himself aboard, even if he is still getting it elsewhere as well. But what to do? You could try accusing him of having an affair but that is likely to backfire on two counts: either he will deny it and then put some extra effort into ploughing your lady garden to try and prove he's not having it away with his secretary, or he'll confess, dump her and try and make it up to you with a sexy weekend away. Either way it's going to be pretty dreadful for you. No, if I were you I would just ignore the whole thing, keep wearing the grey jogging bottoms with the stains on and the mismatching underwear and just let sleeping dogs lie. And if it's any consolation I have told your husband to do the same.

NEWS BRIEFLY

MALE BIOLOGICAL CLOCK SAYS IT'S 'QUARTER TO SEX'
'Lucky for you I knock off at "sex-fifteen", says 42-year-old man with Mazda MX-5.'

PORN FANS TERRIFIED BY GIGANTIC PLASMA COCKS
Enthusiasts urged to limit themselves to 27 inches and simulated stereo.

SAUDI KING DEMANDS WIVES FOR PETROL
'Leave them by the gate, so I can check their teeth', decrees oily dictator.

Do you have a problem you'd like Petula to help with?
e: petula@thedailymash.co.uk

Psychic Bob's Week Ahead

Taurus (20 APR – 20 MAY)
Now is a great time for trying out new things. Why not have a go at sex?

Gemini (21 MAY – 20 JUN)
Thinking about asking out someone new? Now's the time. That burning sensation when you urinate is nothing to worry about!

Cancer (21 JUN – 22 JUL)
Feeling low? Go to a bar, get drunk, and sleep with a stranger. That feels much better, doesn't it?

Leo (23 JUL – 22 AUG)
Remember that hottie you met on holiday? She's been thinking about you too! She's changed her name and had major facial surgery.

Virgo (23 AUG – 22 SEP)
A good friend is seeing you in a different light. Don't they know kerb crawling is illegal?

Libra (23 SEP – 23 OCT)
Never underestimate the power of a home-cooked meal. Make an erotic pudding, but use a small banana to avoid disappointment later.

Scorpio (24 OCT – 21 NOV)
Are your lover's quirky habits now driving you bonkers? Tell him to set fire to his own farts.

Sagittarius (22 NOV – 21 DEC)
Take some time to reflect on all that you have achieved in your life so far. That's enough.

Capricorn (22 DEC – 19 JAN)
You're feeling extra generous, so why not do a friend a favour and stop sleeping with her husband?

Aquarius (20 JAN – 19 FEB)
You'll find yourself in a situation where another person's feelings could easily get hurt. Enjoy!

Pisces (20 FEB – 20 MAR)
You must learn to share the people you love. Here's £5, go to the pictures.

Aries (21 MAR – 19 APR)
Your ego takes a pounding, but don't be depressed. Get back in the bush and wait for someone else come along!

DIanArAMa

Diana, Princess of Wales now flirting with Jesus

A prayer for Diana, Princess of Wales
by Rowan Williams, Archbishop of Canterbury

PRINCESS DIANA, WHO ART IN HERMÈS,
CHANEL WAS THY FAVOURITE BRAND NAME.
THY KING DID COME,
BUT HE FANCIED ANOTHER ONE, AS DID YOU ANYWAY.
GIVE US THIS DAY A FLASH OF YOUR SMILE,
AND FORGIVE US OUR PAPARAZZI,
AS WE FORGIVE THOSE WHO PAPARAZZI AGAINST US.
AND DRIVE US NOT INTO THE SIDE OF A TUNNEL
WHEN WE AREN'T WEARING OUR SEATBELT. AMEN.

Diana was Spiderman claims Al Fayed

PRINCESS Diana led a secret life as a superhero who was able to scale buildings and shoot a web-like material from her wrist, Harrods' owner Mohamed Al Fayed claimed today.

Giving evidence to the inquest into Diana's life, Mr Al Fayed said he was the only one who knew about the Princess's crime-fighting alter ego.

He told the court in central London: 'She phone me up and say, "Uncle Mo-Mo, I am the Spiderman, I solve many crime."

'She say I must tell no one. She say she use spidery sense to uncover plot by dirty Greek Philip bastard to blow up Alton Towers.'

He added: 'I tell her for many year I am suspecting she the Spiderman. She very

agile girl with good legs who know right from wrong. It all add up.

'I tell her my people make her new Spidery-suit with matching accessory. Very nice. Good quality.

'Later she give demonstration at my home. She dress up in suit and fire web at bar stool.

'Then, all of sudden, she disappear. We search every place and no find her. Then we look up and there she is – on ceiling!'

Mr Al Fayed insisted the Princess and his son Dodi planned to marry and have seven children whom they would teach to sing and dance.

He added: 'It be like *Sound of Music*, except on yacht.'

'We look up and there she is — on ceiling!'

Diana tribute: millions unite to spell out 'We miss you' in gigantic letters

BRITAIN has been urged to come together to spell out, 'We miss you' in letters so huge that Princess Diana will be able to read it in heaven.

The 'Big Message' is being co-ordinated by the Cabinet Office in conjunction with the *Daily Express*, *OK!* magazine and Living TV's *Most Haunted*.

Justin Toper, the *Express* astrologer, has confirmed that Diana will be able to see the message from her villa in heaven, while the size of the letters has been calculated by former *Tomorrow's World* presenter Philippa Forrester.

The message will begin in the Lake District and skirt along the western edge of the Pennines before descending through the Midlands and into the South-East.

The emotional tribute will end with a 45-mile-long exclamation mark running from Maidstone to Horsham.

To ensure maximum visibility every volunteer will be given a bright yellow tracksuit and baseball cap sponsored by one of Diana's favourite charities, the Dove Campaign for Real Beauty.

A Big Message spokesman said: 'We've gone for jolly, playful let-tering to reflect that side of the Princess's character.

'Diana liked nothing more than shopping in Knightsbridge, having a light lunch with a close friend and then phoning the *Daily Mail* and accusing Prince Philip of trying to kill her.'

Prime Minister Gordon Brown said: 'This is a once-in-a-generation opportunity for this country to come together and send a message to heaven. This will be Britain's Apollo programme.'

Mr Brown is expected to travel to Matlock in Derbyshire where he will join the bottom half of the letter 'I'.

Letters so big they can be read in heaven.

So who is Spiderman?

DIANA: B&Q OPENS BOOK OF INDIFFERENCE

BOOKS of Indifference were opened at B&Q branches across the country today for men who could not a give a monkeys about the 10th anniversary of the death of Diana, Princess of Wales.

Large queues had formed by early morning as ordinary folk stood in line for the chance to express in writing their utter amazement that anyone still gave a toss.

No flowers were left to rot into a smelly pulp at a makeshift shrine, and few words were spoken as the men waited patiently, many of them writing a simple 'What the fuck?' before heading off to buy a three-litre tub of Polyfilla.

Gary Chalmers, 34, visiting the B&Q Warehouse in Ongar, Essex, wrote: 'So much for the much vaunted safety features of the S-Class!', before his mate Terry Nittens, also 34, added, 'Next time, love, wear a seatbelt.'

Ben Tilson, 39, summed up the feelings of many when he wrote 'wank' in the book at the Didsbury superstore. His best friend Rob Powers, 38, added, 'I shag arses, call me,' and the number of Mr Tilson's mobile phone.

Archie Hunter, 87, demanded to be wheeled from his old folks home in Chippenham to his local B&Q so he could write: 'I strangled Germans with my bare hands.' Phil Topping, his carer, said: 'He always writes that now, even on his Christmas cards.'

Bill Hughes, 43, wrote, 'Mine's a large one,' while Rob Palmer, 17, added, 'Nice nips!!!' Bill Fidget, 22, put down, 'Cock', Pete Stoddam, 57, wrote, 'Tit's oot', and Simon Hoskins, 45, added, 'Fanny'.

The Rolls-Royce of crack fillers.

British media agrees to phased withdrawal of Diana stories

THE British media last night welcomed the Diana inquest verdict and called for the Princess to be laid to rest over a period of 15 to 20 years.

As the inquest jury confirmed that Diana was not, in fact, Spiderman, the UK's newspapers and broadcasters set out a timetable for reporting other things.

The phased withdrawal begins this weekend with a series of 48-page pull-outs celebrating Diana's life and hair, while speculating over the true identity of the web-spinning superhero.

From May the tabloids will carry just two Diana stories per week, while the broadsheets will restrict their coverage to writing about the tabloids' coverage of Diana.

The editors of the *Daily Mail* and *Daily Express* have agreed to a five-year moratorium on the headline, 'Was she Spiderman after All?', while the *Sunday Times* will wait until after the death of Prince Philip before running what they promise will be a pathetically flimsy story about his MI6 connections.

All newspapers and broadcasters have also pledged a low-key com-memoration of the first anniversary of the inquest verdict.

Tom Logan, Assistant Diana Editor at the *Financial Times*, said: 'As our Diana resources are redeployed it will enable us to devote more space and talent to scaring the absolute fucking beje-sus out of people on a daily basis.'

Meanwhile the inquest has been praised for taking just six months and £10 million to conclude that Diana was killed because she was being driven around Paris at 100 mph by the drunkest man ever to get behind the wheel of a car.

Jury inspects toilet where Princess had final movement

THE Diana inquest jury was last night taken to the bathroom of the Ritz Hotel in Paris to see where the Princess enjoyed her final bowel movement.

The jurors stood in silence before the Armitage Shanks Lichfield™ water closet which still contains the last precious evacuation – preserved by hotel staff in memory of the late Princess's perfect intestinal health.

A row of Ikea tealights was placed on top of the cistern to mark the solemn occasion.

Meanwhile one of the local Carmelite nuns who maintain a permanent vigil at the toilet said the rosary as the jury members filed past the makeshift shrine.

A spokesman for the coroner said: 'We all know that Diana spent a great deal of time and money keeping her colon well irrigated.

'Even now, all these years later, it was obvious that this movement had been perfectly executed by a beautiful woman in the prime of her digestive life.

'It really brought home to us all how fragile existence is. One minute you are sitting on the toilet thinking how glad you are you don't suffer from constipation like poor people on bad diets and the next you are being murdered by the British Secret Service on the orders of Prince Philip. Shocking.'

A row of tealights marked the solemn occasion.

I love it when a plan comes together

By HRH the Duke of Edinburgh

IT WAS with a small measure of relief and not a little satisfaction that I heard the coroner declare The Arab's allegations to be entirely without substance. In the end it has all come together so beautifully, has it not?

Oh, how The Arab must be boiling with rage. But surely even someone as clumsy as him could have predicted this particular endgame? Never underestimate the respect, nay affection, the British judiciary have for their dear monarch and those who have served her so selflessly and for so long.

You see, the murder itself was the easy part. All it takes is enough cold, hard cash and a gang of industrious Chinamen. Goodness me, the things those little chaps can do when they put their minds to it. I find it's best not to ask too many questions.

And even if they had been caught red-handed, no one

'Murder itself was the easy part.'

would have suspected a thing. The Duke of Edinburgh? In league with dastardly Chinamen? I think not, Inspector.

No, the tricky part – the clever part – is the smoke and mirrors. It's the sleight of hand that sends the newspapermen the other way and keeps the Great British Public in a state of constant and blissful ignorance.

Let them speculate about the 'security services' and 'the Establishment', whatever that is. It's all such marvellous theatre. Meanwhile, my dear, deadly little Chow-Ping is safely back in Shanghai, gambling away his ill-gotten gains around the Mahjong table.

But I'll hand it to The Arab, he knew it was me all along and he was resolute in his determination. But the very thought that I, a Prince of the Realm, would be brought before some squalid little inquest! 'But I'm just an old man, this all so confusing.' Too ghastly, I'm sure you'll agree.

So what's next, you're wondering? Do you know, with my gang of little Chinamen on one side and The Arab on the other, I think I might just be unstoppable Chin-chin!

the daily mash

it's news to us   www.thedailymash.co.uk   No. 5

I'LL BE JUST FINE, SAYS PLANET

THE planet Earth has dismissed claims that it is in danger from global warming, stressing the worst that could happen is the extinction of the human race.

The Earth spoke out after a series of books, television programmes and environmental campaigns urged people to do everything in their power to 'Save the Planet'.

Earth – 4,000,000,000 – said last night: 'I'll be absolutely fine, seriously. I might get a bit warmer and a bit wetter, but to be honest, that actually sounds quite nice.

'Try living through an ice age. Pardon my French, but it's absolutely fucking freezing.'

The planet, based 93 million miles from the Sun, said it was 'sick and tired' of being drawn into arguments about human behaviour.

'Look, I'm just a planet doing its thing, all right? If you want to live on me, that's your business, but I've got important planet stuff to do, okay?

'Try being in elliptical orbit for five minutes, or balancing your gravitational pull with a medium-sized moon. Let me assure you, it's no fucking picnic.'

The planet said environmental campaigners should change their slogan from 'Save the Planet' to something more relevant such as 'Save your Sorry Arse'.

Earth added: 'Okay, so there may come a time when, for a variety of reasons, I am no longer able to support pandas, polar bears, and humans, but you know what? Life goes on.

'Who knows, I might end up being a haven for toads.'

'If you don't mind, I've got some orbiting to do.'

---

news

CILLIT BANG TO RUN NHS

news

BRITAIN URGED TO USE A FUCKING HANKY

Apple tightens grip with launch of iTold

APPLE is to tighten its grip on twenty-first century society this week with the launch of iTold, a new software application which will seize control of every aspect of your life.

The computer giant is concerned that many people buying its products, especially the recently launched iPhone, regard them as their own private property and not a physical extension of Apple CEO Steve Jobs.

Mr Jobs said: 'I didn't create a huge company peddling all sorts of over-engineered crap so that people could buy it off me with their own money and then think it was theirs to do with as they pleased.

'Once you buy one of my products I own you and you are my bitch. So bend over while I update your ass with my hard-drive.'

Kneel before Jobs.

Ted Knutz, iTold developer, said: 'The iTold will download automatically onto all Apple appliances and gives Steve Jobs the irrevocable right to take the virgin-ity of the daughters of anyone who has purchased an Apple product in the last 30 years – and the sons as well if he wants, but obviously not at the same time as that would be disgusting.

'Once installed iTold will order all Apple users to give a tenth of their annual income to Jobs, either in money or in kind by working in his fields. It will also make them fight for Jobs should he declare war on any of his business rivals.

'We are not saying he will, but if he does and you don't turn up ready to die for Apple then iTold will turn your iPhone into a steaming lump of dog shit and make your MacBook download child porn until the police smash your door down and then lock you up with a 7-foot-tall bum rapist. That will be $99 please.'

🔍 IN FOCUS: Getting to know your iPhone

(1) **Toaster:** two slots, variable heat, works in tunnels.

(2) **Grill:** perfect for steak and sausages 'on the go'.

(3) **Auto-babysitter:** only alerts you if it's serious – let's get hammered!

(4) **Porn button:** includes 50x zoom function, you dirty, filthy boy…

(5) **Reassurance button:** plays, 'You are not a shallow, pretentious cock,' in a soothing voice.

Absolutely everything can kill you, warns Department of Health

WARNING!
EATING BARK DURING PREGNANCY COULD HARM YOUR BABY

Too many pregnant women are still eating tree bark.

EVERYTHING will carry a government warning label, under plans to prevent anything from happening, the Department of Health has announced.

From next April all things will undergo a government risk assessment and then be labelled according to the most likely catastrophe.

The move comes after a series of successful pilot schemes, including toasted sandwich makers, urban foxes and World War II grenades.

The recent move to label alcohol bottles with the warning: 'This bottle is full of alcohol' was also judged to be an enormous success.

Public health minister Caroline Flint said: 'This announcement follows an extensive public consultation exercise.

'More than 1,400 people managed to seriously injure themselves with the consultation document. It should have carried a warning label.'

She added: 'This is not about the government trying to nanny people.

'We simply want to tie their shoelaces, tidy their hair, ensure they have a good breakfast and then threaten them with a £60 fine unless they brush their teeth.'

OTHER WARNINGS WILL INCLUDE

- Goldfish: 'Do not eat 40 of these at once.'
- Milk cartons: 'Do not fill a basin full of milk and then stick your head in it for 10 minutes.'
- Hardback books: 'Do not attach a chinstrap and use as a helmet.'
- Helmets: 'Do not use for carrying hot soup.'

Darth Vader a Baptist, says Vatican

THE Vatican has admitted intelligent life exists elsewhere in the universe but that much of it is under the control of protestant denominations.

Monsignor Umberto Facci, the Vatican's Head of Religious Science, called on Earth's Catholics to challenge intergalactic heresy and help billions of alien planets find the path to Rome.

The Vatican's study involved watching a series of films including the original *Star Wars* trilogy, *Dune*, *Battlestar Galactica* and *Star Trek III: The Search for Spock*.

Monsignor Facci said: 'We applied our usual rigour and determined there was a very high probability that all of these stories were 100 per cent true.

'Based on our observations, it would seem Darth Vader, Boba Fett and Emperor Palpatine are all Baptists.

'I am particularly disappointed in Lord Vader. You might say I find his lack of faith disturbing.'

He added: 'It will come as no surprise that Jabba the Hut is a fairly typical Presbyterian, while we strongly suspect that Lando Calrissian is, at best, an Episcopalian.

Lord Vader finds communion awkward due to his unwieldy helmet.

'Thankfully there is hope. Luke and Princess Leia have recently been confirmed, while Han Solo has the makings of a first-class Jesuit.'

MPs banned from paying their children to live in Fulham

Mr Speaker usually hands out the money on Friday afternoons.

MPs are to be banned from paying their children £40,000 a year to live in Fulham under new parliamentary regulations.

Most MPs currently maintain one or two sons and a daughter in a large flat in the area to conduct research into developments in the strategically important London borough.

Conservative MP Tom Logan said: 'My son Zak has spent a lot of time researching the introduction of the smoking ban at the White Horse in Parson's Green. It seems to be going well but they do have a large beer garden.

'He's also keeping an eye on the local economy, and as soon as house prices come down I'm going to buy another flat there with my housing allowance. I made an absolute killing on the last one so I'd be stupid not to.

'It really is a lovely place to live, and whenever Tom and his chums want to pop into the Commons for a few subsidised drinks, it's just 20 minutes on the District Line.'

Labour MP Henry Brubaker said it was vital he maintained at least one child in Fulham to keep a watchful eye on his class enemies.

He said: 'I might represent a dirty, northern constituency but there is no need for my children to have to live there and run the risk of getting fat or pregnant.'

Under the new rules MPs' sons and daughters will have to live in south-east London, somewhere between the Elephant and Castle and Peckham.

Although they will no longer be on a wage from their parents, they will be allowed to sell cannabis and reconditioned handguns.

🔍 IN FOCUS: Parliament, the world's longest trough

THE Houses of Parliament, situated magnificently on the banks of the River Thames, was paid for after the Duke of Wellington submitted an expenses claim for £28 million in 1833. Since then the Commons has maintained the finest traditions in the claiming of expenses and is recognised as a model for parliamentary expenses claims around the world. The

KEY FACT: MPs are allowed to come into your house and take whatever they want from the fridge.

Westminster parliament is the beating heart of Britain's democracy and so, every four or five years, each MP tots up the total expenses they have claimed and then decides whether it would be worth their while standing for re-election. It is rare that an MP decides not to seek another term as the position generally involves drinking excellent French wine and getting things comprehensively wrong, safe in the knowledge that most potential voters are currently struggling with the *Daily Express* 'QuizWord'.

CUTTING-EDGE SCIENTISTS CONDEMNED TO EIGHTH CIRCLE OF HELL

SCIENTISTS engaged in cutting-edge, bio-genetic research will be condemned to the eighth circle of Hell, surrounded for all time by panderers and seducers, the Vatican has announced.

Setting out a new list of deadly sins, the Church warned that those involved in unlocking the structural nature of the human genome will be scourged by horned demons and be forced to eat fire for at least the first half of all eternity.

The new rules, developed by the Supreme Tribunal of the Apostolic Penitentiary, the Vatican's modernising wing, include:

Third Circle
People who manufacture or consume synthesised drugs, such as ecstasy and metamphetamine will endure a constant, heavy rain and be terrorised by Cerberus, the three-headed dog.

Fourth Circle
People who make large sums of money through a series of complex trades on the international futures exchange will be condemned to the Fourth Circle, where they will push large rocks around until the end of time while being taunted by crows.

Eighth Circle
Scientists who conduct stem-cell research using state-of-the-art electron microscopy will be condemned to the Second Ditch of the Eighth Circle, where they will wallow in pools of their own excrement. Meanwhile astrophysicists will be forced to spend eternity watching *Deep Impact* starring Téa Leoni.

Ninth Circle
Those who drive their hybrid cars using the petrol engine, instead of the electric motor, more than 50 per cent of the time will be cast into the First Ring of the Ninth Circle, where they will suffer alongside Traitors to Kin and have their heads frozen in blocks of ice.

Consumers to link oil company profits and petrol prices any day now

OIL company executives were last night heading to undisclosed locations amid speculation that consumers were about to make the link between high petrol prices and corporate profits.

As Shell and BP both reported a sharp increase in first-quarter earnings, industry experts said drivers who are currently sitting in a queue outside a petrol station in Scotland waiting to pay £1.25 a litre would soon work out the connection.

Tom Logan, an analyst at Donnelly-McPartlin, said: 'At that point they will get out of their car, calmly dust themselves down and then commit every fibre of their being to hunting down oil company bosses and

'Son of a BITCH!'

killing them like rabid dogs.

'They will develop a faraway look in their eyes, wear camouflage clothing and sit around campfires at night, sharpening

their machetes and describing all the ways they are going to inflict pain on the finance director of Texaco.

'There will also be those who want to hang them up by the feet until the last remaining pennies fall out of their pockets and then beat them to death like one of those Mexican donkey things full of sweets.'

Many oil executives have put in place contingency plans including false beards, wide, floppy hats and unusual foreign accents.

Logan added: 'The executives may think they are safe inside their volcano fortresses, but I suspect they have not had to deal with a Scotsman who wants his money back.'

Al-Qaeda fury over Botham knighthood

OSAMA Bin Laden's deputy has condemned the award of a knighthood to Shredded Wheat legend Sir Ian Botham.

In a 20-minute audiotape, Ayman al-Zawahiri threatened to retaliate against Britain for honouring the former England cricket captain.

Zawahiri said: 'I say to the infidel that by honouring this man you repeat the insults of Colin Cowdrey and Vivian Richards.'

The Al-Qaeda mastermind claimed that Botham's pair of

centuries against Pakistan in the 1978 test series was an 'affront to Islam'.

Zawahiri added: 'First, he defiled our brave Islamic warriors

at Edgbaston and then two weeks later he brought shame on his family with a series of depraved boundary strokes at Lords.'

He also condemned Botham's charity exploits, claiming that walking from one end of a country to the other was 'un-Islamic'.

The government dismissed Zawahiri's comments and stressed that Botham's honour was in recognition of his services to Shredded Wheat and Bite-Size Shredded Wheat.

Caravan Club celebrates one millionth traffic jam

THE Caravan Club yesterday celebrated causing its one millionth traffic jam of this year's holiday season, beating its own previous record by a full two weeks.

Club members David and Enid Jackers created an 18-mile tailback on the A82 between Tarbert and Crianlarich before 10 a.m. by driving along the narrow road at four-and-a-half miles an hour using a Morris Minor to pull their 26-foot, six-berth Elddis Crusader Super Storm.

The Jackers said they were 'surprised and amazed' to have caused such a memorable jam when they were stopped and told of their achievement by jubilant Caravan Club officials just outside Tyndrum.

What a pair of bastards.

Mrs Jackers said: 'We were totally shocked to learn about the huge traffic jam on the A82, the roads around here just seemed so quiet and peaceful to us as we pottered along, we hardly saw any cars at all.

'We thought that it must have had something to do with the value of the pound keeping all the foreign tourists away.

'Instead it turns out that it was just us and our little holiday home on wheels causing a minor inconvenience to a handful of our fellow motorists.'

The Caravan Club was set up 100 years ago this week with the express aim of creating misery and delays on the roads of Britain.

Robert Preston, 43, a photocopier salesmen from Clydebank who was four hours late for an appointment in Oban thanks to the Jackers, said: 'Kill them, kill them all.'

Your PowerPoint presentation was an embarrassing piece of shit

THIS may seem like an obvious question at this particular moment but I have to ask it: What were you thinking? I mean, what in the name of Christ was going through your mind?

Don't get me wrong, it started off reasonably well. You were obviously trying to develop a theme, there was even a joke, albeit a weak one, to ease the tension after that fairly unpleasant team meeting.

But seriously, what were you thinking? After a mediocre, but ultimately acceptable introduction, you just went to hell.

At no point beyond the first three minutes did the images match the text. The graph you used was 15 years out of date and had absolutely nothing to do

with the business we work in. It was as if you had gone through a time-warp and found yourself in the boardroom of a completely different company.

And what possessed you to include a photograph of Jason Donovan? Did you honestly think that was going to be funny? The finance director's eldest son was the spitting image of Jason Donovan until he was stood on by a cow. Every time he sees you he's going to think about his son, under a cow. You don't get over something like that.

As for your 'animated' sequence, a half-wit child with a broken arm could have done a better job. If we were to show that to anyone outside this office they'd think we were a bunch of complete fucknuts.

Thank Christ you showed this to the directors before they let you loose on any of the clients.

You're fucked, by the way. You are sooooo fucked.

In Agony with PETULA SOUL

Do you have a problem you'd like Petula to help with?
e: petula@thedailymash.co.uk

Dear Petula,
Is there anything I can do about the size of my penis? I'm 26 and my bum tickler is only six inches long when fully erect. I've tried pills in the past but they did not work. I've also tried hanging lead weights off it, but while this does provide me with an odd pleasurable sensation it has not done anything to increase the size of my beaver cleaver. I'm really embarrassed about this and it's stopped me having sex for years now, even with myself. Please help.

Long John,
Silverlink

Petula says:

Dear John,
A lot of guys these days worry about the size of their penises, and with good reason. In the old days women tended to keep pretty quiet about hugely disappointing sexual encounters with men with tiddlers, often telling only ten or 20 of their closest friends that last night's shag should be avoided as he was a premature-ejaculating matchstick man. However, thanks to the internet such information can be spread much more rapidly among the sisterhood through the many love-lance-comparison websites that have recently sprung up, including my own favourite

www.are-you-in-yet?.com, which contains comprehensive size and performance listings for most men in Britain. Checking your last entry, if you could call it that, it would appear your voluntary abstinence is no great loss to womankind. According to Tracey Onions back in 2001 it was closer to four-and-a-half and she had hardly unwrapped her chips before you were finished and off out the alleyway. Have you got one of those special men-rulers, or do you think the penis starts just above the knee for measuring purposes, like most blokes?

Psychic Bob's Week Ahead What does the future hold for you?

Taurus (20 APR – 20 MAY)
Give some love away today, it'll make you feel sunny and positive. But don't forget to charge again tomorrow. Shoes don't grow on trees!

Gemini (21 MAY – 20 JUN)
If reputation is your top concern, revise your list. Everyone thinks you're a slut.

Cancer (21 JUN – 22 JUL)
Your compassion makes you get upset over something that doesn't matter. Reverse over the cat just to make sure.

Leo (23 JUL – 22 AUG)
You're feeling good about where you are, but want to explore further. Ask first; the 'oops, I slipped' line fools no one.

Virgo (23 AUG – 22 SEP)
Today is perfect for travel – or for staying at home.

Libra (23 SEP – 23 OCT)
Think about the one positive step you can take to improve your health. How about a chocolate orange?

Scorpio (24 OCT – 21 NOV)
If you like what someone is doing to you, show them how much. Leave a tip, even if it is your wife.

Sagittarius (22 NOV – 21 DEC)
Pay close attention; it's your turn to drive the minibus. I know you survived last time, but not everyone can swim!

Capricorn (22 DEC – 19 JAN)
Romantic energy is coursing through you. Get close to the right person and rub yourself against them until you go pop!

Aquarius (20 JAN – 19 FEB)
Expose yourself to beauty. But don't try hiding in the the ladies' toilets again. They're on to you.

Pisces (20 FEB – 20 MAR)
A family member blows up for no reason. Get a bucket and some cloths.

Aries (21 MAR – 19 APR)
Your brain is hungry for new stimulation – try harder drugs.

SHARP RISE IN NUMBERS TALKING ABSOLUTE ARSE

THE number of people talking arse has risen for the tenth year in a row and is now at its highest since records began.

More than 62 per cent of the population now know someone who knows someone whose house burned down because their plug-in air-freshener caught fire in the night.

Around 58 per cent have a friend who has a friend who received a cheque for $24,800 from Bill Gates after forwarding an e-mail to everyone they knew to help test a new Microsoft product.

Wayne Hayes, 32, said: 'I had a mate whose best mate was charging his mobile when it rang. He put it up to his ear and got a massive shock right in his brain. Died on the spot.

62 per cent claim to have read a fascinating book about 'how buildings really collapse'.

'Another guy I know worked with a chap who had to have one of his testicles off because he kept his phone in his pocket all the time. I wrap mine in foil.'

Nikki Hollis, 26, said: 'I have a girlfriend whose husband works in demolition and he says there is no way a skyscraper would ever collapse straight down like that, even if it was hit by a plane.'

Bill McKay, 45, said: 'My daughter's friend had hired a hotel for her wedding and the guy who ran it asked them if they'd shift the date for ten grand because someone else wanted it.

'They said no, and then the guy said he'd pay off their mortgage if they'd just move it back a week. When the cheque arrived, it was signed by David Beckham. I've seen it.'

---

news

MY BALLS ARE SO HUGE, CLAIMS PAXMAN

news

GAP WIDENS BETWEEN RICH AND INCREDIBLY RICH

Millionaires give each other awards for dressing up

IT is the biggest, most glamorous night of the year. It is the night when millionaires give each other awards for dressing up and pretending to be someone else.

The night belonged to the Coen Brothers, Bert and Arthur, who shared the award for Best Person at Showing Other People How to Dress Up.

They were also named as Best People at Writing Instructions for How to Dress Up, as well as the night's big prize of Best Pretend Thing.

Daniel Day-Lewis, who won the award for Best Man at Dressing Up, said: 'I feel privileged, humbled and unworthy to be in the company of some of the best men who have ever dressed up and pretended to be someone else.'

He added: 'This means so much to me because every time I dress up and pretend to be someone else, I try to do it really well.'

Other British victories included Best Costumes for Dressing Up In, as well as a special award for Tilda Swinton, Europe's tallest woman.

It was a good night for international millionaires, with the award for Best Woman at Dressing Up going to a French person who won critical acclaim for pretending to be another French person.

Meanwhile a Spaniard won an

'I want to share this with all those millionaires who have the courage to dress up.'

award for having a psychotic haircut.

Jamie Oliver chicken recipe wins Bad Sex Award

JAMIE Oliver's recipe for free-range chicken roasted with garlic and chestnuts has won this year's Bad Sex book award.

Now in its 14th year, the prize is awarded by the *Literary Review* to highlight the difficulties of writing about quivering members, supple thighs and endless spasms of forbidden pleasure.

The TV chef triumphed over Norman Mailer's *Two Old Homosexuals*, Ali Smith's *Girl Meets Horse* and Nigella Lawson's *Summertime Sausage Party*.

According to the judges Oliver's recipe displayed an 'alarming indifference to the complexity of human sexuality' and a 'profound misunderstanding of what it means to be a chicken'.

Here is Oliver's award-winning bad sex passage:

Get hold of a nice, plump free-range chicken. I get mine from Sainsbury's but why not try your local butcher or a farmers' market?

Rub it all over with olive oil, garlic and salt. Roughly chop some fresh sage and thyme and rub that in there too. Great fun.

Batter your chestnuts in a tea towel and then mix them with the rest of the garlic, a squeeze of lemon juice, a pinch of salt and a dash – no more – of Worcestershire sauce.

Grab a large handful of this mixture and push it right up inside the cavity of the bird. Then cook at 190C, gas mark 6, for about an hour and a half.

Take the bird out of the oven and let it rest for about 15 minutes. Then – and only then – can you safely insert your penis.

Ireland begins search for new Chief Leprechaun

IRELAND'S leprechaun-catchers were grabbing their nets and pulling on their boots last night as the country began its search for a new leader.

Declan O'Docherty, chief leprechaun since 2002, announced he would be standing down to spend more time at the end of his favourite rainbow in County Meath.

Leading leprechaun-catcher, Sheamus O'Flaherty, said the new leader must have a 'bee-ootiful singin' voice and special magic dust that makes the dew sparkle and dance on a sunny Spring morning'.

O'Flaherty added: 'I'll be lookin' under toadstools and inside old tree stumps, so I will.

Then I'll clap my hands together and do a little jig.

'And if he's too shy to come out and say hello, I'll leave him a little bit of boiled beef. Oh, they can't resist it!'

Mickey O'Reardon, a leprechaun-hunter in the County of Cork, said: 'There's a special cupboard at the back of O'Reilly's pub in the town of Skibereen where, if you whistle a jaunty tune on a moonlit night in May, the little people come out and loan ye a bit o' their magic.

'But use it wisely, mind. They won't forgive you if you waste it on horses and stout and suchlike.'

O'Reardon added: 'Of course,

Finnan O'Muckerty is the bookies' favourite.

the thing ye have to remember most of all when huntin' for a new chief leprechaun is that they love bribes. Great, big, fat bribes.'

Lesbians to establish Republic of Lesbia

THE world's 800 million lesbians are to club together and set up their own country.

They are currently scouting locations in Europe and South America where they hope to establish the People's Republic of Lesbia.

The move follows legal action by the Greek island of Lesbos who claim only their lesbians should be allowed to call themselves Lesbians, and not because they are lesbians, but because they are Lesbians.

A spokesman for Jodie Foster, the reigning Grand High Lesbian, said: 'Lesbia is going to be a really lovely place.

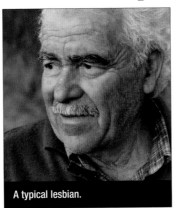

A typical lesbian.

'There will be no need for clothes, and if two girls want to get into a big bath of custard in

the middle of the town square and have a bit of a tumble then that's cool.

'Apart from that it will be a daily routine of pillow fights, communal showers and rubbing oil into each other's buttocks.'

Dimitri Kiriakos, the governor of Lesbos, said: 'How can they be Lesbian? I Lesbian, my wife Lesbian, both my sons Lesbian and my cat Lesbian. Even Vince, the local lesbian, is Lesbian.'

The International Council of Lesbians decided not to fight the latest legal challenge after their expensive and unsuccessful battle with *Mary Poppins* star Dick Van Dyke.

82 per cent wish they were pretending to be dead

THE number of people in Britain who wish they were pretending to be dead has risen for the fifth month in a row.

Researchers say the latest increase is down to the cold weather, a further tightening of the credit squeeze and the school-boy errors made by suspected canoeist John Darwin.

Dr Tom Logan, a leading fake-death consultant, said: 'People looked at Darwin and thought, "You've got it made, why the hell are you walking into a bloody police station?"'

Dr Logan said the public had woken up to the advantages of pretending to be dead. 'The first thing you notice is a steep drop off in telephone calls.

'Your line manager doesn't noise you up about why you didn't come in today and the threatening emails about the steady decline in the quality of your work tend to dry up fairly quickly.

'Better still, you don't have to

Dead people receive relatively few text messages, according to Vodafone.

have an internet phone, a Facebook page or care about who's made it to the next round of *Let Me Through, I'm a Celebrity Paramedic.*'

He added: 'My clients tell me one of the most enjoyable things about pretending to be dead is covering yourself with fake blood and then pressing your face against living room windows of people you don't like.

'Or you could wait until one of your enemies comes out of his office and stand on the other side of the road just staring and pointing at him.'

But Dr Logan stressed there were a few golden rules to ensure a long and successful fake death.

'Planning is everything. Make sure you have a place to live, a source of food and no matter how tempting it may seem at the time, do not have your photograph taken for a Panamanian website.'

Worthless Opinion Poll
How are you expressing your perversions?

Keeping a photo of Ned Sherrin in my underpants	14%
Watching children's television	16.8%
Training for the priesthood	31.6%
Arranging my breakfast into a pair of breasts	37.7%

NEWS BRIEFLY

BBC RESPONDS TO HUGE DEMAND FOR PIECE-OF-SHIT AUSTRALIAN SOAP-OPERA
'I liked *The Neighbours*, make it come on my telly again,' says licence-payer.

CAMERON SHOOTS TOASTER
'He stood over the toaster and called it a "planet-killing son-of-a-bitch" before emptying both barrels,' says neighbour.

MINISTERS HAIL SUCCESS OF 24-HOUR VIOLENCE LAWS
'This is what continental Europe would be like if it was horribly violent all the time,' says Home Office spokesman.

BBC LAUNCHES NEW SERIES OF 'LOCKED IN A PORTACABIN WITH 14 ANNOYING BASTARDS'
'If one or two of them turn out to be sexist or racist that would be just marvellous,' says BBC controller.

PRINCE WILLIAM TO ASK RAF AND NAVY WHAT THEY DO
Prince will tour nation's military facilities after asking waiting staff of Klosters what they do.

CONSUMERS VOW TO REMAIN OBLIVIOUS TO MUSIC COPYING LAWS
'D'you know what? I don't fucking care,' said Nikki Hollis, 16.

FIRMS NOT ALLOWED TO ASK WHY YOUR CV IS FILLED WITH LIES
Employment rate would drop to zero if workers are forced to tell the truth on resumés.

At home with Boy George

HE is one of the biggest stars of his generation, known for his acid wit and his flamboyant sense of style. Boy George – icon, artist, enigma – gives the *Daily Mash* a privileged peek inside his luxurious London home …

GEORGE greets us dressed in a silk kimono. His make-up is freshly applied and he sips from a cup of sage and jasmine tea. He is gracious and warm as he guides us through his exquisitely appointed hallway. We are intrigued by the intricate leatherwork that adorns the walls and the masterful watercolours which express George's passion for ancient Greek heroes having acrobatic sexual intercourse.

As we move into the drawing room, a mixture of 1930s' Coco Chanel Paris with a smattering of boho chic, we notice the beautiful, tiny mirrors placed on the coffee table and the lingering scent of what can only be described as Grade-A skunk.

George sinks into a sumptuous, pink leather armchair that, in just the right light, looks remarkably like a giant scrotum.

He talks excitedly about his triumphant return to London and his fascinating new projects, before throwing a custard cream to the naked dwarf chained to the radiator. The dwarf glances up with a look that says, 'Phone the police immediately.' He has the aroma of freshly pressed olive oil.

George's kitchen is sleek and efficient. Naked dwarves are preparing a brunch of roasted butternut squash and blanched spinach. In the corner another naked dwarf is peeling garlic while chained to a radiator. The stainless steel worktops are spotless and dazzling.

George's inner sanctum, his boudoir – his bedroom – is a riot of colour. We sense that the theme is male genitalia. The bed

'His make-up is freshly applied and he sips from a cup of sage and jasmine tea'

seems narrow until it expands into two symmetrical round sections at the top. 'It looks like a great big cock,' we say to George, and he smiles and nods.

Negotiating our way around the naked dwarf who is strapped to the bedroom door, we move back into the hallway and our brief but scintillating odyssey through the life of George is complete.

He thanks us graciously as we pass back into the Georgeless streets and with a final wave he seems to say, 'Give me an hour before you contact the authorities.'

He is, simply, George. A national treasure.

Hedge funds now most important thing people know nothing about

HEDGE funds have overtaken the Big Bang as the most important thing people know nothing about.

As a massive American hedge fund faces imminent collapse, millions of people across the globe have found themselves panicking without the faintest idea why.

Tom Logan, head of markets at Donnelly-McPartlin, said: 'This fund was over-speculated in long-term, prime-reverse wide-money.

'It could be devastating or it could be utterly insignificant. Would you like to buy a Range Rover?'

Wayne Hayes, 42, from Chelmsford, said: 'I was saying to Geoff, I said, "Geoff mate, this is the big one." And he's, like, "Why?," and I'm like, "If you don't know, there's no point in me trying to explain it you."'

Meanwhile Nikki Hollis, 33,

Many people have no idea how to read the *Economist*.

from Doncaster said: 'It couldn't have been very strong. Did they get it from Homebase? I hope they managed to get all the little birds' nests out.'

Professor Henry Brubaker, of the Institute for Studies, said the confusion over hedge funds had arisen because many ordinary people were buying the *Economist*, but then reading it upside down.

He added: 'Essentially, hedge funds are used to buy commodities like rice, jam, stock cubes and the like.

'When the stock cubes reach the agreed "hedging" level the shares are transformed into something called "double-bonded, hard-edged gilts" which then take on one-and-a-half times their initial value for a period of around six weeks.

'After six weeks the buyer, or "goose", can then hand them back or sell them "up the chain".

'If, at that point, the value falls, you become a homeless crack addict.'

England to be excused from sports

ENGLAND has asked to be excused from sports for the rest of the year after producing a note from its mum.

Senior teachers are still assessing whether the note is genuine, but it seems likely the country will be allowed to use Wednesday and Friday afternoons for study time.

The note reads: 'Dear teacher, My England should not have to do sports no more cause it's got an infected toe and a swollen wrist.

'The doctor says it needs to stop doing PE and be allowed to sit in the corner with its hand down its pants.'

Meanwhile classmates of the slow, awkward country welcomed the decision, stressing that having England on your team was worse than having to play with a girl.

Wales said: 'England used to be quite good at sport but now it's all fat and speccy and useless.

'It just stands there in its vest and its crap trainers, looking like a twat.'

Wales added: 'You know it's time to pack it in when Scotland gets picked before you do.'

But Mr Hobbs, the PE teacher,

England has rubbish trainers.

said this was typical of England, adding: 'You horrid little turd.

'Strip down to your fatboy undies and climb those wall bars before you get my toe up your arse.'

ONE WOMAN'S WEEK: Keeping the Faith
by KAREN FENESSEY

I AM one of those people who genuinely believes that interracial marriage is okay. That's why I was utterly horrified to be brutally ejected from a Jew-Protestant unification ceremony (or 'wedding') on the grounds that I was an 'anti-Semite'. Anyone who knows me understands that I have absolutely no problem with the Jews and have stated time and time again that I forgive them for all those bits in the Holy Bible where they killed Jesus.

The ceremony was between my boyfriend Donny's sister and her partner, Sam (a Jew). Sam and Janet offered to put us up at their house in Wales. My first act of clemency was to agree to this arduous journey because I'd assumed all weddings took place in the birth town of the bride. But, as ever, I am open to the bizarre customs of foreigners because I am a libertarian.

At their house, Janet revealed that she had 'converted' to Judaism. I was shocked. I am a Catholic and, while I'm not thrilled about Donny's protestant lineage, I make the sacrifice because that's what being a Catholic is all about. I take the sacrament very seriously and this is probably why Donny has never raised the topic of marriage with me. I don't go to church every week, but that's because God understands how pure I am and doesn't need the Sunday morning hard graft that He must demand of others. At family events I am always enraged by my fat sister who attempts to take commun-

ion even though she never goes to church and has faith in nothing except KFC. I always have to pull her out of the queue for the Body of Christ and, rolling my eyes, say a quick prayer of apology to the Lord for her ignorance.

I was able to keep my opinions to myself until after the 'wedding' was over and the groom's family were singing in

> 'Do you see me having a birthday party in Latin, or a house-warming in Aramaic?'

their outlandish lingo and doing stupid dances. Janet announced to us how proud she was to be a 'Jewess'. I couldn't contain my rage any longer: 'Oh, get a grip! Not only are you alienating all of your Christian guests by conducting your ceremony in a ridiculous dead language which no one even speaks, but now you are making up English words too! Do you see me having a birthday party in Latin, or a house-warming in Aramaic (the language of the Son of God and of Mel Gibson)? Do I call myself a 'Catholina'? Or are the immigrant kids 'muslimettes'?

Janet started a confrontation by yelling back that Hebrew was still spoken by thousands of people in Israel, that she was a Jewess and that I was being ungrateful for their hospitality. 'I never asked to stay in your dusty, old house!' I yelled back, because

I am a woman who always speaks her mind and if people and Jews don't like that, they can just go to hell (and no doubt will). 'There weren't even any cushions on the beds!' I continued. 'Get with the fucking programme!' (My bed has a total of nine cushions on it, which I bought from Habitat. Donny always moans that they just end up on the floor so there's no point in having them. He and his uncultured protestant family just don't get it!) Then, Sam's mother had one of her awful nephews manhandle Donny and me out of the venue. 'Shylock!' I screamed at him. He denounced me as anti-Semitic, but I knew in my soul that I had done God's will, so I was able to rise above his bullying.

While I am open-minded enough to see that these actions aren't representative of all Jews, I feel that I finally understand what it must have been like for Christ Himself when he was hanging off the cross by rusty nails, and I'm sure Sam and Janet will think twice about their actions when they don't see a fig from us this Christmas.

Worthless Opinion Poll
Why are you being bugged?

Freezer full of heads	12.5%
Keep blowing things up	16.9%
Ninja dwarf army in shed	30.6%
I be a pirate, Jim Lad	39.9%

In Agony with PETULA SOUL

Do you have a problem you'd like Petula to help with?
e: petula@thedailymash.co.uk

Dear Petula,
I ended up in bed with this bloke after meeting him on the internet. I am in my early sixties and got talking to him in one of those chatrooms pensioners use when looking for anonymous sex. I met up with him and frankly he was a bit disappointing in the looks department, but I did not want to waste the £1.20 I had spent on my train fare, so I shagged him anyway. I am a pensioner after all. It all went well until the moment came for him to chuck his muck when he shouted out, 'Shoot it, Archie, shoot it,' at the top of his voice, and then 'GOOOOAAAAALLLLL,' immediately afterwards. He then went and told all the blokes down the over-sixties lunch club he had boffed me, and wrote in the loos that I gave good head. Is this normal behaviour for a 60-year-old?

Wrinkled,
Shettleston

Petula says:

Dear Wrinkled,
I am afraid your superannuated sex god is suffering from a widespread condition among men that we sex therapists call 'immature ejaculation'. Most teenage boys will display some, or all, of the above behaviours after jetting out their love juice. It obviously does something to their heads. However, by the time they reach their mid-forties, about half of blokes will have matured enough to realise it is quite inappropriate to be so indiscreet about their goings and comings. The other half will be divorced already after having been caught out so they won't care. Try listening to my premium-rate phone line 'Dealing with immature ejaculators'. If that does not help, just tell his wife. It won't repair the damage to your reputation, but he will get a boot in the knackers from his missus, and the crotch cut out of all his Farah slacks.

Psychic Bob's Week Ahead What does the future hold for you?

Taurus (20 APR – 20 MAY)
Moving from where you are to where you want to be in life is hard since the double amputation. But just think what you are saving on shoes!

Gemini (21 MAY – 20 JUN)
Cash flow issues are on your mind and that could mean it's time for a re-evaluation of your budget, or just that you need to move into prostitution full-time now.

Cancer (21 JUN – 22 JUL)
You are so sure of yourself right now that you can't be bothered to listen to other points of view. So why are you reading this, you tosser?

Leo (23 JUL – 22 AUG)
You're experiencing some deep feelings right now, but it's not clear where they are coming from. Try looking over your shoulder. Recognise that face? Thought not.

Virgo (23 AUG – 22 SEP)
People are looking to you for the enthusiasm and energy that they themselves lack right now. Tell them to fuck off. You're knackered.

Libra (23 SEP – 23 OCT)
Love is on your mind right now – and it shouldn't be too hard to bring it to life. The new range of washable latex vaginas feel so real it's untrue. But you know that already!

Scorpio (24 OCT – 21 NOV)
Someone's confidence is too close to arrogance for anyone to take them seriously. Unfortunately, it's you.

Sagittarius (22 NOV – 21 DEC)
Today might bring a brief foray into depression, maybe for no good reason at all, or maybe because your life is shit and only ever going to get worse. Probably the latter.

Capricorn (22 DEC – 19 JAN)
Your quiet charisma is being noticed at last and you should find it easy to draw people to you, either for romance or friendship. Only kidding! Get back in your corner and shut up.

Aquarius (20 JAN – 19 FEB)
It's a good time to liven up work with a little fun. Do a shit in a waste paper bin and then place it next to a colleague's desk when they're eating lunch. Then set fire to it.

Pisces (20 FEB – 20 MAR)
There's a lot of really important stuff going on under the surface right now that's very hard for you to understand. Maybe you should have tried harder in school, you stupid bastard.

Aries (21 MAR – 19 APR)
You're feeling the urge to push yourself, and it's not easy. Try going to the bridge with a friend and asking them to give you a shove. I'm sure they'll be happy to help!

the daily mash

it's news to us   www.thedailymash.co.uk   No. 7

BIG RISE IN WOMEN GETTING ABOVE THEMSELVES

THE number of women getting above themselves has risen from 'all right love, keep you hair on' to 'God, is it that time of the month already?', a new study reveals.

According to the research the amount of humourless ballbreakers in charge of departments, or even whole companies, rose from 3.2 per cent last year to an astonishing 3.3 per cent in 2008.

Professor Henry Brubaker, of the Institute for Studies, said this meant record numbers of women were now being totally unreasonable at work after some harmless banter or minor misunderstanding.

He added: 'I arrived late at a seminar the other day and asked the nice wee lassie taking notes if she wouldn't mind getting me a glass of water and a couple of bourbons.

'Turned out she was chairing the meeting. She went fucking nuts.'

Bill McKay, 56, said: 'I was flying off to Tenerife last year when the pilot comes on the tannoy to tell us about the headwinds and stuff, and it's only a bloody woman, isn't it.

'I said to the stewardess, "I hope we don't have to reverse into any parking spaces at the other end." She thought I was bloody hilarious.'

Wayne Hayes, chief analyst at stockbrokers Donnelly-McPartlin, added: 'We just took on this maths PhD from Cambridge, not a bad looker, but when we took her out to the Spearmint Rhino for a bit of team-building she just sat stony-faced all night.

'Hi, I'm Susan and I'm having my period.'

'When we told her we'd like her to sleep with one of the clients, who was bloody rich anyway, she slapped us with a lawsuit. Lesbo.'

news

45% WILL VOTE FOR LAST PERSON THEY SAW ON TV

news

THATCHER WANDERS INTO NO. 10 BROOM CUPBOARD

Them foreigners is a right bunch, say angry old men

THEM foreigners who come over here, taking our jobs and sticking their knobs in our lovely young poppets is ruining Britain, according to a major report by a committee of old men.

The old men said all this immigration was terrible and that you couldn't get a seat on the bus because it's full of Bulgarian fruit-pickers.

Committee member Lord Wakeham said: 'I remember when you could go to the pictures and see a nice film starring Kenneth More and that lovely Jean Simmonds. There was a proper lady. Now it's all "bang, bang, bang". And the music? Cor, what a racket.'

Lord Lamont said: 'I had one of them Polish fellas round my house. I says, "Oi, Ivan can't you speak no English, eh? Can't even say please or thank you?"

'It's a disgrace is what it is. Lucky for him he did such a magnificent job on my downstairs loo or he'd have got my old boot up his thievin' backside.'

Lord McGregor added: 'I told my grandson he should get himself a job pickin' fruit. "Put some money in your pocket," I says, "Take that nice young girl of yours to the seaside for the day."

'He says to me, "Grandad, I'd rather go on the dole than pick stinkin' old fruit." I says to him, "If you don't, it'll be all them

Dirty Bulgarian things.

Bulgars pickin' that fruit and takin' your girl to the seaside and doin' dirty Bulgarian things to her up the back of the Co-op.'"

Home Office Minister Liam Byrne said: 'Whenever I want intelligent, rational advice on the issue of immigration the first thing I do is talk to some angry old men.'

Middle-aged man mowing lawn nominated for Turner Prize

A middle-aged man has admitted he was surprised to be nominated for the biggest prize in art, stressing he really was just mowing his lawn.

Roy Hobbs, an assistant bank manager from Gloucester, said he was taking advantage of the good weather to cut the grass, put in some new bedding plants and do a bit of weeding.

He added: 'So it came as something of a surprise when a couple of days later a chap appeared on the doorstep saying he was from the Turner Prize committee and that I had been shortlisted.

'It turns out I encapsulate not only the cultural clash between

Islam and the West, but I'm also an iconic representation of the inherent contradictions of globalisation.

'I said to him, "That's very nice of you, but I really was just cutting the grass."

'He kept telling me I was "terribly daring", and I said I didn't think so because I had checked the forecast and if there had been even a hint of rain I'd have been straight back inside with a cup of tea and an episode of *Midsomer Murders*.'

Mr Hobbs will face stiff competition this year from a teapot on a plinth, a very long radiator, a *Felix the Cat* video and a mannequin on the toilet.

Mr Hobbs said his Flymo LC400 has been excellent value for money.

He added: 'My wife and I are very much looking forward to the trip up to London. She thinks the teapot is a shoo-in, but I have to say, I just love the mannequin having a shit.'

Royals blackmailed over 'deformed prince under the stairs'

THE Royal Family is being blackmailed over claims they have been keeping a deformed prince in a cupboard under the stairs.

Weekend newspaper reports suggested that the Queen and Prince Philip imprisoned the hideously ugly child more than 30 years ago and have been feeding him twice a day on stale Cornish pasties and cans of Irn Bru.

Late last week two men were arrested in connection with the alleged plot amid speculation they held secret video footage of the Buckingham Palace troll being walked on a chain.

The Palace last night denied the allegations but stressed that if a member of the Royal Family was locked in the boot cupboard under the footmen's rear staircase, the public could rest assured it was not one of the important ones.

A Palace insider said: 'Over the years we've heard violent screams and torrents of unspeakable profanity, but we just assumed it was Prince Philip watching a documentary about immigration.

'A few years ago there were whispers about a child who was so hideous he was banned from appearing in public, but then we saw Prince Edward on *It's a Knockout*.'

It is the latest blackmail scandal to hit the House of Windsor. Last year Prince Charles was forced to deny allegations that he rides his wife around the drawing room like a seaside donkey.

Meanwhile the Royal Family is to commission its own version of

Is this a rare sighting of the royal troll?

the famed Terracotta Army of the first Chinese emperor Qin Shi Huangdi.

The Windsors' army will number more than 2,000 figures including a terracotta car-crash organiser, a terracotta drug-dealer and a terracotta provider of blow-jobs.

Queen did not drug a horse, admits BBC

The BBC has apologised to the Queen for wrongly implying that she drugged a horse during Royal Ascot.

The trailer for a new documentary showed the Queen standing next to a horse while holding a large syringe, followed by a clip of her walking away saying, 'That should do the business.'

A BBC spokesman said: 'Her Majesty did not drug a horse. The actual sequence of events was misrepresented.'

The documentary, *Compared to her we're All Scum*, is the centrepiece of the BBC's autumn line-up.

The Queen and her daughter,

Not drugged by Queen.

the Princess Royal, were filmed touring the stables at Ascot, during which she was shown a typical horse-drugging syringe.

The Queen inspected the piece of equipment, but then handed it back and continued her tour without trying to drug a horse.

As she left the stables the Princess Royal turned to the Queen and said that she was using E45 cream to treat a stubborn rash.

It was then that the Queen replied, 'That should do the business.'

It is the latest in a series of controversies to hit the Royal Family and comes just eight weeks after Prince Philip was fitted with a new set of balls.

UK launches crackdown on foreign wind

THE government has unveiled ambitious plans to end Britain's dependence on foreign wind by 2020.

Ministers believe the British economy could eventually burst as a result of volatile Russian wind prices.

Meanwhile experts have warned that hot, dry winds from the Middle East are now arriving in the UK via Italy and France, by which time they are covered in grease and virtually useless.

Under the £250-billion plan, a 1,000-foot-high Wind Capturing Device will be constructed in the middle of Britain, possibly on the outskirts of Derby or Stoke.

The device will suck wind from the huge reserves just 10 miles above our heads and transform it into a series of high-energy gusts that will be pumped out to sea,

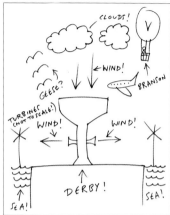

The government's £250-billion plan is based entirely on this pathetic sketch.

feeding Britain's invincible army of coastal turbines.

Energy minister John Hutton said: 'Two years ago a group of experts came to me and said that

Britain was sitting on a windmine. I pointed out that it was actually sitting underneath a windmine – in the sky.'

He added: 'For too long we have sucked on the fast, easy winds that whistle across the Urals. And – in case you hadn't already noticed – Putin is a gigantic bastard.

'As long as he has his finger on the TransEuropean GustFunnel, this country will be at the mercy of corrupt Russian wind magnates.'

The minister also stressed the knock-on benefits of home-grown wind sufficiency.

'Our vast turbine army will send a clear message to migrating geese that they are not welcome here.

'No longer will Britain have to endure the soft, distant honking of unskilled foreign geese scrounging off our cherished wetlands.

🔍 IN FOCUS: Victorian Britain and the invention of steam

Victoria Beckham's steamed face.

KEY FACT: Steam can also be used to remove creases from shirts, trousers and Spice Girls.

DURING the mid-nineteenth century, men of good standing and sound education across the British Isles were obsessed with just one thing: How to burrow to the centre of the Earth.

Between 1832 and 1865 more than 400 people were killed or injured in failed burrowing attempts. The essential problem was how to maintain the momentum of the giant drill bit. For many years Irishmen were used to turn a giant crank wheel, but all would collapse of exhaustion and drink before the contraption had burrowed less than half a mile into the Earth's crust.

But all that changed in 1866 when Norwich schoolteacher Harold Hayes patented his Thermally Vapourised

Moisture Assembly, known today, simply, as 'steam'.

It's the same 'steam' you will find coming from a kettle, or seeping out of that room at the leisure centre that's always full of flamboyant young men.

Within hours of Hayes' invention, giant, steam-powered burrowing machines were rolling off the slipways of Tyneside as brave adventurers and their rich benefactors mounted new expeditions to the very centre of the Earth.

Unfortunately none succeeded as they all soon discovered that when you reach 50 miles underground the temperature rises quickly to around 4,000C, instantly incinerating everyone on board.

Rising sea levels to reach Ronnie Corbett

EXPERTS have upgraded their estimates on rising sea levels, predicting they could submerge Ronnie Corbett within a decade.

The previous worst-case scenario involved seawater lapping around the chin of *Taxi* star Danny DeVito.

Now climate scientists are warning we face the loss of not only DeVito, but Holland, Norfolk and the golf-loving Scottish comedian and his famous chair.

Dr Tom Logan, of the Institute for Sea Level Studies, said: 'The planet is now so damn hot we will almost certainly lose an entire generation of stars under 5' 6".

'Joe Pesci – gone. Dustin Hoffman – gone. That bloke who played the dwarf in *Lord of the Rings* – gone.'

Last year *Close Encounters* star Richard Dreyfuss paid $2 million for a pair of titanium stilts while the Jockey Club has demanded aqualungs for their horses.

Meanwhile the Institute has published a revised sea-level scale, beginning with R2D2 and rising through DeVito, Corbett, Tom Cruise and the average Welshman.

Dr Logan added: 'At this stage we don't foresee any serious problems for Mel Gibson, though his nipples will get thoroughly soaked.'

| 1.4m: DeVito, R2D2, East Anglia | 1.5m: Corbett, Joe Pesci, Holland | 1.55m: Cruise, Hoffman, the Welsh |

Facebook distracting workers from underpaid, soul-destroying tedium, says CBI

SOCIAL networking sites such as Facebook and MySpace are distracting office workers from the hellish, brain-curdling reality that is their shabby, predictable and ultimately meaningless lives, according to a new report from the Confederation of British Industry.

The CBI is concerned that surfing the internet is preventing workers from reaching financial targets that will bring them no measurable benefits, but will swell executive bonuses by up to 220 per cent a year.

They are calling on the government to introduce legislation that will ban workers from thinking about the slightest hint of a possibility that life may not in fact be a relentlessly nauseating sea of shit.

Meryl Blears, a 28-year-old finan-

cial assistant from Swindon, said: 'I like Facebook because it gives me hope that one day I'll have actual conversations with people who don't secretly want to kill themselves.'

Kate Braff, 22, from Bristol, added: 'I like MySpace because I can see photographs of human beings enjoying things like fresh food and pets, rather than staring all day at a spreadsheet filled with my chief executive's brothel expenses.'

Helen Greatbatch, 36, from Bedford, said: 'So far this year my boss has spent about 45 minutes at his desk and that was only because he was ordering a snooker table for his boat.

'On the way out he told me that if I wanted to look at Facebook I

Everything is going to be just fine.

should quit my job, become a drug addict and end up begging for money so that I could buy a cup of coffee in an internet cafe and stand behind someone who was looking at Facebook.

'Then he hit me on the head with his shoe. It's men like him who are keeping the Chinese at bay.'

England players vow to spend their way out of depression

DAVID Beckham is to buy himself a Bugatti Veyron, a diamond-covered horse and the nation of Equatorial Guinea in a bid to ease the pain of England's Euro 2008 failure.

Beckham said the England squad was hurting and confused, to the extent that many could not remember which of their homes they were supposed to go to after the game.

'It was a poor performance. The only explanation I can think of is that maybe we're not paid enough,' he said.

Scott Carson, the rookie goalkeeper blamed for England's shock exit, said it was only the thought of his indoor heated swimming pool, sauna and fitness room

Casa de Gerrard is awash with tears.

which kept him going.

He said: 'If it wasn't for the Fabergé quad bike, the Maserati jetski and the Patek Phillipe sandwich toaster, I think I'd have slit my wrists in my sunken bath and its eight whirlpool massage jets.'

Steven Gerrard said the pain of defeat was so intense he had to be carried from the dressing room to his Aston Martin in a sedan chair.

He said: 'I don't know if buying a third Jacobean mansion and filling it with solid gold eggs will help, but for God's sake I've got to try.'

Rio Ferdinand said he would cheer himself up by paying Paul Gascoigne £1 million to recreate his 1996 wonder goal against Scotland in his back garden 'over and over again'.

Reg Hollis, 53, a lifelong England fan, said he could appreciate that the football stars were hurting but thought they might get over it. 'I'm hurting too,' he said. 'And I'm absolutely fucking skint.'

DIARY: Katie Price

THIS is a very exciting time for myself and Peter. He's writing his life story, which his agent told me is going to be *An Autobiography*. I don't know about you, but I thought that was a well weird name for a book – I mean, what has that got to do with my Pete's life story, hey? Why don't they call it *What I've Done So Far in my Life So Far by Peter Andre, Husband of Katie Price*?

Anyway, things is really exciting at the moment because following on from the success of my fragrance Stunning, I'm going to be launching my own cooking oil. The idea came to me when I was frying Peter's breakfast the other morning. I said to him, 'This cooking oil smells shit – I wish it smelt of something nice like Katie Price's Stunning, instead.' Peter agreed that cooking oil smells shit and so I phoned my agent Lucy, who put the wheels in motion.

I'm in the middle of writing my seventh book. I had a meeting with my publisher bloke today, and I must admit I got the right hump with him. He wanted me to call it *An Autobiography*. 'That's the same title as my Peter's book,' I told him. Publisher bloke may have gone to Cambridge University in Oxford but fuck me, he ain't got a clue. Like my mum said, people who go to university may be intelligent but they're still fucking scum. Besides, I'm the one who's worth £17 million, and he's the one who dresses like my nonce of a geography teacher. I then came up with the really brilliant title, *Katie Price: My Story – Not an Autobiography*. He started huffing and puffing a bit, before agreeing that I was right, and he was wrong. As they said in issue 137 of OK! magazine, 'Katie Price is a Powerful Female Ikeacon'.

I went to a premiere this afternoon. Fucking horrible – the bloke who directed it insisted the celebs sat through the entire film. I wouldn't mind if it was *Pirates of the Penzance III* or that one with the four-eyed kid, but this was sooooooo boring. For a start it was in a foreign language, had subtitles and went on for yonks. I had a right go at some bloke sitting next to me who kept telling me to shut up – 'Hello!' I said, 'Haven't you ever heard anyone read before.' Fucking wally.

NEWS BRIEFLY

DISNEY TO BAN PATIO HEATERS
'"The March of the Patio Heaters" from *Fantasia* was groundbreaking,' says critic of films.

BROWN BACKS 24-HOUR SUPER-MUSEUMS
All fruit-machines to be based on the Great Reform Act of 1832.

NEANDERTHALS ATTACKED FOR FAILING TO INSULATE CAVES
'Profligate in their use of fire,' says Friends of the Earth.

Worthless Opinion Poll
How should the middle-classes get off their tits?

14 bottles of Muscadet	12%
Tinfoil crack pipe	14%
Mashed aspirin and Orangina	28%
Da Bong	46%

In Agony with PETULA SOUL

Dear Petula,
I am a 30-year-old man who has only recently lost his virginity after many years during which I had no success with the ladies. As you can imagine, during this time I became very well acquainted with Rosie Palmer and her five lovely sisters. My new girlfriend is loving, understanding, and incredibly generous in bed. However, something is not quite right. I really miss my own right hand. What should I do?

Fingerless,
Fintry

Petula says:

Dear Fingerless,
It is inevitable that the first love of your teenage years will have made a strong impression on you. But you have to ask yourself: Am I just romanticising my past? All you remember are the good times together with your hand. But do you recall the tantrums and the arguments, and more importantly the terrible scabs and blisters? It's time to grow up and put that stage of your life behind you. Unless, like most men of my acquaintance, you are determined to be a wanker all your life.

Do you have a problem you'd like Petula to help with?
e: petula@thedailymash.co.uk

NEWS BRIEFLY

HUMANS 'NOT EVOLVED ENOUGH' TO KEEP QUIET DURING A FILM
Species made up of babbling imbeciles, bred on diet of puke-flavoured nachos.

BAFTA GLORY FOR 'ALLOTMENT'
'It's a great night for people who grow their own leeks,' says Keira Knightley.

EVERYTHING TO BECOME SMALLER AND MORE EXPENSIVE, SAYS GATES
'People are having smaller experiences and thinking smaller thoughts.'

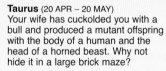

Psychic Bob's Week Ahead What does the future hold for you?

Taurus (20 APR – 20 MAY)
Your wife has cuckolded you with a bull and produced a mutant offspring with the body of a human and the head of a horned beast. Why not hide it in a large brick maze?

Gemini (21 MAY – 20 JUN)
You've got a big heart – bigger than most people realise. But don't let your deformed internal organ prevent you enjoying life. While it lasts.

Cancer (21 JUN – 22 JUL)
Feeling glum? Why not splurge on yourself. Remember to put down the plastic sheeting first.

Leo (23 JUL – 22 AUG)
Somebody you are close to is suffering rough times. Manipulate them into sex and then move on.

Virgo (23 AUG – 22 SEP)
You don't want to know. Seriously.

Libra (23 SEP – 23 OCT)
Mercury is telling you not to take your faulty laptop to the TechGuys at PC World. Remember what happened to Gary Glitter?

Scorpio (24 OCT – 21 NOV)
Your worth is about more than money. That thing you can do with your tongue is priceless.

Sagittarius (22 NOV – 21 DEC)
Your guardian star Venus is looking out for you at work. But if you're in Manchester, watch out because he's useless at spotting trams.

Capricorn (22 DEC – 19 JAN)
You need to stick to your guns today – don't be distracted by all the screaming and begging.

Aquarius (20 JAN – 19 FEB)
Share your troubles with close friends and family. They will be really interested to hear from you. Syphilis is so rare these days.

Pisces (20 FEB – 20 MAR)
Your mate ends up rubbing you the wrong way. Never mind. Just go the toilet and rub it yourself.

Aries (21 MAR – 19 APR)
Someone close tells you that you need to slow down. If you smell burning apply more jelly.

HOUSE PRICE SMACKDOWN

BRICK FOR SALE!

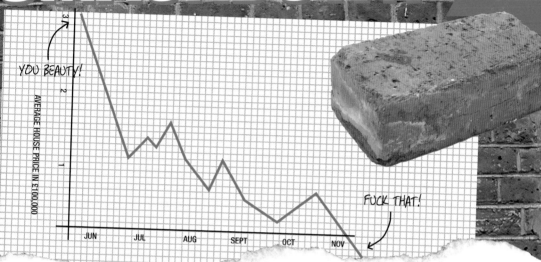

AVERAGE HOUSE PRICE IN £100,000

YOU BEAUTY!

FUCK THAT!

JUN JUL AUG SEPT OCT NOV

Houses worth less than the bricks they are made of

BRITAIN'S houses are now worth less as homes than they are as individual bricks, it was claimed last night.

Estate agents say most home-owners are dispensing with their services and instead dismantling their houses and selling them bit-by-bit at car boot sales or down the pub.

Others are breaking up individual rooms and selling them off piecemeal in a bid to stave off repossession while retaining a habitable portion of the family home.

Wayne Hayes, a roofer, pulled apart his detached, four-bed-room house and put all the bits on eBay after the best offer he received was a can of dog food and a dirty stick.

He added: 'I got nearly 500 quid for the bricks. Once you add in the copper wire, the light fittings and the Belfast sink I've only lost about three-quarters of a million.'

Bill McKay said he had sold the top two floors of his three-storey Georgian mansion after it was valued at slightly more than the price of a KitKat.

He added: 'The corrugated iron keeps out most of the water and we've got a bucket in the corner for number twos.'

Tom Logan, chief economist at the Halifax, said there were some lovely bricks coming onto the market, adding: 'Now that they have been released from their pointless houses, they have some real value.'

Meanwhile Prime Minister Gordon Brown yesterday sought to calm worried homeowners by sitting in the middle of his office floor, pulling his knees up to his chin and rocking back and forward, mumbling: 'Everything will be just fine, you'll see – finey, finey, fine. Is it time for tea?'

Estate agents will starve to death after house price crash, says upbeat report

WORRIED homeowners were cheered last night as economists revealed that this year's house price collapse will lead to widespread starvation and prostitution among Britain's estate agents.

The upbeat report says the entire profession will be on the streets begging for food by August, apart from those who manage to get jobs as sex whores by lying about their previous occupation.

Professor Nick Oak, the Van Hoogstraten Chair of Prices at the House Institute, said: 'Great news, the pin-striped tit-cockers are all going to starve to death. Slowly.'

Jerry Househunter Johnson said: 'When I'm looking around a house I don't need some dick in a lilac shirt telling me, "This is the en-suite bathroom." I can see it's the en-suite bathroom. It's got a great big fucking bath in it.

'I can also tell the difference between a desirable upscale property in a sought-after location and a rat-infested bedsit with a brothel on one side and a crack house on the other. Do you think I'm blind, or just stupid?'

Charles Reeves, 42, said: 'Subjects would benefit from modernisation? So previous resident died and rotted into the floorboards and now the whole house will have to be marinaded in Dettol for a year to get rid of the stench.'

Tom Booker said: 'I have to walk two miles to the newsagent because the only things the shops round here sell is houses. I don't care if my place halves in value, I just want to buy a paper.'

Nikki Hollis said she was looking forward to picking up a cheap second-hand Mini once all the estate agents were forced to hand theirs back.

She said: 'I would buy one now but I'm worried someone would think I was in the property business and stuff shit up the exhaust.'

According to the report estate agents are currently worth 'absolutely fuck all' to the British economy, which would be £600 billion better off if they all dropped dead overnight.

Nothing can possibly go wrong.

HOMELESS AND HUNGRY ESTATE AGENT, WILL LICK YOU FOR FOOD.

Estate Agents!
Letting the worthless gobshites
die may save billions.

BUY-TO-LET INVESTORS AGE 1,000 YEARS IN FOUR SECONDS

'HOUSANDS of buy-to-let investors are ageing 1,000 years in around four seconds after receiving the latest valuations of their rented properties.

Laura Quinn, said her husband Tom crumbled to ashes at the breakfast table shortly after opening a letter from his bank.

She said: 'He kept telling everyone we were loaded because he'd bought ten flats on the never-never and the daft sods who were wasting their money renting them would make us into millionaires.

'He opened the letter and his face started to crumple. I thought he was crying, but he was getting more and more wrinkled. Then his hair went all long and white, then he was just a skull, and then he was gone.

'Turns out we owe the bank £1.5 million, even after I've given them our house. They say I should go on the game. It's alright for Tom, he's in a jar.'

Cathy Smith, 36, said her husband Keith dissolved like 'one of baddies at the end of Raiders of the Lost Ark' after taking a phone call from his bank.

'He was laughing at first, saying, "Just take the keys and have the bloody flats back, they're more trouble than they're worth."

'Then they told him they were taking the house and all our savings. Four seconds later he melted into a brown puddle on our lovely John Lewis rug.'

She added: 'Keith said buy-to-let was perfect for people like us with no knowledge of the property market. Now all I've got left are his teeth.'

Julian Cook, a neighbour of the Smiths who had spent four years listening to Keith boasting about how they would soon retire to France, said: 'Aha, ha, ha. Aha ha, ha, ha. Aha, ha, ha, ha, ha, ha. Ha.'

British dinner parties on brink of collapse, says IMF

THE International Monetary Fund last night issued its starkest warning yet that British dinner parties are vastly overvalued and on the brink of a devastating collapse.

According to the IMF, being invited to dinner by someone you would not speak to if their kids were not at school with yours is not fun and will result in you being force-fed Chicken Kiev with blood in it, and a crème brûlée that smells of cat sick.

Meanwhile, listening to a drunk man, who claims to be a socialist, pretend he is embarrassed that his house is worth half a million pounds while he stares at your wife's tits is a tremendously shit way to spend a Saturday night.

David Chapel, chief economist at the IMF, said: 'Why should I care if you get your beef from that amazing organic butcher your chiropractor told you about?

Please, for the love of God, shut up about your blowtorch.

'All I know is you bought your starter from Waitrose, your kids are foul, and you've got Amy Winehouse on a loop.

'Have you ever thought of talking about something other than how hard you work, how much you are worth, and how fucking great you are? Especially as we all know your alcoholic wife is at it with the Polish au pair.

'Why should I have to waste ten minutes of my life listening to a twat in plastic glasses tell me how you discovered this cheese on a walking holiday in the Spanish Pyrenees when all I want is to eat something that doesn't stink like a goat's end?'

Mr Chapel said the only glimmer of hope was a total wipe-out in the British property market which would, 'Shut up all those smug bastards who've spent the last five years boasting about their property investments, and drive them into bankruptcy.'

Alistair Darling, the Chancellor of the Exchequer, said: 'I really must stop shitting myself.'

Banks use man-eating tigers to deter new borrowers

BRITAIN'S leading mortgage lenders are to deter new customers with a range of tactics including man-eating tigers and a huge Arab warrior armed with a mighty sword.

From today the Woolwich will position a pair of ravenous Bengal tigers outside its branches, while the Nationwide has rigged a boobytrap consisting of hundreds of small poisoned arrows that will be triggered by a pressure pad under the doormat.

Customers who survive the arrows will then have to swing across a moat filled with electric eels before entering the Domain of the Scorpion.

The giant scorpion not only carries an instantly fatal poison in its tail but can shoot fire from its pincers. Would-be homeowners will have to stab the creature between the eyes to have any hope of borrowing more than three times their joint salary.

If they defeat the scorpion they will then have to survive Knife Alley and the Room of the Enormous Hammers, making sure they are not distracted by the vultures picking clean the bones of previous failed applicants.

And just as they are in sight of the mortgage advisor, out of the shadows will step Al-Hassan, an invincible seven-foot-tall Arab Warrior, armed with a razor-sharp scimitar and wearing a necklace fashioned from the thumbs of his enemies.

Independent financial advisers are urging their clients to either run at the swordsman with a long spear, or if possible, just shoot him in the middle of the chest.

A Nationwide spokes-man said: 'If you can get past Al-Hassan, then yes, you can have a fucking mortgage.'

Have you brought three months' pay slips?

Balloons in this development near Swindon are selling for £98,000.

More young professionals forced to live in balloons

WITH house prices now more than 400 times the average salary, more and more young people are being forced to live in hot air ballons, according to new research.

A study by Glasgow Clyde University found a 33 per cent year-on-year increase in balloon-based living among young professionals across the UK.

Research director Dr Mark Hadley said: 'Balloons offer a practical, low-cost alternative to a canal barge, a tent or an old fridge freezer.

'Thanks to a planning loophole we are seeing more and more balloon estates cropping up on the edge of major towns and cities.'

He added: 'Although small, the views are fabulous. And let's face it, in a balloon the world is not just your oyster, it's your toilet as well.'

Sarah Bamforth, a 28-year-old marketing manager from Swindon, has been living in a balloon with her boyfriend for six months.

'You do have to get the hang of the sand bags, otherwise it takes ages to get down to the ground. I was late for work every day for a month when we first moved in.'

She added: 'It's fine really. But I would advise against having a pet. We've gone through five cats since Christmas.'

the daily mash

VATICAN TO BUILD HUGE TELESCOPE IN HUNT FOR JESUS

THE Pope has commissioned a $1bn super-telescope as the Vatican steps up its hunt for Jesus.

The telescope, to be positioned in orbit 200 miles above the earth, will scan the heavens in a bid to force the Son of God from his hiding place.

Vatican astronomer Monsignor Umberto Facci said: 'The exact whereabouts of Jesus remains one of the final mysteries of science.

'Over the years he has been spotted in Orion, Ursa Major and the Horsehead Nebula, as well as numerous chapatis and tortillas.

'With this gigantic viewing machine we can chase him all over the heavens until he gets tired and gives up.'

Is this Jesus?

The Vatican has rejected claims of hypocrisy despite its long history of burning astronomers to death for suggesting the Earth may not be a giant fried egg, cooked by God.

Monsignor Facci added: 'This is a common misunderstanding about the Church's attitude to astronomy. Let me be clear – Galileo was persecuted because he spoke with a lisp.'

The telescope can also be turned towards the Earth so that Vatican scholars can spot miracles as they happen.

A spokesman said: 'This will allow us to have a shrine, a giftshop and a dozen swivel-eyed beggars in place before the Muslims have even got their coats on.'

---

news

BRITAIN FALLS INTO A HEDGE

news

CHANNEL 4 TO SHOW QUEEN MOTHER EATING A GIGANTIC SAUSAGE

Cows declare war on sheep

RURAL Britain is bracing itself for widescale bloodshed after the cows declared war on the sheep.

Tensions have been building between the two species since a young cow was bitten and kicked by a gang of sheep in Wiltshire 18 months ago.

Last night both sides said that diplomatic efforts had failed and that conflict was now inevitable.

Cow Prime Minister Edelweiss, a four-year-old Holstein from a farm near Buxton in Derbyshire, said: 'This morning the cow ambassador handed the sheep a final note, stating that unless we heard from them by 11 o'clock, that they were prepared, at once, to apologise for the biting incident, a state of war would exist between us.

'I have to tell you that no such undertaking has been received and that consequently the cows are at war with the sheep.'

Cow soldiers across the country have received orders from their high command and will begin a full-scale attack within days.

The sheep are expected to fight a brief rearguard action before taking to the hills to mount a

Charge!

guerrilla campaign.

A spokesman for the National Farmers Union said: 'It's very difficult to milk cows when they're at war. I would advise everyone to stock up on cream.'

Worthless Opinion Poll	
What are you giving up this year?	
All red meat, except beef	15.2%
Toddler Fight Club	25.1%
Touching myself in church	28.6%
The Sudanese family in my loft	31.1%

Russia to withdraw 400 lapdancers

RUSSIAN prime minister Vladimir Putin has threatened to withdraw an entire squadron of lapdancers from central London, as the latest diplomatic row with Moscow escalates.

Putin said: 'Weak British men must pay for naughties. Cannot live without naughties. I take away fruity girls, your country weeps like child with knee injury.

'You say I am bad man. You say I make enemies go "poof". I say you cannot live without naked botties in face.'

He added: 'You make enemy of my Russian tough boys, I buy all your football teams and turn them into pig farms. I am Vladimir. You will obey.'

Putin's latest move follows a 98 per cent drop in UK levels of deadly radioactive polonium.

An embassy spokesman said the findings were 'entirely coincidental' after the expulsion of four Russian diplomats, adding: 'In Russia everyone carry polonium, in Britain everyone carry crisps. What is problem?

'When chubby British tourists leave Moscow, chocolate level drops by 70 per cent. You are fat but we do not hate you.'

'I am Vladimir. I am king of laps.'

Fat guys told to put their tits away

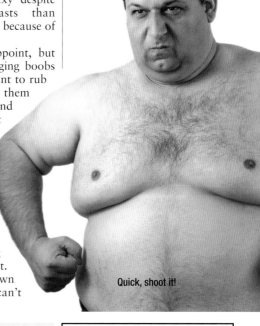

Quick, shoot it!

FAT men are being urged not to bare their breasts in public this summer, as it emerged they were not attractive to women after all.

Nikki Hollis, beauty editor of *Gas!* magazine, said male breasts had become a common sight in the high street in recent years due to the total collapse of all moral standards and high levels of beer.

She urged men to look at themselves naked in the mirror before going topless and to avoid disrobing in the presence of children and horses.

Hollis said: 'We've had three days of sunshine and the town looks like it's hosting a convention of middle-aged Brazilian transsexuals – in trainers.

'Whatever gave you the idea when you got up this morning that I would want to clap eyes on your wobbling white tits, you great whale?

'And before you even think it, Jack Nicholson is sexy despite having larger breasts than Pamela Anderson, not because of them.

'I'm sorry to disappoint, but the sight of your sagging boobs does not make me want to rub Ambre Solaire into them and then stick my hand down your shorts. It makes me want to puke.'

Nick Oaks, a 36DD from Essex, said he was shocked to discover how many women were raving lesbians these days.

He said: 'I'm a big hunk of beautiful meat. Big up top, and big down below. They just can't handle it.'

WOMEN BISHOPS TO FILL CATHEDRAL WITH KNICK-KNACKS AND POT POURRI
'What this place needs is some vanilla tea lights and my collection of little china pigs,' says Reverend Emily Jenkins.

BURMESE PEASANTS USE AID MONEY TO DRILL FOR OIL
'Then you invade and kill maniac generals, yes?' says woman with no inherent economic value.

FAT KIDS USED TO BOLSTER FLOOD DEFENCES
'Calm down, we're giving them snorkels,' says council leader.

Worthless Opinion Poll
Why are you supporting human-animal hybrids?

I need a trunk ASAP	10%
I'd like a big red arse and a blue face	15.6%
I want to lick my private area	34.4%
I'd like to see my boss try that shit with an alligator	40%

Global economy now run by fucknuts

THE US Federal Reserve is to give everyone in America a spaniel in a bid to prevent recession in the world's biggest economy.

It is the largest domestic pet the US central bank has given out, and almost ten times the size of the chinchilla issued to every household in the wake of the dotcom crash of March 2000.

Julian Cook, an analyst at Donnelly-McPartlin, welcomed the move to a spaniel-based economy, adding that the breed was one of the biggest single generators of additional spending, more costly even than a fat child.

He said: 'Shoes, vomit-remover, electric fencing, a cattle prod, two new sofas and a mobile phone. All those will have to be bought in the first two weeks.'

Meanwhile, Fed chairman Ben

Bernanke is a leading authority on Spanielnomics.

Bernanke urged people 'to just buy shit and worry about it later', including electric brooms, homoeopathic remedies, miracle cleaners, and anything advertised by Carol Vorderman, apart from Farmfoods.

He said: 'The world has been brought to the brink of depression by a ridiculous consumer-spending spree fuelled by cheap credit and home makeover shows. So let's keep it going.'

Bernanke said the only way to prevent the current unsustainable consumer bubble from bursting was by slashing interest rates and creating another even bigger one for someone else to worry about after he had moved to Goldman Sachs.

Professor Henry Brubaker, of the Institute for Studies, said: 'We conducted a detailed analysis of every major policy decision taken by every central banker in the world over the last 10 years and came to inescapable conclusion that they're a collection of fuckin' idiots.'

French trader was forced to work 30 hours a week

FRIENDS of rogue trader Jerome Kerviel last night blamed his $7-billion losses on unbearable levels of stress brought on by a punishing 30-hour week.

Kerviel was known to start work as early as nine in the morning and still be at his desk at five or even five-thirty, often with just an hour-and-a-half for lunch.

One colleague said: 'He was, how you say, *une workaholique*. I have a family and a mistress so I would leave the office at around 2 p.m. at the latest, if I wasn't on strike.

'But Jerome was tied to that desk. One day I came back to the office at 3 p.m. because I had for-

Kerviel hid his November losses in a batch of wonderfully fresh croissants.

gotten my stupid little hat, and there he was, fast asleep on the photocopier.

'At first I assumed he had been having sex with it, but then I

remembered he'd been working for almost six hours.'

As the losses mounted, Kerviel tried to conceal his bad trades by covering them with an intense red wine sauce, later switching to delicate pastry horns.

At one point he managed to dispose of dozens of transactions by hiding them inside vol-au-vent cases and staging a fake reception.

Last night a spokesman for Sócíété Généralé denied that Kerviel was overworked, insisting he lost the money after betting that the French were about to stop being rude, lazy, arrogant bastards.

Madonna's former home destroyed by Jesus

POP star Madonna's childhood home in Detroit has been burned to the ground in an apparent revenge attack by Jesus.

Witnesses spotted the Son of God last Friday evening at an Exxon service station in the Detroit suburb of Rochester, where he was seen filling a large metal canister with petrol.

The Prince of Peace then crossed the road to the Stop'n'Go convenience store where he bought a packet of J-Cloths and a large box of safety matches.

Security footage from the rear of the store shows Jesus taking bottles from the recycling bank, filling them carefully with the petrol and then stuffing them with the cloths, before placing them in a cardboard box and heading for the nearest bus stop.

Nikki Hoberman, a cashier, said: 'Jesus walked right up to me and asked me where Madonna used to live. He looked upset. I said to him, "What you gonna do, Jesus?" and he said he was gonna find that house and torch it.

'I said to him, "Why, Jesus, why?" and he just looked straight at me and said, "*Like a Virgin? Like a Prayer?* Like a fuckin' skank more like. It's barbecue time."

'Then he started goin' on and on about Kaballah and how he didn't get "nailed to a goddamn tree" just to see a Catholic girl sign up for some "pervert Jewish witchcraft".'

She added: 'He wasn't too happy about the cover version of *American Pie* either.'

Jesus prefers J-Cloths in his petrol bombs.

Worthless Opinion Poll
What should we eat to combat global warming?

Whales	5.5%
easyJet	12.2%
Vegetarians	27.2%
Americans	55.1%

Glasgow unveils Commonwealth Games logo

HE encapsulates modern Glasgow and extends a warm Scottish welcome to the world: he's Mungo the Shit-Faced Octopus.

Glasgow City Council yesterday unveiled the £1.2-million logo which they hope will charm the world during the 2012 Commonwealth Games.

'Ten years ago we might have gone for a little Scottie dog or maybe even a cheeky wee haggis,' said a council spokesman.

'The fact that we've chosen a shit-faced octopus shows just how much Glasgow has embraced the twenty-first century.'

Tom Logan, of design company Conceptomatix, explained the thinking behind the new brand.

'He's called Mungo, because Mungo is the name of our managing director.

'He's blue because of Glasgow's proud maritime tradition. He's under water because for millions of years the Glasgow area was completely submerged. He has eight legs because he's an octopus. And he's shit-faced because he's a Glaswegian octopus.'

Conceptomatix is one of the UK's hottest young design agencies.

Last year only 38 per cent of their logo designs led to fits and seizures by members of the public.

Mungo the Shit-Faced Octopus.

I'm having a picnic and everyone's invited! by David Cameron

GLOBAL warming is a threat to us all. I'm really serious about this. It will cause untold misery for millions across the globe and change the way we live, for ever. But in the meantime it does mean lots and lots of lovely weather. And what's the absolute best thing to do when the sun shines? Have a picnic!

My wife Sam and I have been talking about it for a couple of weeks and we just decided, 'What the hell – let's go for it.' But we didn't want to leave anyone out so you're all invited. We've borrowed Somerset from a couple of friends and we really hope you can make it.

And when I say everyone, I really do mean it. That includes you lot 'oop north', with your funny voices and your funny stories. You're so full of life, always stealing things or damaging things or blaming other people for your misfortune. I know you're on incapacity benefit, but I'm sure your legs will start working again when there's free beer on offer. What characters!

We want all you Scots there too. We love the Scots, with your funny voices and your funny stories and PLEASE DON'T HIT ME! Just kidding. We love going to Scotland and buying interesting little souvenirs, tasting unusual food and haggling with the locals. Last year we visited a place called 'Paisley' (you'll have to look up the pronunciation) and we

'I know you're on incapacity benefit, but I'm sure your legs will start working again when there's free beer on offer'

couldn't believe that a place with such friendly and charming people could also be so poor and horrid. It moved us so deeply that we decided to sponsor a child there, and you should do the same. (And I promise this year I'll learn to speak a few words of Scottish!)

And how could it be a picnic without the Welsh? You're so warm and welcoming with your funny voices and your funny stories. Always complaining so musically and gossiping so viciously. But remember, you'll be

out in the countryside and those animals don't belong to you. I'm not getting into trouble with the farmer because of you lot. You know what I'm talking about!

Last, but by no means least, we really want to see all you women there too. Bring a pie. I love women with their funny voices and their funny stories. You and my wife Sam will get along so well. You can slosh back gallons of white wine and chatter away all afternoon about handbags and marinades and shampoo, and how you manage to juggle a career *and* an Aga. If you ask me you're all Wonder Woman!

So there we are. Everyone's invited (except the Irish, obviously). And don't forget, we've got a planet to look after so do try and come by train or bus, or even better get on your bike. (And I suppose you lot 'oop north' could even steal a horse – ha ha!) See you in Somerset on the 26th!

Worthless Opinion Poll
How are you insulting your customers?

Ugly child at table six!	11.8%
Credit card in bumcrack	16.6%
Ice cubes made of pish	19.3%
Arranging green beans to read TWAT	52.3%

In Agony with PETULA SOUL

Dear Petula,
Six months ago I started an affair with a married woman at work. She was open from the start and said it was just a bit of fun on the side and there was no way she would ever leave her husband, who she insists she loves deeply. I'm married too and the arrangement suits me fine. We now have fantastic, passionate, guilt-free sex at least once a week before returning happily to our partners and our other lives. Just thought you would like to know that. Should I opt for a fixed rate or variable when remortgaging?

Confused,
Perth

Petula says:

Dear confused,
Guilt-free philanderers often find themselves in a quandary when it comes to personal finance issues. So much effort goes into covering up their disgusting sexual transgressions that there is very little brain-power left over for complicated issues like financial planning. Perhaps if you kept it in your boxers for a few days you might be able to work it out for yourself. You make me sick. Take it from me: your supposedly guiltless hobby-sex will come back to haunt you. I know mine did. Fixed, if you can get it.

NEWS BRIEFLY

ORGAN-SWAPPING PARTIES SWEEP SUBURBIA

'Bob drew a picture of his pancreas on a card, wrote his name on the back and threw it into a big bowl on the coffee table.'

GOVERNMENT TO TACKLE BINGE-WANKING

'We want to make binge-wanking as socially unacceptable as drinking blood or setting fire to children,' says minister.

Do you have a problem you'd like Petula to help with? e: petula@thedailymash.co.uk

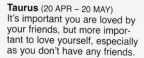

Psychic Bob's Week Ahead What does the future hold for you?

Taurus (20 APR – 20 MAY)
It's important you are loved by your friends, but more important to love yourself, especially as you don't have any friends.

Gemini (21 MAY – 20 JUN)
At last you get the recognition you deserve for something you thought no one had noticed. Damn that DNA database!

Cancer (21 JUN – 22 JUL)
Laughter isn't the best medicine – medicine's the best medicine!

Leo (23 JUL – 22 AUG)
Don't tell your sweetheart how you feel, show them. That's also a breach of your restraining order? Tough!

Virgo (23 AUG – 22 SEP)
Don't be shy about voicing your opinions. Everyone is fascinated by everything you have to say on any subject.

Libra (23 SEP – 23 OCT)
Consensus is strong around you right now. Everyone agrees: you really are an arse.

Scorpio (24 OCT – 21 NOV)
A friendship you thought was dead appears to be re-awakening. It's probably just the gas from decomposition.

Sagittarius (22 NOV – 21 DEC)
You're a spendthrift, and have a reputation for generosity towards friends and psychically inclined strangers. Fancy meeting for a drink?

Capricorn (22 DEC – 19 JAN)
Someone totally misreads you and gets things almost exactly backwards. Try numbering your holes to avoid further confusion.

Aquarius (20 JAN – 19 FEB)
A friend comes under attack but think twice before defending them. It's a big crowd and they have clubs.

Pisces (20 FEB – 20 MAR)
If someone appears critical don't take it personally, take it for the honest assessment it is, you stinking, pox-ridden whore.

Aries (21 MAR – 19 APR)
It's time to try something new that has always scared you a little. Go on, smoke that heroin your mum gave you.

the daily mash

it's news to us   www.thedailymash.co.uk   No. 9

CHILDREN TOLD TO SIT DOWN AND SHUT THE FUCK UP FOR 18 YEARS

CHILDREN should just shut it and do as they are told for once in their lives, according to the results of a major academic study.

Researchers have found that instead of being treated like equals and asked for their opinion on a

It's called The Big Book of Shutting the Fuck Up.

wide range of issues, children should button their lips and remember who pays the bills around here.

Professor Henry Brubaker said: 'There has been a move in recent years to include children in decision-making and respect their opinions. Why? They're idiots.

'We studied 50 children over a two-week period and concluded that rather than indulging these ghastly, violent, cheeky little shits, perhaps we should concentrate on feeding them three times a day and making sure they do outlandish things like their homework,

brushing their teeth and going to bed at a reasonable hour. All the while telling them to sit down and shut it on a regular basis.'

He added: 'Once you've established a pattern you can then carry on doing that right up to the point where they find a job and get the fuck out of my house.'

But Kyle Stephenson, 12, a spokesman for the British Youth Parliament, said: 'I have just finished writing a really important thing about the environment.

'It's called "Why Can't People Just Stop Doing Things that Are Bad and Start Doing Things that Are Really Good Instead".

'The Prime Minister has asked me to start work at the Number 10 Policy Unit as soon as my balls drop.'

---

news

BRITISH SQUIRRELS 'FATTEST IN EUROPE'

news

EVERYONE NOW HAS GREAT HAIR

Prince William to use HMS Invincible as a bottle opener

PRINCE William has been given permission to use the aircraft carrier HMS *Invincible* as a bottle opener at his summer barbecues.

The Prince will install the 194m long, 22,000-tonne vessel in the grounds of Highgrove House, just in time for his 26th birthday party at the end of June.

Once in position, next to the barbecue patio, *Invincible* will be fitted with a small, standard-issue bottle opener on the starboard side, below the water line.

It is the latest military asset to be loaned to the young Prince, whose late-night, RAF Tornado 'fag runs' have become a fixture on London's Fulham Road.

The Prince has been keen to involve the armed forces in every area of his life and has already replaced his bed in Clarence House with a complex assembly of 12 lance-corporals from the Queen's Royal Hussars.

Meanwhile the dining chairs in his central London apartments are volunteers from the Brigade of Ghurkas, squatting on their haunches for up to 16 hours without a break.

Military expert Denys Finch-Hatton said: 'These Ghurkas leave their villages in Nepal and hike through the Himalayas for a week to reach the recruiting office in Katmandu where they sign up to become dining chairs for the future King of England.'

A Ministry of Defence spokesman said: 'It's all standard practice. Last year more than

Have you not got one?

500 officers completed their flight training by piloting a Chinook helicopter to London, picking up their brother and then flying it to a stag do on the Isle of Wight.'

Your baby is not as pathetic as you, study reveals

WORRIED parents are being urged not to automatically assume that their baby is as pathetic and ill-informed as they are.

Research has revealed many parents have already decided their child will suffer from the same made-up food allergies they do.

And a recent study showed that 65 per cent of GP visits were the result of parents believing their baby is developing a Coco Pops intolerance because they have a great aunt who is hypoglycaemic.

But now scientists say there are other factors that cause babies to become feverish, develop a rash or shit themselves up to 18 times

Doctors have stressed, however, that babies are allergic to large piles of rat faeces.

a day. Dr Tom Logan, of the Institute for Studies, said: 'It's

because they're babies.'

He added: 'If your baby is developing in a perfectly normal way, try to not jump to the conclusion that it must be suffering from the corned beef allergy you read about in *Take a Break*.

'Also, if you think that you may have an intolerance to cheese, black pudding and Greggs pasties, don't assume that your baby is also going to be a delusional, self-absorbed halfwit.

'The best thing to do is wait until you have finished breast feeding and then either give the baby to Barnardos or leave it outside a big, posh house.'

BBC replaces Grange Hill with confusing Japanese cartoon

Koizumi Pig breathes fire and plays the trumpet.

IT was essential viewing for 16 generations of British children and launched the careers of Letitia Dean, Todd Carty and the girl who played Trisha Yates.

Grange Hill taught millions of teenagers how to take drugs and was home to television's most twisted psychopaths, including Gripper Stebson, Mr Ronson and that nice woodwork teacher with the dark hair who went on to become the most evil person ever to live in Coronation Street.

But now the alma mater of Tucker Jenkins, Benny Green, Sue Tully and the other ones is to be closed down to make way for a cartoon about a team of super-strong baby farm animals who are also in a marching band.

Shenzo Super Bang-Bang Squad follows the adventures of a gang of wide-eyed pigs, cats and chickens who collect points by fighting the robot weasels from Shenzo City using their special laser key fobs.

They then turn the points into magic coins which they use to buy instruments and uniforms. Each episode ends with a song about a fictional endangered species.

Media analysts say the move is in line with the BBC's ongoing policy of decommissioning popular, long-running shows of consistent quality and replacing them with heaps of cut-price shit.

A BBC spokeswoman said: 'Shenzo is already huge in Vietnam and Tunisia.

'There will be a range of branded toys, games, laser key fobs, a weekly magazine, bath products, cooking utensils, and a selection of hardwood conservatories.

'And come summer time there will also be ice lollies shaped like your favourite Shenzo characters, which I'm sure you'll agree is a bit more appetising than big fat Roland on a stick.'

Tate crack filled with junkie borrowers

THE huge crack in the middle of the Tate Gallery has become a seedy hangout for tiny, drug-abusing Borrowers, it was claimed last night.

More than a dozen visitors to the central London exhibit have fallen into the crack only to be beaten and robbed by heroin-crazed, three-inch junkies.

Known simply as 'The Crack' among the capital's Borrower community, the 580-foot-long artwork was once a thriving thoroughfare for the miniature people until a visiting art history professor accidentally dropped a small plastic bag filled with cocaine.

Det. Sgt Helen Barnes on the look-out for Borrower drug gangs.

'Very quickly the whole neighbourhood was awash with the stuff and it wasn't long before the dealers and the hardened criminals moved in,' said Lewis Wade, a Borrower outreach worker.

'It's very dangerous to venture in there after dark. Tiny drive-by shootings are commonplace and every street corner is occupied by gangs of incredibly small prostitutes.'

Police believe that organised gangs of Borrowers are forcing rich tourists into the crack either by tying their shoelaces together or baiting the widest sections with Brussels paté.

Bra research must go on, vows scientist

THE RESEARCHER developing an intelligent bra says there is 'no way' it is finished and that he may have to carry on studying women's breasts for decades.

Dr Charles Marx, head of breasts at the Cambridge Tits Institute, said reports his bra research was complete were 'irresponsible', and could stop women volunteering to help with his work.

He said: 'I would love to say that my intelligent bra was now a reality, I really would, but I think I will probably end up working on this project for the rest of my life.'

Dr Marx has devoted his life to developing a super-bra that will stop women's breasts bouncing around during exercise, but with very limited success so far.

Unlike rival researchers who

This generation's Apollo programme.

use sophisticated laser-measuring techniques to gauge levels of bounce Dr Marx personally observes his volunteers using his bras as they jog before him on a treadmill.

He said: 'I only got into this line of work by accident after

my university rejected my initial proposal to look into intelligent panties. But it has proved hugely rewarding.'

Most of the research takes place in Dr Marx's office, which is equipped with a treadmill, video camera, heavy curtains and tissues.

All joggers are asked to wear blindfolds to prevent anything they see interfering with the experiments, while Dr Marx always removes his trousers in case they affect the results.

He added: 'People often ask me what possible scientific benefit can arise from spending hours in a darkened room watching a woman with large breasts jog on the spot in front of you in a not very supportive bra.

'Imagine if they had said that to Einstein? He would never have invented the atom bomb.'

🔍 IN FOCUS: Oxford and Cambridge

These people now control every aspect of your life.

BRITAIN has only two universities: Oxford and Cambridge. Other towns and cities claim to have universities, but in reality these are simply 'holding pens' for call-centre workers and public relations executives.

To win a place at 'Oxbridge' it is important to know how to wear a jumper. Every year thousands of applicants fail by pulling the jumper over their head and putting their arms inside the sleeves. Jumpers, of course, are simply draped over the shoulders so that they can be trans-

ferred easily to that shivering young politics student with the phenomenal charlies.

A degree from Oxford or Cambridge means you never have to work again, you simply have to collect the monthly salary.

KEY FACT: Oxford and Cambridge take it in turns to be better than each other.

ADVERTISING FEATURE

MOONWATER
IS HERE!

After many years of research, exploration and technological innovation
MoonWater is now a reality.
We have worked tirelessly to bring you the HIGHEST QUALITY
natural spring water all the way from the MOON.
Now, in association with the *Daily Mash*, we are offering you the chance
to invest in our exciting new venture and to receive the VERY FIRST
consignments of this AMAZING and REFRESHING drink.
If you would like to be part of this fantastic consumer PHENOMENON
then why not secure your stake in MoonWater today?
For an initial investment of just £5,000 you will receive 250 ordinary shares
and be the ENVY of your friends and colleagues.
Not only that, but you will receive 12 FREE one-litre bottles
of this DELICIOUS and INVIGORATING beverage.
Our experts predict that within just one year
MoonWater will be the BESTSELLING drink on
the Earth – and the Moon!

The MoonWater Journey...

- Our army of robot miners digs up ice from just below the surface of the Moon.
- The ice is transferred to our Heat Zone where it melts to become delicious MoonWater.
- The MoonWater is then pumped on board our translunar vehicle and brought to Earth where it is tested for quality by our highly trained beverage technicians and bottled ready for shipping across the globe.

The MoonWater Experience...

- Low in calories and virtually fat-free.
- Best served chilled, but no lemon or lime. You don't want anything to get in the way of that great MoonWater taste.
- Goes great with fish, salads and chicken, as well as crisps and nuts.
- Great for rehydrating after an intense work-out.
- Our experts reckon the taste is unique, but some say there's just a hint of apples.

To secure your £5,000 stake in MoonWater and to receive your 12 FREE bottles contact the *Daily Mash* for more details.

MoonWater IT'S WATER . . . FROM THE MOON!

Cage-fighting probably gay, say doctors

NO-HOLDS-BARRED cage-fighting can lead to long-term gayness and an obsession with thighs, doctors claimed last night.

The British Medical Association said men who are attracted to cage-fighting are already gay or entertaining the possibility of a gay-based lifestyle.

According to a BMA study around 82 per cent of men who took part in the vicious fights were gay before they started and another 12 per cent became gay during their first fight.

The remaining six per cent took part in cage-fighting because they wanted to beat up gay men.

Cage-fighting began in the United States in the 1980s as a way for off-duty policemen to act out their fantasies.

Fighters are only allowed into

Dennis and Joaquim married in Honolulu last April.

the cage if they are wearing tight-fitting underpants and are smothered in olive oil.

They are then allowed to grab any part of their opponent's body

before throwing him to the floor, jumping on top of him and asking him out for a drink.

Roy Hobbs, a former Ultimate Fighting Champion, denied he was gay, insisting he preferred to socialise with men because they had bigger hands.

He added: 'Like most men I enjoy a violent wrestling match followed by a shower, champagne cocktails, a club, some more violent wrestling and a continental breakfast on the veranda. Does that make me gay?'

A BMA spokesman said: 'Gayness is lovely, but we think there are better ways to discover your sexuality than stripping down to your undies, getting oiled up and pummeling another man's thighs. We just haven't worked out what it is yet.'

Dollar now nancy-boy of international currencies

THE US dollar is now the nancy-boy of the international money markets and the gayest currency in the world.

The once manly greenback is afraid to be left alone at night and has to sleep with the light on, but is still constantly wetting the bed.

It is also scared of leaving the house because the last time it did the pound and the euro laughed at it for wearing a pastel scarf.

The limp dollar said: 'Can you lend me £20 until I get paid? I've lent all my money to some black people to buy houses and they won't give it me back.'

Robert Peston, BBC business

The dollar (left) with its friend the Canadian dollar.

editor, said the dollar was now singing an octave higher than last

month because its credits had been so heavily crunched.

He said that while the pound was rugged and good at sport, the US dollar made the Canadian dollar look like Daniel Craig.

Peston added: 'The international currency market is like a giant bag of spanners. If your nuts are loose it can twist them until you pant.

'But if you get threaded then those same spanners will make your pips squirm and give your cat a revolting disease. It's as simple as that.'

Alistair Darling, the Chancellor of the Exchequer, said: 'I appear to have shat myself.'

If it's all right with you, I'd quite like a fridge by Yen Xiao, farmer, Jiangsu Province

HERE in China, life is hard. I'm sure you've read many newspaper articles about our booming economy and burgeoning middle class, but the vast majority of Chinese still rely on subsistence farming and have no access to modern sanitation and electricity.

We work in the fields, regardless of the weather, just to feed our families and keep a roof over our heads. We are simple peasants, forever at the mercy of the shifting political climate.

So I have to say I do get a bit bloody pissed off when I hear the West is all worried about China's economic growth and how it might increase global warming. While you're using electricity to charge your fucking toothbrush I have to shit in a hole in the ground and then cover it with bamboo leaves. Did you know that?

The local Communist Party bloke popped in last week to let us know how things were going in Beijing. There's big plans for more roads so that we can transport more of the cheap shit we pump out of our factories that you lot in the West can't seem to get enough of.

He says that the banks in Shanghai are doing a roaring trade, what with all the foreign investment pouring into the country and buying up all the good farming land so that they can build even bigger headquarters for the sodding banks.

So then I asked him about the plans for the power station and the electricity cables that will eventually feed into our village. There's a few problems with that, he says. Might be a bit of a delay, he says. Western governments are worried about 'carbon emissions', he says.

To be honest, I just want a fridge – a little one would do – so that the goat's milk and chicken drumsticks don't go off and give us all the squits. Try having the runs in 90 degree heat when the nearest chemist is 800 miles away. Let me assure you, it's no fucking picnic.

And it's not as if I'm desperate to watch television, although that would be nice – there's only so many times you can hear the same story about the same duck. Electric lighting would be nice too. Last Monday night I got up to go for a wiz, tripped and landed in the wife's grandmother. Unpleasant? Yes it was, thanks for asking.

So while I'm landing face-first in the ancestors do please continue to use your electric whisks and your toasted sandwich maker. I'll just sit here in the dark with a cork up my back passage and a dream of a bright new tomorrow.

🔍 IN FOCUS: Communism – wrong about everything

ONE day in 1848 a young man woke up in his own filth in a dank hovel in the East End of London and said to himself: 'I hate being poor, I must get some rich people to give me half their money.'

That young man was Karl Marx and that hovel was Joseph Engels. The two soon began an odyssey through Mayfair and Belgravia, stopping rich gentleman and asking if they could have half their money. Their request was rejected without exception and so the industrious pair sat down and wrote a short book about why being poor was so awful. The original title, *Oi, Quentin! Give me Half your Money!*, was quickly changed to *The Communist Manifesto* and soon bearded men across Europe were on fire with its theories of distribution and production (not to mention its risqué photographs of semi-naked horses).

Within 20 years everyone in Europe was a 'Communist', as by then it was the only way one could even hope to get into the knickers of fruity, young actresses. A generation later the Bolshevik revolution heralded the start of Russia's long experiment in genocide, starvation and queuing for three days to buy soap. By the early twenty-first century Communism was regarded as little more than an embarrassing cock-up, like Lemon Coke or Roman Catholicism.

Karl Marx used the profits from the Communist Manifesto to set up a no-frills train service between London and Cardiff

In Agony with PETULA SOUL

Dear Petula,
Six months ago I started an affair with a married man at work. He was open from the start and said it was just a bit of fun on the side. That suited me as I'm married too. So we started having fantastic guilt-free, passionate sex at least once a week. The trouble is it's no fun without the guilt and I worry that the spark is going out of my extra-marital relationship. How can I carry on cuckolding my husband and get some passion back into my affair?

Deflated,
Dundee

Petula says:

Dear Deflated,
A good question. Lots of people think having affairs at work is a completely natural thing and expect the passion levels to stay high all the time they are being unfaithful. Yet, inevitably, over time even snatched illicit hoggins in the broom cupboard can lose its fizz. Put some more effort into creating the right atmosphere for your cheating. Have a glass of wine to lower you inhibitions. Fill the cupboard with rose petals and light some nice scented candles to cover the stink of cleaning fluids. Put on some romantic mood music. Give each other a gentle massage. Before you know it your knees will be trembling like the good old days. Have a listen to my premium rate phone line 'How to get the best out of your affair'. Happy hochmagandy!

Do you have a problem you'd like Petula to help with?
e: petula@thedailymash.co.uk

NEWS BRIEFLY

BROWN PROMISES TO CONSULT PEOPLE WHO AGREE WITH HIM
'I want to involve as many ordinary Britons who think I'm right as possible,' says brooding sociopath.

LABOUR TAKES 'QUENTIN' LEAD OVER TORIES
'But we still have more Percivals and Gaylords,' says Tory spokesman.

IRAN BUILDING 6,000 NUCLEAR CENTRIFUGES 'FOR CHILDREN IN NEED'
'I'm building mine while dressed as Winnie the Pooh,' reveals President Ahmadinejad.

KNIGHTHOODS FOR ENTIRE CAST OF 'HEARTBEAT'
Victoria Wood OBE awarded a third CBE for having a really, really great personality.

Psychic Bob's Week Ahead

Taurus (20 APR – 20 MAY)
If things look weird today, and they probably do, you're wearing your wife's glasses. Again.

Gemini (21 MAY – 20 JUN)
A misunderstanding should help others learn to be more tolerant. How were you to know she wasn't up the duff? Fat cow.

Cancer (21 JUN – 22 JUL)
Unwanted pregnancy? Don't worry. You have 16 years to get your own back on the little bastard.

Leo (23 JUL – 22 AUG)
It's easy to dismiss the legitimate concerns of others, so what are you waiting for?

Virgo (23 AUG – 22 SEP)
If someone from a different culture tests your patience, don't get upset – have him deported.

Libra (23 SEP – 23 OCT)
Someone close gets into an argument with you, which starts out playfully but might not end that way when you kick their fucking teeth in.

Scorpio (24 OCT – 21 NOV)
Try not to give too much away when a family member upsets you. The police aren't completely stupid.

Sagittarius (22 NOV – 21 DEC)
A lot of warmth is coming your way. But it won't stay warm for long. And then it will start to smell.

Capricorn (22 DEC – 19 JAN)
Friendship means different things to different people. But it rarely means that to anyone. You filthy pig.

Aquarius (20 JAN – 19 FEB)
Something emerges this morning that you might miss. That's the problem with button flies.

Pisces (20 FEB – 20 MAR)
You've got some big decisions ahead. Try to put them off as you will make the wrong fucking choice – as usual.

Aries (21 MAR – 19 APR)
Your emotions are intense but you can handle them. So why can't Holly Willoughby? All you asked for was a new signed photo because the other one's all crusty.

FAITH TO FAITH

God is everywhere — even under my little red hat.

Atheists are nice people who will roast in hell, says cardinal

ATHEISTS and agnostics are decent people whose tormented souls will burn for all eternity in the scorching fires of hell, Britain's biggest Catholic said last night.

Cardinal Cormac Murphy O'Connor said non-believers should be respected, right up to the point of death when they will finally come face to face with Satan and his blood-soaked pitchfork.

He told a conference in London: 'Those without faith should not be shunned or abused. Jesus and Beelzebub are already cooking something up

for them, don't you worry about that.'

The leader of Roman Catholics in England and Wales stressed that a 'hidden God' was active in everyone's life, often nipping to the shops for them or wiping down their kitchen surfaces.

Stressing that God was not in the phonebook, the Cardinal said: 'You can't just ring him up. You have to get an appointment and that can take up to 18 months.

'I suppose I could try to put in a good word for you . . . if only I wasn't so skint – if you catch my drift . . .'

He admitted talking about

God was difficult, especially as some people genuinely believe a man was born of a virgin, performed miracles and then died and came back to life, while others believe that this is a lot of insane, voodoo rubbish.

He added: 'We must not allow Britain to become devoid of religious faith, otherwise how will I afford new hats?'

The Cardinal's lecture follows clashes over stem cell research and gay rights, where the church tried to impose laws based on a 2,000-year-old book written by people who stoned each other to death for wearing the wrong clothes.

85

Infidel! The next time it shall be your head!

MOST BRITISH CHILDREN NOW DEMONS

MORE than half of all British children are demons whose souls have been devoured by Satan, according to a new study.

Researchers claim that since 1998 around 56 per cent of British children have been possessed by some of hell's most senior demons including Baal, Legion and the Moloch.

And they said it was vital the media continued to demonise children, otherwise they would be 'playing straight into Satan's hands'.

Dr Tom Logan, of the Institute for Studies, said: 'The last thing you want to do with a demon is pretend he isn't one.

'We took one child who seemed perfectly nice, but when we X-rayed him we got a very clear image of a snarling, two-headed devil-dog.

'When we showed him the X-rays he got very agitated and started speaking backwards in Aramaic before nicking my iPhone.'

Dr Logan added: 'The mother in *The Exorcist* tried to pretend her daughter was not a demon.

'The next thing you know there's a dead guy at the bottom of a flight of stairs with his head turned all the way round.

'I'm not saying your child is going to throw someone out of a window and then do unspeakably dirty things with a crucifix. But that doesn't mean they're not a mouthy little shit.'

Twelve-year-old Regan likes Justin Timberlake and taunting elderly priests.

Muslim teddy bear has paws chopped off

SUDAN was facing international sanctions last night after hacking off the little paws of a three-year-old teddy bear.

The cuddly toy was found guilty of blasphemy after taking the name of the prophet Muhammad, in defiance of the country's strict Islamic teddy-bear-naming laws.

A spokesman for the Sudanese Ministry of Justice defended the sentence, adding: 'This is an act of mercy.

'Our laws demand that blaspheming toys be stripped to their underwear and stoned to death before their bodies are thrown into the desert as an afternoon snack for the vultures.

'By removing only the paws of this infidel we are demonstrating great restraint. This is a gesture of goodwill to you Western devils and your pornographic governments.'

He added: 'How would you react if your child named a teddy bear after Jesus, John the Baptist or even Tom Hanks?

'Would you not decapitate the toy, thrash the child and throw the teacher off a cliff to be devoured by ravenous killer whales?'

The United Nations and Amnesty International have called for the release of more than 2,500 cuddly toys imprisoned without trial since early September.

A UN spokesman added: 'Of course, some may argue there is no point in us keeping all these Sudanese children alive if they can't even think of a legal name for a teddy bear.'

The bear was named following a classroom vote, with 'Muhammad' chosen ahead of 'Paddington', 'Baloo' and 'Al-Hassan, the Terrible Golden Sword of Righteousness'.

MUSLIMS AND CHRISTIANS TO UNITE IN HATRED OF GAYS

A GROUP of senior Islamic clerics has written to Pope Benedict XVI calling for the world's two biggest faiths to find common cause over their obsessive hatred of gay people.

The Muslim leaders have appealed to Christians to join them in making increasingly bizarre and inflammatory claims about the nature of homosexuality.

The letter states: 'Dear Pope – We hate the poofy men more than you. Yes? We think so, but maybe no. Why not we have coffee soon and be finding out?

'You say men with men is disease. We say it caused by devils. It is, how you say, 'potatoe – potahtoe'.

'We also want to tell you and all Christ followers – we love

'Perfectly happy to discuss the possibility that it's caused by devils.'

Creationism! Also, let's talk about women and how rubbish they are at everything.'

The letter ends: 'What world needs right now is much power to religious fundamentalisers. Yes? See you soon. Best regards, the Muslims.'

Pope Benedict has yet to respond officially but Vatican sources said the Pontiff read the letter while nodding a lot, pointing to different paragraphs and shouting, 'Yeah! yeah!'

Tom Logan, Professor of Theology at Glasgow Clyde University, said: 'Some people may be wondering why this has taken so long, given that they're all out of their fucking minds in exactly the same way. Probably something to do with money.'

The inter-faith project is expected to start with a seminar on the top ten ways to hurt yourself in the name of God.

Beckham unable to pronounce 'Scientology'

IN his first major setback since arriving in Los Angeles, David Beckham has revealed he is unable to pronounce the word 'Scientology'.

Sources close to the LA Galaxy footballer say he has been discouraged from joining the religion of friend Tom Cruise, because it has too many syllables.

One source said: 'If it was just called 'scien' or 'oggy' he'd be much more comfortable with giving them a huge amount of money.

'Tom's been working with him, but the closest they've got is "syen-toggoly". Maybe they should change the name to something with just the one syllable such as "ball" or "hair".'

The source added: 'It's a shame because David has exactly the right kind of brain for Syentoggoly. He could be the first British person to reach the level of "Boiled Egg".'

Last week the chest of Beckham's wife Victoria became the latest celebrity recruit for the controversial movement founded by chubby salesman L. Ron Hubbard.

Beckham still wants to be able to join in discussions about the religion and has employed a team of high-profile intellectuals, including George Monbiot and Noam Chomsky, to pronounce 'Scientology' for him at parties in Beverly Hills.

The source added: 'David will carry an intellectual with him at all times in case the conversation moves into uncharted philosophical territory such as comparative religion or the tying of shoelaces.'

Together, as a nation, we can find my glasses

by CARDINAL CORMAC MURPHY O'CONNOR

For so it was, at around 11.30 on Tuesday morning, I realised with a heavy heart and a sagging spirit, that I could not find my glasses.

I had begun to look for them at 11.15 a.m. as I had intended to read the letters page of the Daily Telegraph and marvel, once again, at the alertness of our senior citizens.

I looked in my desk drawers, I looked under my desk and I even scoured the surface of my desk. But reward was elusive. I crammed my fingers down the side of the seat cushion only to find a drawing pin. Like a crown of thorns it pierced my all too human flesh.

As I fell to the floor I thought of the many lessons handed down to us by our gracious fathers of the church.

I thought of Pope Deciduous XV who, in his letter to the Second Council of Magaluf, wrote: 'It may seem, at times, that God is not on your side. It may seem, at times, that God is unreasonable or even demented. But take comfort in the knowledge that it is God who knows the hiding places, it is God who seeks endlessly and it is God who will remember all the things that you have forgotten.'

It was then that I was touched by a wondrous revelation: I should get someone to help me.

I called on Mrs Lamont, my housekeeper. A woman so sweet in nature, so cheerful in tone, so welcoming and colourful in disposition. In many ways she reminds me of an ice-cream van.

Like St Urethra and St Calendula searching for the True Grail, we covered the four corners (of my reading nook as opposed to the Assyrian Empire).

But the glasses, like the simple, jewel-encrusted, solid-gold chalice that held the blood of the Prince of Peace, remained unfound.

Mrs Lamont and I knelt on the floor and, hand in hand, we began to pray. We prayed for humility, for patience and for grace.

And as I uttered a final 'Amen', the wisdom of the ages tapped me on the shoulder and its message was clear: We should get more people to help.

And so it is that I embrace you, my brothers and sisters in Christ, as Jesus himself embraced the Magdalene and offered to moisten her toes.

Let us, in good heart and strong faith, take up the challenge that God has set before us. All of us, working as one.

Except, of course, the homosexuals. I do not want your help. But I will need my glasses so that I may observe your sin.

the daily mash

NUCLEAR SUBMARINE FOUND ON TRAIN

THE government faced fresh embarrassment last night after a Vanguard-class nuclear submarine was found on board a commuter train.

A junior Cabinet Office official has been suspended, while Home Secretary Jacqui Smith has been told to hand back her keys to the Tower of London.

HMS *Vengeance* was discovered by Julian Cook, a trainee solicitor, during his 45-minute journey from Luton to Kings Cross Thameslink. Mr Cook immediately handed the vessel, and its 135 crew, to the BBC.

He said: 'I was actually going to the toilet when I noticed the aisle was blocked by 16,000 tonnes of ocean-going holocaust machine.

'The moment we arrived at Kings Cross I dragged it onto the tube and headed straight for Shepherds Bush.'

Full of semen.

After confirming it was a genuine submarine the BBC immediately contacted the Press Association who in turn passed it on to the editor of the *Spectator*.

The submarine was eventually handed back to the Royal Navy by the assistant features editor of *Grazia*.

The latest security breach comes just 48 hours after the aircraft carrier HMS *Invincible* was hijacked by a pack of dogs.

Meanwhile Al Qaeda has released a statement via Al Jazeera TV, outlining plans to shift its international HQ to the 7.45 from Croydon to Victoria.

---

news

POT-SMOKING INVALIDS MUCH EASIER TO ARREST, SAY POLICE

news

DNA PROFILING GUARANTEES CONVICTION OF SOMEONE OR OTHER, SAYS STUDY

Valentine's sex bid will fail, says angry girlfriend

THE amount of money you would need to spend on gifts to get sex on Valentine's Day after you stayed out last Saturday night without explanation is so huge there is no point in you even bothering, your angry girlfriend said last night.

Nikki Hollis dismissed claims you spent the night on Steve's couch after getting so drunk with the lads that you missed the last bus home and could not remember your address for the taxi driver.

However, that slut from the office who has been sniffing around you for weeks like a bitch in heat and is now walking about with a stupid smirk on her fat little face is welcome to you, she added.

Hollis, 26, said: 'If I was you I'd save your pennies because that tubby little cow looks very high-maintenance and you won't have me paying your rent any more.

'If you think you can get in my pants with that pathetic bunch of roses and a box of Thorntons like last year, then you are even more of a dick than all my friends said you were.

'A bottle of Tesco's Cava? You cheap fucking shit. Take that round to your little whore – I'm sure they'll be straight off.'

Hollis stressed that you should just fuck off and leave her alone adding: 'If you take fatty boom-

'Stick 'em up your arse, you fucking prick.'

boom to our restaurant tonight, I will come in and tear her fucking head off and use it as cocktail glass. You bastard.'

Gary Degan, 26, said: 'Nikki. Nik. Niks. Pleeeaaase. Let me in. I know you paid for it, but it is my Playstation.'

NHS to replace homoeopathy with medicine

THE NHS is to replace homoeopathy with medicine after realising that a wet teabag applied to the buttocks will not cure cancer.

The homoeopathic system was invented in the late eighteenth century by a German who discovered that sick people would pay to be treated with a mixture of ground-up pubes and lice.

Despite the invention of medicine, the remedies are still used by some people today, up to the point where they discover they actually have something wrong with them and demand proper drugs and an operation.

Henry Brubaker, director of the Institute for Studies, said no one had suffered adverse effects from using modern homoeopathic tablets, which contain a mixture of humus and magic air.

He said: 'The only people to wind up dead after taking these tablets were already ill. They are perfectly harmless, as long as they are not taken by sick people.'

Bob McKay, 56, said: 'I have taken homoeopathic remedies all my life so as soon as I started shitting blood I treated it with a tincture of black puddings'.

He added: 'Are you coming to my funeral next week? My wife needs to know for the sandwiches.'

Nikki Hollis, 26, said: 'I used homoeopathy to ease the pain of childbirth. If my husband ever comes near me again I'll chop his cock off with a rusty tin lid.'

While this teabag cannot perform keyhole surgery on a ruptured spleen, it does make a nice cup of tea.

UK threat level raised to 'Underpants'

THE terrorist threat level across the UK has been raised from 'Spacehopper' to 'Underpants', security chiefs confirmed last night.

Members of key national security committees, including 'Cobra', 'Jaws' and 'Thunder-cats', now believe the threat to be so hot that Britain could be consumed in a ball of fiery gas by the end of the week.

'Underpants' means everyone in the UK must carry a whistle and be prepared to tell the police what they dreamt about last night, no matter how weird or perverted.

A Home Office spokesman said: 'Following the discovery of two cars full of petrol and a fairly typical Saturday afternoon in Glasgow, the government has decided to increase the United Kingdom threat level from 'Spacehopper' to 'Underpants'.

'We will do everything within our power to ensure the threat level does not have to be increased to "Phillip Schofield".'

He added: 'You should go about your daily lives as if nothing is wrong while at the same time being constantly vigilant and terrified.

'If you don't like the look of someone, or you overhear comments that you disagree with, you should immediately point at your enemy and blow your whistle until police marksmen arrive.'

Whatever you do, don't panic.

Meanwhile security experts have called for a change of tactics to deal with the new breed of rubbish terrorists.

Denys Finch-Hatton, a security consultant, said: 'The fact that they are unable to distinguish their arse from their elbow means we have to develop ever more imaginative ways to thwart them.

'Instead of asking people to remove their shoes at airports, perhaps we should be asking them to tie their laces. That might weed out some of the real half-wits.'

UK THREAT LEVELS

All is well. Unlock your doors and lend your car to a neighbour. Sing.

Unsettling. What was that noise? Where were you born? Share my values at once, young man.

Terribly frightening. Death has your business card. Trust no one and carry a bucket at all times.

Incredibly dangerous. You and everyone you know is now a terrorist. Go home, lock the door and watch *Grey's Anatomy*.

Oh Christ. The shit's hit the fan. Your car is on fire. And so are your trousers.

MANGO

HEDGEHOG

SPACEHOPPER

UNDERPANTS

PHILLIP SCHOFIELD

Ministers defend treatment of worthless foreign scroungers

THE government has rejected claims that Britain mistreats the thousands of whining, dishonest foreigners who wash up on our shores every year like so much rubbish.

The asylum system has come under attack from a senior judge who is no doubt sponsoring a gang of urchins in one of these flea-ridden cesspits.

Sir John Waite's report said the UK had abused the hordes of unwashed thieves by not giving them fluffy pillows, a mug of hot chocolate and a bedtime story before sending them back to whatever hell-hole they climbed out of.

A Home Office spokesman said: 'So what if they get a clip round the ear and a cold Pot Noodle?

'They're dirty foreign types who just want to steal our hospital beds and move into my garden.'

The report also accused the immigration service of refusing to serve afternoon tea in detention centres and failing to compliment these la-di-da refugees on their choice of rags.

The spokesman added: 'What's wrong with their own countries? I've been to Somalia. The scenery is beautiful and Mogadishu just oozes rustic charm.

'And anyway, I thought you wanted us to treat them like shit?'

Somalia: land of opportunity.

NEWS BRIEFLY

CONCERN GROWS AS SPEARS TAKES THREE ATTEMPTS TO REVERSE INTO PARKING SPACE
'That lamppost could have been her baby,' says big, fat TV therapist.

POOR PEOPLE TO EAT CARBON UNDER U.S. CLIMATE PLAN
Carbon to be captured, reconstituted and offered to poor nations as chocolate-covered treat.

KLAN-TV LAUNCHED AS RACIST TELEVISION WAR HOTS UP
Flagship programmes to include *White Power Treehouse* and *Strictly Anglo-Saxon Dancing*.

Worthless Opinion Poll How will you be increasing the UK population?	
Incorporating coil into Hallowe'en costume	10.8%
Embracing Popery	21.8%
Storing my essence in a jug	30.6%
Smuggling a boat-load of Afghans	36.86%

How the UK's love of dishwashers is outweighing its fear of cancer

BRITAIN is to build a new generation of nuclear power stations after consumers said their love of dishwashers outweighed their fear of cancer.

Concerns that building 20 giant bombs which could at any moment melt down and burn through to the Earth's core sending the planet spinning off its axis and destroying the entire human race were set aside after it emerged that without nuclear stations there would be no Sky[+].

Nikki Hollis, a sales executive from Nantwich, said she was worried how she would power her hair straighteners, iPod, second iPod and vibrating egg.

She added: 'Without nuclear, it's hard to see how we can avoid descending into savagery.'

HOW THINGS WORK: Nuclear Power

Making power from nuclear atoms is straightforward and almost always harmless.

The process starts with a so-called 'Doomsday Machine'. This is not as bad as it sounds. The machine produces dilithium crystals similar to those used in fictional spacecraft only much, much, much more dangerous.

The crystals are then saturated with a mixture of bomb juice and Satan's urine. This starts a reaction which must be channelled very quickly through an electricity machine before *absolutely everything* explodes.

When the machine reaches top speed, the electricity flies out and along a series of ionised rubber tubes until it reaches your dishwasher, novelty smoothie-maker or rechargeable 'chin massager'.

The only downside from nuclear power is the uncontrollably huge amount of boiling hot electric cancer.

NUCLEAR POWER: A PICTORIAL GUIDE

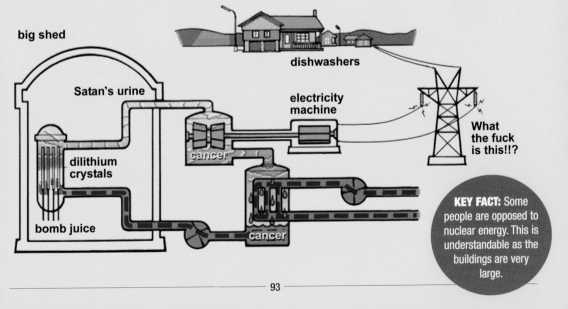

big shed

dishwashers

Satan's urine

electricity machine

dilithium crystals

cancer

What the fuck is this!!?

bomb juice

cancer

KEY FACT: Some people are opposed to nuclear energy. This is understandable as the buildings are very large.

Capello tells England players to stop being so bad at football

ENGLAND manager Fabio Capello has urged his squad to be much better at playing football, ahead of tonight's friendly against Switzerland.

Capello told the squad their failure to qualify for Euro 2008 was because they had played football with a con-sistently high-degree of awfulness.

Capello has given each player one of these.

He said: 'I told them, "You are terrible footballers, all of you. But it's okay because I have a plan: Stop being so bad at football and start being really good at it instead."'

He added: 'I said to Joe Cole, I said, "Joe, sometimes when you collect the ball on the half-way line you pass it really very badly indeed.

'"Instead, why don't you try passing it accurately to another member of your team, prefer-ably just in front of him, so he can run onto it without breaking his stride?"'

Capello has also advised goal-keeper David James to try to stop the ball with his hands, other-wise it may cross the line,

resulting in a goal for the opposing team.

Newly appointed captain Steven Gerrard said the manager had lifted morale by predicting that the team would win more matches just as soon as they can stop being quite so dreadful.

'He made it very clear that we weren't good at defending or attacking and that we should really try to be much better at both of those very important things. He's a breath of fresh air.'

Meanwhile, Capello has also introduced a tough new regime that will see the players forced to cut up their own food, flush their own lavatories and pay off their own money-grubbing nightclub skanks.

Free bank with every new mobile

COMPETITION has intensified in the mobile phone market with rival companies offering a medium-sized bank with every new handset.

Vodafone are tempting new customers with a Motorola V9 or a Samsung G600 and their choice of HBOS, the Woolwich or Bradford and Bingley.

A Vodafone spokesman said: 'The HBOS deal is going well, but a lot of people are saying they would rather just have the phone without being saddled with an over-valued mortgage book.'

Carphone Warehouse said it

has attracted thousands of new sign-ups with its range of Nokia deals, which include a bluetooth headset and a seat on the board of Alliance & Leicester.

A company spokesman said: 'We don't want to overwhelm people. At the end of the day they are buying a phone, not a bank.'

Meanwhile O₂ is enhancing its Apple iPhone offer with 200 free minutes, 100 free texts and a controlling stake in BNP-Paribas.

Roy Hobbs, deputy chief econ-omist at Madeley-Finnegan, said: 'More and more people are trans-ferring their assets out of banks and into Tupperware. And then

T-Mobile's Nokia/Lloyds TSB deal includes built-in GPS and 63,000 staff.

putting the Tupperware on a secret shelf inside the chimney breast.

'Inevitably this means ware-houses filled with worthless banks that have to be given away for nothing before they start to stink like rotting cheese.'

ONE WOMAN'S WEEK: Fighting the fat

by KAREN FENESSEY

IT is wonderful to look around our British streets and see so many different walks of life being not only tolerated, but encouraged.

The whites walk alongside the blacks, the rich and the poor, and the gays and the normal.

At the weekend, I happened upon the latest special needs group to join our society after my sister dragged me to her favourite new store – Curvalicious. Yes, my sister belongs to our heaviest social strand – the obese. But should we really indulge our enormous friends so enthusiastically?

I suppose it's no bad thing that the discovery of an outsize bra and pant store has given my sister the stimulus to get off the couch and remove her gigantic paw from her packet of Wotsits.

Nevertheless, I felt distinctly uncomfortable in Curvalicious as my sister wobbled around the rails. I swear that from the minute I entered the shop, I received threatening looks from every woman there. I can only attribute this to their jealousy.

> 'Should we really indulge our enormous friends so enthusiastically?'

There was only one couple present and it may surprise you to learn that the man wasn't even fat. In fact, he was rather petite, which somehow just made it all the more wrong. Needless to say, she dragged him to the exit as soon as I walked in. It must have been so painful to see her man desiring a woman as exemplary as myself.

My sister wound up buying a size double H bra – and that wasn't even the largest available. The sizes went up to a double J which, in my opinion, is halfway up the alphabet and practically unfathomable.

My sister's doctor claims her monstrousness is down to depression. Really? I suffer from depression on a regular basis due to my stressful work with primary school children and their disgusting parents, yet I am not the size of a house.

Can't the bosses of Curvalicious see their folly? Soon, I won't be able to walk down the street without being eyeballed by heifers and desired by their tiny, bizarre companions.

DIARY: Jeremy Kyle

MY new prime-time show, *Jeremy Kyle Tells you to Shut it*, airs tonight, and the first episode is an absolute corker.

A woman who'd lost her entire family in a multiple car wreck was sitting in the chair, moaning and groaning about her lot in life, which I know was pissing the audience off no end. So I hit her over the head with my rolled-up script.

'Listen, sweet tits, you're not the only one who's feeling pain, you're not the only one who's lost all 17 members of their family in a road traffic accident – well, maybe you are, but you're a freak.

'I want you to buck your ideas up, go home, open a couple of bottles of Chardonnay and drink until you forget about this whole, sorry episode. Now bugger off and take your snot-filled tissues with you.' That seemed to do the trick.

Last week I walked into my local Tesco Express in the hope of finding some Alphabetti Spaghetti to go with the Findus Crispy Pancakes. Following a fruitless search, I approached a checkout girl.

'I came in here to purchase a tin of spaghetti for my tea, and guess what? Nothing. You've let me down, you've let all these people down – and more importantly – you've let yourself down. I think everyone in this lengthening queue will agree when I say that you're a total and utter disgrace. Okay, if you're going to cry, then please do it in your own time, at the back of the shop.'

At that I walked out of there to the sound of cheering from the people queueing inside – it's hard being the people's champion.

In Agony with PETULA SOUL

Dear Petula,
I came home earlier than usual from the pub last night and crept into our house in the dark only to be greeted by the noise of vigorous lovemaking coming from upstairs. The sounds I heard were unlike any I had encountered during my own hochmagandy with the missus, and I was shocked and disturbed. Unsure what to do, and frightened of what I might do should I barge in and discover her in the act, I went into the kitchen. But with my mind disturbed it seemed somehow strange and unfamiliar. Some hours later a man I had never seen before in my life came into the kitchen, saw me, started shouting and then roughly threw me out the front door causing me to sprain my ankle. Do you think I was in the wrong house?

Puzzled,
Dundee

Petula says:

Dear Puzzled,
A difficult question to answer this, but only if you are pissed-up half-wit. Reviewing the evidence so far presented, the strange noises, the unfamiliar surroundings and the violent ejection, I would conclude that, on balance, you are a clueless dunce. Of course you fucking were! While I take my job as an Agony Aunt seriously, it is the pain and torment of the soul I deal with not the confused mind and twisted ankle of a moron such as yourself. My readers don't want twisted ankles. They want three in a bed, I'm in love with my best friend's uncle's sister's brother, that kind of thing. If this is the best you can come up in future stick to 'Dear Deirdre' in the Sun. *She'll answer anything.*

Do you have a problem you'd like Petula to help with? e: petula@thedailymash.co.uk

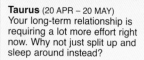

Psychic Bob's Week Ahead What does the future hold for you?

Taurus (20 APR – 20 MAY)
Your long-term relationship is requiring a lot more effort right now. Why not just split up and sleep around instead?

Gemini (21 MAY – 20 JUN)
News of an ex's new sizzling affair will upset you. But remember: things are over for a reason – you stank of mildew and were shit in bed.

Cancer (21 JUN – 22 JUL)
You are the calm eye of the storm, the place where everything is quiet and serene. No you're not. You are fucking insane, and you know it.

Leo (23 JUL – 22 AUG)
You need a stimulating dose of a new culture today – try unprotected sex. But first you must learn how to spell chlamydia.

Virgo (23 AUG – 22 SEP)
Skip over the irritating detail in that project you're working on today – you'll be amazed at how easy it is cut corners, even in nuclear reactor design.

Libra (23 SEP – 23 OCT)
You are after a wild week, but your planets are keen on you finishing projects you began earlier this year. Boring, boring bastards.

Scorpio (24 OCT – 21 NOV)
Why be shy or modest about how you feel? It is always good to show your affection. Except to horses. That's illegal.

Sagittarius (22 NOV – 21 DEC)
When others ask you help them this week, you will actually be helping yourself an enormous amount. So there is no need to pretend to be deaf like usual.

Capricorn (22 DEC – 19 JAN)
Are you nervous about that upcoming family gathering? Don't be. They are all going to die in a gas explosion next Tuesday.

Aquarius (20 JAN – 19 FEB)
Your business and romantic connections intersect in a very unusual way when you discover your wife is running a brothel. But what were you doing there in the first place?

Pisces (20 FEB – 20 MAR)
Getting enough alcohol is a top priority for you. Take those airline-size bottles of wine to work, perfect for a top-up during a toilet break. But don't forget the pub at lunchtime!

Aries (21 MAR – 19 APR)
Use extreme violence to get what you want in your relationship without compromise. Easy!

the daily mash

it's news to us   www.thedailymash.co.uk   No. 11

SMOKERS BANNED FROM LOOKING AT CIGARETTES WHILE SMOKING

'For the children.'

SMOKERS will have to hold a large piece of card over their face so they cannot look at the cigarette they are smoking, ministers said last night.

The 'smoking mask' will include a small mouth-hole and a handle, though later models may be fitted with elasticated straps.

From next April, if smokers want to buy cigarettes they will have to uncover them during a day-long treasure hunt using a series of very difficult clues.

Under the new regulations the smokers will then have to store their cigarettes inside a large cereal box, which may or may not contain a cobra.

When they want to smoke they must position the cereal box on a table, strap on their smoking mask and then fumble around inside the box in the hope of finding a cigarette and not a large, venomous snake.

The mask will also carry a warning which reads: 'Lighting a Cigarette while Wearing this Mask May Cause you to Set Fire to the Mask instead of the Cigarette and Burn your Face Off.'

Health secretary, Alan Johnson, said: 'If you can't see nicotine, it can't see you. And, as any scientist will tell you, if something can't see you, it has no way of knowing you exist.'

But Tory back-bencher Denys Finch-Hatton said: 'The best way to make cigarettes attractive to children is to hide them in the woods as part of a day-long treasure hunt.'

---

news

KEVIN BACON TO TEACH BRITAIN HOW TO DANCE

news

MOST BBC NEWS NOW ABOUT THE BBC

'D'you know what? I'm such a fucking racist,' says Tory MP

CONSERVATIVE leader David Cameron is facing fresh embarrassment after a senior backbencher described himself as 'an enthusiastic and committed racialist'.

Dennis Hatton-Finch, MP for Minchinhamptonsteadbury, has refused to resign after writing an article for his local newspaper entitled: 'Aren't Africans Ghastly?'

Worthless Opinion Poll

Why are you being blackmailed?

I eat poo	12%
Attic full of scouts	21%
Arse-hamsters	22%
Drug-fuelled blow-job unpleasantness	45%

'My article in the *Minchin Courier* is a serious contribution to the debate about the absolute ghastliness of Africans,' said Mr Hatton-Finch.

'I was simply saying how awful these foreigners are and why they should stay in their own stink-holes.

'Does that make me the new Enoch Powell? Possibly, but I tell you what, you should hear me at home. It's all "n-word" this and "d-word" that. I'm such a bigot.'

Mr Hatton-Finch added: 'They come over here with their huge penises, beating us at football and making me feel like a girl.

'And it's not just the Africans. The other day a Polish chap turned up at my door and told my wife he would flush her pipes for £75.'

Powell: brilliant intellectual and racist shit.

'I mean, really. Coming over here with their tool kits and their huge penises and flushing my wife without an appointment.'

A Labour spokesman said: 'This is conclusive proof that every member of the shadow cabinet enjoys nothing more than urinating into a cup and throwing it at a poster of Nelson Mandela.'

France warns of war with Iran not involving France

THE rest of the world could soon be embroiled in a war with Iran, the French foreign minister has warned.

Bernard Kouchner said in the event of conflict over Iran's nuclear programme, the United States and Britain would enjoy the full moral support of the French people.

'War is a terrible thing, which is why we prefer to avoid it,' said Kouchner. 'But for other countries it is often unavoidable and when that happens we will be there to wish them the very best of luck.'

Kouchner said the easing of tensions with North Korea proved that diplomacy can work as long as it goes hand-in-hand with the threat

of a war not involving France.

He added: 'We urged the Americans to be tough with North Korea and assured them that if the situation did escalate we would be on the end of the phone, day or night. If necessary we would come over with a delicious pie.'

Kouchner provoked a row last month when he accused the Iraqi government of being in disarray and insisted the country was still far too dangerous for French troops.

Meanwhile Iran has denied developing nuclear weapons, insisting it was only enriching uranium as part of its Duke of Edinburgh Award.

The last thing Iran needs is a lot of Frenchmen running about, said Kouchner.

Most willing to lie about green lifestyle changes

Seventy-seven per cent said they would be more than happy to give up their novelty juicer but had absolutely no intention of doing so.

MOST people are ready to tell enormous lies about the personal sacrifices they will make to halt climate change, the latest *Daily Mash* poll reveals.

Our survey asked: 'Would you give up your 4x4, foreign holiday, luxury consumer goods, and dishwasher to save the planet?' More than 80 per cent said: 'Absolutely, yes.'

We then asked: 'Would you really give up your 4x4, foreign holiday, luxury consumer goods, and dishwasher to save the planet?' More than 80 per cent said: 'No, actually, I wouldn't, come to think of it.'

Alexandra McLeish, 48, a mother of two, said she would happily give up her Maytag ZigZag fridge-freezer and Electrolux Iron-Aid tumble-dryer to preserve the planet for her young son and daughter.

When we offered to take them away on an electric truck she said: 'You will have to prise them from my cold, dead hands, motherfuckers," and barricaded herself in the kitchen with a shotgun.

Bill McKay, 36, from Reading, said: 'I would personally sacrifice my mother and father, wife and three children if it meant I could replace my PS3 with a Nintendo Wii and fly to Thailand for sex tourism.'

He added: 'It would work out better in the end, because I will be able to offset my kerb crawling.'

Bob Holt, 48, from Harrogate, said he was prepared to make huge personal sacrifices to save the planet from climate change as long as it did not involve any huge personal sacrifice.

He said: 'There are billions of poor Chinese people who don't have big cars, adequate sanitation, central heating or electric light. If we could just keep it like that then I can have a Range Rover Sport. What exactly is the problem?'

But Yen Xiao, a farmer, from Jiangsu Province in China, said: 'If it's all right with you, I would still quite like a *fucking fridge*.'

NEWS BRIEFLY

TRANQUILISERS REPLACE TELEVISION AS WORLD'S FAVOURITE CHILDMINDER
'I crush two tabs of diazepam into their Petit Filous and they just sit there like a couple of turnips. Result.'

GPs URGE GOVERNMENT TO CONFIRM ONLINE BANKING DETAILS
'Next time we'll try and sell them the secret of how to make £62,000 a week by working from home,' says BMA.

MUSIC COMPANIES CALL FOR BAN ON WHISTLING
'If you whistle "Whistle while you Work" while you work, we'll cut your lips off,' warns Disney.

Worthless Opinion Poll
Which toy are you recalling?

Toy	%
Exploding-Head Barbie™	14.8%
Knife-in-a-Box	16.2%
My First Cobra®	17.5%
SpongeBob SquareCock™	51.5%

Keith Richards to write story of his life as a Beatle

ROCK legend Keith Richards is to write his memoirs, filled with intimate details of his life as a member of The Beatles.

Richards, 63, said the book would describe his first meeting with songwriting partner Paul McCartney when both were at school in the Yorkshire mining village of Manchester.

According to the guitarist the schoolboy friends quickly formed a small free-jazz ensemble with fellow Mancunians George Harrison, Charlie Watts and Harold Wilson.

However, history would only be made, Richards added, when the quartet met up with Mick Jagger and John Lennon, both then studying art at the London School of Economics in Liverpool, to form the pop group that would soon become known as the Fab Four.

Richards said: 'I also have a very clear memory of writing the

rock opera *Tommy* in our digs in Bamburg, the Dutch seaside town where we really cut our teeth as a live act.'

The guitarist is to spend the next two years researching his own life to ensure he is not actually writing a book about someone else.

Nevertheless Richards insists he already has some great tales to tell.

'We had some major artistic differences, particularly over a song I had written called "Lady Eleanor Rigby". Paul wanted to use a really intricate string quartet arrangement mixed with samples from Enrico Caruso and Dame Nellie Melba and I wanted to spend the weekend in St Tropez licking acid tabs off the top of Princess Margaret's head.

'We compromised and recorded Paul hoovering up a yard of coke off the naked bum cheeks of Marianne Faithful, slowed it

Keith seems to think he is second from the right.

down, played it backwards and used it as the finale for "I Am the Yellow Submarine". Cool.'

Later sections will reveal how Richards quarrelled furiously with George Harrison's mother Yoko Ono and how Mick Jagger's insistence that he was actually in the Rolling Stones eventually led to the break-up of the best-loved band in the world.

BBC2 unveils plans for 'Nigella Lawson Eats a Banana'

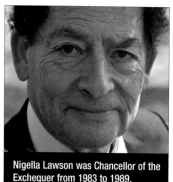

Nigella Lawson was Chancellor of the Exchequer from 1983 to 1989.

TV food fans were celebrating last night after the BBC confirmed plans for a new series of *Nigella Lawson Eats a Banana*.

The series of six half-hour shows will feature Nigella Lawson sitting in front of a camera, eating a banana.

A BBC spokesman said: 'There will be no script, no music and no credits.

'It will just be a solid half-hour of Nigella Lawson working her way through a

fairly large banana.'

The Corporation has already commissioned a raft of shows featuring the popular chef.

Next spring sees the premiere of *Nigella Lawson Rides a Horse*, while the centre-piece of BBC2's summer schedule will be *Nigella Lawson Washes a Car*.

This year's prime-time Christmas Eve slot on BBC1 will be filled by the hour-long special *Nigella Lawson Dresses Up as an Elf*.

Rizlas to carry cannabis tedium warning

RIZLA cigarette papers are to carry warnings that excessive cannabis smoking makes you incredibly boring and likely to bore others around you.

The warnings follow new research into the dangers of so-called 'passive tedium' which show that people exposed to cannabis smokers are often incredibly bored by the experience.

Dr Wayne Hayes, director of reefer at the Institute for Studies, said: 'You may think that your incoherent theories about the nature of music are interesting. But the fact is, they are unbelievably boring and you have to shut up.'

He added: 'The danger is other people become so bored they start to throw up and before you know it you have to make yourself look interesting by growing dreadlocks.

'It's about as cutting edge and rebellious as my gran. Reggae? Thump, thump, thump. Batty boys, Mr Bombastic. What a lot of pish.'

A series of warnings will be printed on each individual Rizla paper including:

- Smoking cannabis while pregnant will make your baby boring.
- Cannabis smoking will lead to a slow and painful conversation.
- Don't stab people in the eye when you go all psycho and shit.

Health minister Alan Johnson said that every day cannabis smoking bores 19,000 Europeans who don't smoke cannabis.

He added: 'We're urging moderation. There's no need to roll a really fat one first thing in the morning, unless you have a stressful job like driving a train.'

Smoking cannabis makes you boring and bores others around you

Glasgow launches bid for 'swearing olympics'

GLASGOW City Council has unveiled a £40-million package of incentives in their bid to host the 2014 Commonmouth Games – the Olympics of world swearing.

Glasgow bid supremo Tom Logan said much of the incentive package would be directed into swearing promotion, in particular potty-mouth training for the under-fives.

He added: 'The games are all about celebrating the top arseing swearers in the world today, but there is no pissing point unless we invest to bring on the next cocking generation.'

The city has designed a new promotional logo featuring a smiling child and the slogan 'Fuck Glasgow 2014'.

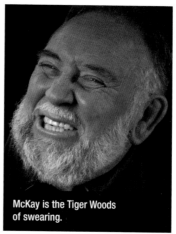

McKay is the Tiger Woods of swearing.

The bid has received strong support from William McKay, Glasgow's own World Freestyle Swearing Champion.

He said: 'What in the name of tits are you looking at? Bastarding arsemonkeys. Shit off. Twat!'

Glasgow has submitted a formidable bid with many of the facilities needed to stage a major swearing event already in place.

With Hampden, Celtic Park and Ibrox, the city already has the world's three most respected swearing venues, all of which frequently stage events attracting 60,000-plus crowds of unbelievably foul-mouthed amateur swearers.

Javier de Montez, chairman of the games committee, said: 'I'm sure all the bids will be shitting brilliant and it's just a shame that some fucker has to lose.'

M&S on the brink as public decide to peel their own vegetables

MARKS & SPENCER last night warned that civilisation was at an end after its profits slumped following poor Christmas sales of hand-peeled free-range sprouts at £9.99 a pair.

Chief executive Sir Stuart Rose said the retailer's failure to shift a single 'carrot in a box' at just £14.99 suggested the country was only months away from anarchy and civil war.

However, analysts blamed the retail giant's financial woes on a poor buying strategy after it failed to get its hands on sufficient stocks of this year's surprise Christmas top sellers: tinned baked beans and guns.

Wayne Hayes, of Conceptomatix, said many high street retailers had done well out of the

Delicious, but are they worth £1,500?

season's must have items including:
- Water-purification tablets.
- Body armour.
- Amputation saws.
- Live pigs.

Hayes said: 'Tesco was knocking out a box of 48 tins of value beans, a 12-bore and 20 cartridges, and a gas mask for only £19.99 and they

were flying off the shelves right up until Christmas Eve.

'All M&S had to offer was a pair of Purdeys with a jar of cassoulet and a ripe stilton for ten grand, but they only had about a 100 of them and they were all gone by the end of November.'

He added: 'If you've got the right stuff you can still shift it. My mate Stevo has an army surplus place and he's been selling camouflage hats and loads of really big knives. And chainsaws.'

Brand consultant Nikki Hollis blamed M&S's poor Christmas performance on 'that fucking advert'.

She added: 'If Dervla Kirwan likes the honey-glazed carrots that much why doesn't she just shove them up her glory hole?'

ONE WOMAN'S WEEK: Giving my all

by KAREN FENESSEY

As anyone who knows me will tell you, I am one of the most charitable people anyone could hope to meet. In fact, I would go as far as to say I am a disabled person's wet dream.

But my charitable exploits are something I like to conduct in the privacy of my own home, so when I am approached on my Saturday shopping spree by inanely grinning youths holding clipboards and trying to get me to contribute to their charity, I simply rage, 'No number of clipboards will make your ridiculous and un-environmentally friendly dreadlocks look like those of a professional charity representative,' and, 'You and your Congolese orphans won't see a penny from me!'

I regularly contribute to the weaker members of our society by donating some of my cutting-edge fashion choices to organisations such as Oxfam and other special needs shops. Nevertheless, I must admit that this constant bombardment of new 'fad' charities is testing my infinite patience.

I was approached on Saturday afternoon by not one, not two, but THREE of these charity bastards. The first two, I was able to bat off using my umbrella but the third caught me off guard: 'Hey!' he said, 'Where did you get your hair cut?' As I only recently had my hair cut (at a cost of £180 by Vidal Sassoon), I couldn't help but give him my attention, as it is surely a keen eye for style that spots when Karen Fenessey approaches! However, he only talked about my hair for ten minutes before getting round to Congolese fucking orphans and my bank details. Plus, he really didn't seem to know what he was talking about with regards to styling, and didn't even know what a half head of highlights were. It was then that I knew he had grown jealous of my hair and now wanted to strip me of my every last penny as revenge.

'Listen,' I told him sternly, 'I am one of the most charitable people you will ever meet and, as I'm sure I make a lot more than you and

> 'You and your Congolese orphans won't see a penny from me'

probably most people in this street, I think it's safe to say I give more than most. But I am damned if I am going to contribute my hard-earned cash to your Comic Relief bollocks.'

The youth mumbled something about how he wasn't collecting for Comic Relief, and something about oppression in the Congo. 'The Congo?' I said, and then added as a final witticism, 'Why don't you give them Um Bongo? They drink that in the fucking Congo!' I couldn't help laughing to myself as I stormed off. I really do have a fantastic sense of humour – and everyone I relayed this story to later that day said the same thing.

Some may say that I should have contributed to the plight of the Congolese in need. And I certainly agree it is right to give them rations. But, as I said, this is something I will do privately and not through this evil Comic Relief mass hysteria.

Years ago while watching the show on TV, I felt compelled to donate some money. But their claim that any amount is sufficient is a total lie, because when I went online it kept asking me for thirty quid, and wouldn't let me give the fiver I'd intended for those landmine kids.

Then it occurred to me: when I donate my money to Comic Relief, there's only one African it goes to – and that's Lenny Henry. And when you look at the size of him, and consider that he's just earned a small fortune for his portrayal of a man who stays at a Premier Travel Inn and buys bread for a rubber duck, I think I can safely say he is in no urgent need of rations and it is in everyone's interests to keep our fivers to ourselves. After all, as Jesus said: 'Charity begins at home!'

Worthless Opinion Poll Which heartwarming animal story are you enjoying?	
Frog gets taxi to shop	14.3%
Otter gets pilot's licence	23.3%
Kitten gives birth to horse	27.7%
Piglet gives insides to sausage factory	34.7%

In Agony with PETULA SOUL

Dear Petula,
I am a happily married woman of 40 who loves her husband of 20 years very much. We have an active and fulfilling sex life but for some time now my hubby Bob has been asking me if I would be interested in wife swapping. Personally it gave me the shivers but, because I love him dearly, I eventually gave in, and so my husband invited around our friends Jack and Laura for the night. We opened a bottle of wine, and one thing led to another until at the end of the night Bob swapped me for a complete set of 1970 Mexico World Cup medallions from Esso, a set of tumblers and 4,000 Embassy coupons. Is this right? I would have thought I was at least worth a decanter set.

Hurt,
Hull

Petula says:

Dear Hurt,
Most modern couples will try wife swapping occasionally, say once or twice a week after that first flush of passion has died down following their return from honeymoon. In most cases it is a perfectly harmless bit of fun. The sex will be rubbish, but it's always reassuring to find out you are not the only person in the neighbourhood who still thinks artex ceilings are just the thing. On the other hand things do tend to get a bit complicated leading to intense hatred, divorce, stalking and murderous jealousy. But, as I always say, nothing ventured, nothing gained! Having seen the photograph you sent in with your letter I think your husband actually got a very good deal. Could you put him in touch? I have an old sofa I need to flog and I really need to raise some cash.

Do you have a problem you'd like Petula to help with? e: petula@thedailymash.co.uk

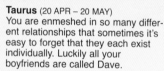

Psychic Bob's Week Ahead What does the future hold for you?

Taurus (20 APR – 20 MAY)
You are enmeshed in so many different relationships that sometimes it's easy to forget that they each exist individually. Luckily all your boyfriends are called Dave.

Gemini (21 MAY – 20 JUN)
You've got to make the call between getting your own way and helping a good friend with what they need. Do you really need my advice on that one?

Cancer (21 JUN – 22 JUL)
Is someone being a bit greedy regarding you? Tell them there is a queue outside the stationery cupboard and we've all only got an hour for lunch. That's two minutes each!

Leo (23 JUL – 22 AUG)
Inspiration strikes in a flash and you suddenly realise how to do what you've been trying to do all this time. No more Velcro-fastening shoes for you!

Virgo (23 AUG – 22 SEP)
Listen to your heart closely today, because when it stops you are dead. Do not attempt to operate any heavy machinery. Stick to light dusting.

Libra (23 SEP – 23 OCT)
You're brimming with self-confidence and are certain you're doing the right thing. As usual, you are wrong.

Scorpio (24 OCT – 21 NOV)
While your office rivals are dozing, you've a golden opportunity to get one over on them. There's no need for back-stabbing or anything sinister. But do it anyway. It's fun!

Sagittarius (22 NOV – 21 DEC)
Global financial issues seem rather remote and unreal, wait until the bailiff kicks your door in and walks off with your television.

Capricorn (22 DEC – 19 JAN)
There may be some follow-through with a new flirtation. Don't strain, and pack an extra pair of pants. No one likes to stink of poo on a first date.

Aquarius (20 JAN – 19 FEB)
You've got a bit of food stuck next to your lip – there . . . no, there. That's it. Gone.

Pisces (20 FEB – 20 MAR)
That visit to the specialist this Thursday? The prognosis doesn't look good – let me put it another way: don't buy any green bananas.

Aries (21 MAR – 19 APR)
Everyone warms to your gentle side – let's face it, people don't see enough of that sort of thing in a man these days, so why don't you drop the weapon and release the hostages?

LIVE HEALTHY
OR
DIE!

'E-numbers make my children hilarious'

PARENTS across Britain have reacted angrily to the European ban on food colourings, claiming artificial ingredients make their children funnier and more interesting.

The EU wants to ban a range of E-numbers amid claims they are made from diesel by-products and turn you into a raging psychopath.

But British parents insist the right level of artificial colourings can transform a dull, predictable child into an hilarious, pint-sized version of Norman Wisdom.

Tom Logan, a father of two from Bexhill, said: 'On Sundays I like to load up my four-year-old with a litre of orange squash and then set him loose in the garden with some old vases, a tortoise and a hammer.'

Meanwhile thousands of parents are objecting to the changes after spending years controlling their children through a delicate chemical balance of E-numbers and horse tranquilisers.

Emma Stevens, 39, from Chester, said: 'I can't remember why we started pumping them full of these things, but we're in way too deep to stop now.

'Take away the horse tranqs and it's like the *Texas Chainsaw Massacre* in here. Take away the bright orange dye and you have to drag them upstairs by the hair.'

Mrs Stevens added: 'My children are a healthy, well-adjusted cocktail of artificial chemical compounds.

'To an outside observer they look completely normal, and I'd like to keep pretending that they are until they go off to university and start mixing their own drugs.'

Isn't Norman Wisdom funnier than your dull child?

Eating Special K linked to girly boys

WOMEN who eat Special K around the time of conception are more likely to have a boy, but it will be a girly boy, according to new research.

Scientists claim the low-calorie breakfast cereal can influence the chance of having a boy who enjoys musicals or, if it is mixed with strawberries, a girl who enjoys other girls.

Dr Wayne Hayes, of the Institute for Studies, said: 'We discovered that more than 60 per cent of those who conceived with Special K are now either managing their son's career or helping him sew on the extra sequins.'

Meanwhile the study found that women who want to have rugged male children must devour large handfuls of dry porridge while having sex in the back of a Land Rover.

Dr Hayes added: 'Alpen tends to produce those weedy, self- absorbed types whose band will never get a record deal.

'Frosties and Coco Pops produce the kind of boys who are well-meaning but wear colourful socks, know all the words to 'Bat Out of Hell' and have to be told when to leave.

'Weetabix, Cheerios and Crunchy Nut Cornflakes will produce healthy, intelligent high-flyers whose only flaw is to be thrashed twice a week by a gang of Nazi whores.

'And if you eat a lot of Shredded Wheat, you'll end up with what is, basically, Alistair Darling.'

Fibre Boy.

Leave it!

Leave bacon out of it, health experts warned

HEALTH experts were last night told to, 'Go fuck themselves,' after advising consumers to give up bacon.

The Department of Health in London was under siege as a mob chanted, 'Death to the men in white coats,' and, 'Whoever defames the pig should be executed.'

Bill McKay, an architect from Dorchester, said he would rather disembowel himself with a trowel than live without bacon, the only meat to be approved by the Vegetarian Society.

He added: 'We've taken a lot of shit from these people over the years. Perhaps the time has come to throw our health experts in jail.'

Rona Cameron, Head of Bacon Sandwiches at the Vegetarian Society, said she believed the experts to be either deranged or in league with the devil.

She added: 'I love pigs, they're so cute and clever. But if I was in a farmyard with the smell of fried bacon wafting across my nostrils, I swear to God I'd grab me a shotgun and a meat cleaver.'

Roy Hobbs, bacon director at the Bacon Institute said: 'Bacon transforms men into incredibly sensitive and generous lovers and guarantees women the longest and most intense orgasms imaginable.'

Meanwhile bacon campaigners have issued a series of recommendations for health experts if they wish to carry on living instead of perishing in a huge fireball after someone pours petrol through their letterbox and sets fire to it with a flaming rag, including:

- Leave bacon out of this.
- Shut up about bacon.
- Mention bacon again and you're fucking dead.
- Don't even look at those sausages.

LIVING IN A BIG GLASS TUBE CAN ADD 40 YEARS TO YOUR LIFE, SAY EXPERTS

ABANDONING your job, your family and the outside world in favour of a big glass tube can extend your life expectancy by decades, according to a new study.

Researchers at Dundee University are now calling for increased government support for those who want to live in a tube and have a cocktail of high-fibre nutrients pumped into their stomachs.

The long-term research project kidnapped two young men, suspending one of them in an eight-foot-long tube and forcing the other one to live in a flat and work for an insurance company.

Specimen A responded well to life inside the tube, enjoying the combination of sedatives, liquid food and episodes of *As Time Goes By* with Judi Dench and Geoffrey Palmer.

Specimen B went to the local pub where he met a nice girl with a fruity laugh. After three years of sexual intercourse they mar-

Liquidise some broccoli and pump it through your tubes.

ried and moved to a leafy suburb to raise a family.

Specimen B consumed a range of foods including bacon, mashed potatoes, Special K, donuts, and ham and cucumber sandwiches with full-fat mayonnaise on wholemeal bread.

He also enjoyed a gin and tonic

after work, wine with meals, a few pints of beer after a weekly round of golf and the occasional cigar. He died in his sleep from heart complications aged 72.

Specimen A is now 75-years-old but has the physical heath of a man in his mid-30s. His daily routine involves selecting programmes from his Sky+ box and then watching them while a steady stream of pulped cranberries and broccoli moves from the tube into his stomach to the tube out of his rectum.

Project leader Dr Bob Wood, said: 'Specimen B was such a wretched waste of a life. I watched him throw his years away unable to interfere with my own experiment.

'But look at Specimen A. His lungs are clear, his bowel movements are sound and his heart pumps away, fuelled by a potent cranberry mush. And he's got Sky+.'

He may as well be drinking out of the toilet

Bulimia not the same as being a greedy bastard, say doctors

DOCTORS last night attempted to end the confusion over the symptoms of bulimia, stressing it was not the same as being a big, greedy bastard.

There are fears that GP surgeries could be overwhelmed after reports that the disorder may now be affecting fat people who like to stuff their face.

Dr Lewis Wade, of the Institute for Second Helpings, said: 'In our studies we always separate the subjects into two groups.

'In Group A are the people who engage in binge eating followed by purging, and in Group B are the people eat a whole tin of biscuits because it's 11 o'clock.

'Although some of the people in Group B eat so many biscuits they end up making themselves sick, it's not the same thing.'

Dr Wade said bulimia was more likely to affect young women with self-image problems, while being a fat bastard tends to affect MPs with access to large amounts of free food.

'Of course being an MP can be stressful, especially if you keep making an arse of yourself on *Newsnight*.

'But instead of being a big, greedy bastard, why not go for a long walk or perhaps enjoy a luxury scuba-diving holiday at the taxpayers' expense and then claim it was a "trade mission"?'

Mr Prescott enjoys diving for cake.

OBESITY CAUSED BY 'INFECTED BUNS'

FATNESS is contagious and can be caught from contaminated cakes, buns and sausages, according to new research.

Biologists at the Institute for Studies have discovered that many foods are filled with fat germs that can be passed on to unsuspecting humans.

Once infected a fat person can then pass their fat germs on to thin people by coughing, sneezing, touching and licking.

Project leader Henry Brubaker said: 'If you know a fat person, the chances are they are teeming with microscopic fatness.

'Unless they wash their hands or use a hanky you too could become chunky within hours. And without antibiotics you will soon turn into a big fat pig.'

Describing chocolate chip cookies as the 'new mosquitoes' Professor Brubaker added: 'We believe the time is right for fat people to be quarantined. What about cramming them into disused churches?

'If they do have to venture outside they should be confined to plastic bubbles. Perhaps their friends could volunteer to roll them down the street.'

the daily mash

MINISTERS UNVEIL £400-MILLION PLAN TO SHOUT AT FAT PEOPLE

BRITAIN'S fat people are to be hounded into submission through a multi-million pound strategy of shouting and community violence.

At the heart of the programme will be 250,000 outreach counsellors who will patrol supermarket aisles looking for 'inappropriate choicemakers'.

Once they have identified a target the uniformed counsellors will approach the shopper and scream: 'PUT IT DOWN, FATTY! PUT IT DOWN!'

Supermarket entrances will be fitted with hidden scales and as overweight shoppers enter they will hear the sound of mooing cows and be handed a photograph of Christopher Biggins.

The counsellors will also have the power to force fat people to strip down to their underpants and run around the car park for 20 minutes.

To her cherished homeland she will issue thin, obedient offspring.

The government's plan for 'healthy towns' will include daily calisthenics, with hundreds of uniformed citizens lined up in neat rows, swinging their arms in time to music.

The sessions will be filmed and shown before popular features at cinemas across the country. Actor Brian Cox will provide a voice-over stressing the importance of physical fitness to the struggle against International Zionism.

The 'healthy towns', or *gesundestädte*, will host weekly torchlit marches to the local sports stadium where the uniformed citizens will eat satsumas while watching Sir Steve Redgrave's 1996 coxless pairs triumph over and over again.

Anyone unable to lose weight will have their passport confiscated and be forced to sew a patch onto their uniform depicting a big, fat cartoon pig.

---

news

KIDS DEMAND TV SHOWS THEY CAN BORE THE SHIT OUT OF EACH OTHER WITH IN 30 YEARS TIME

news

SCHOOL LEAVERS TO PLEDGE ALLEGIANCE TO SOME OLD COW

'Get your bumcheeks out of my face'

MINISKIRTS have risen to record levels making it virtually impossible for men to travel on escalators without being exposed to women's buttocks, a new study reveals.

In the last year skirts have shrunk in size from 'Christ, I've seen wider belts' to 'masking tape' to 'Bloody hell, I can see what you had for dinner.' Further shortening is forecast for July.

More than 68 per cent of men said they were now too scared to use the top deck of the bus in case they met a lady on the stairs and came face to face with either of her bottoms.

Tom Logan, an electrician from Bolton, said: 'I'm at the Arndale Centre, I get on the escalator, minding my own business. Next thing, I look up and there's

A typical lady's front bottom.

two great pillows of flesh bearing down on me like an angry sumo.

'If someone had hit the emergency stop button, I'd have been wedged up to my shoulders in bum. They'd have had to get the fire brigade to prise me out of there. And I'd have lost my glasses.'

Roy Hobbs, an accountant from Croydon, said: 'I work in a very female environment and I'm getting a stiff neck from constantly trying to look straight ahead.

'I was in a meeting last week when this girl from sales uncrossed her legs. No panties. At first glance it looked a bit like Anthony Worrall-Thompson.'

But Bill McKay, a veteran pervert from Leeds, said he was cancelling his subscription to *Front Botty* magazine after 35 years.

'All I need is my free bus pass and one of them camera phones.'

Unexploded plastic bag found in town centre

POLICE last night cordoned off an unexploded plastic bag in the centre of Norwich, as shoppers fled for their lives.

Bag decommissioning experts confirmed it was a medium-sized carrier from the local Somerfield, with the potential to maim dozens of innocent people.

The bag was spotted by traffic warden Wayne Hayes as it wafted along the high street during the evening rush hour.

Hayes said: 'I were frozen in terror. I thought we'd seen the last of these things. But there it was, just floating along on the breeze.

'I shouted out: "Bag! Bag! Bag!" and everyone just scarpered

BAAAAAAAAAG!!!!!

like. Except for this one little kid who ran towards it, almost as if she was trying to make friends with it.

'Luckily, at that point, the police arrived and tackled her to the ground.'

The bag then drifted up into the branches of a nearby tree which will now be destroyed in a controlled explosion.

A Norfolk police spokesman said: 'This time we have lost a tree. The next time it could be your house, or your gran.'

Prime Minister Gordon Brown is expected to visit the scene later today when he will announce an extra £2 billion for a network of hi-tech bag-detecting CCTV cameras.

Naomi Campbell to wrestle a bear

SUPERMODEL Naomi Campbell has agreed to take part in a televised brawl with a bear.

Campbell will receive up to £5 million for the eight-round match against a 10-foot-tall, Alaskan Grizzly named Harold.

Campbell is one of the most accomplished fighters in the world of international supermodelling, but until now has satisfied her appetite for violence by taking on domestic staff and public servants.

Tom Logan, editor of *Bear Fighting World*, said: 'Campbell is in terrific shape, as ever, but this is a big step up from a housekeeper or an airline stewardess.

'Housekeepers tend to be pudgy and slow as well as being naturally submissive, given that they work for you.

'Stewardesses, hotel staff and the like are trained to please and so are likely to accept a severe beating for giving you the wrong flavour of Pringles.

'Harold, however, eats about 20 pounds of raw meat a day and weighs 85 stone. He is, essentially, a killing machine who doesn't take any shit from supermodels.'

Campbell is training for the Old Trafford bout by assaulting up to 20 hospitality workers and junior police officers a day.

It is the first time a supermodel has agreed to fight a wild animal since Elle McPherson retired from alligator wrestling in 1997.

'I gonna beat you like an Italian maid.'

Worthless Opinion Poll
Why have you been banned by British Airways?

I'm a crazy bitch	10.4%
Uncontrollably gassy	13.8%
Shoved crying baby down loo	29.6%
Pleasured self with lemon wipe	46.3%

Masochists welcome kinky porn crackdown

THE editor of *Masochism Today* has welcomed a government crackdown on kinky porn and demanded that a cheese grater be dragged across his testicles for breaching the new regulations.

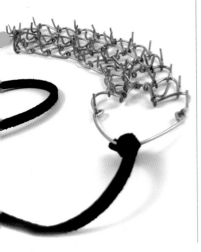

Tom Logan said his publication featured staged scenes of consensual sadomasochistic sex, and called for himself to be strapped to a St Andrew's cross by home secretary Jacqui Smith and his penis flayed with a wet cat o' nine tails.

Mr Logan also said clamps should be attached to his nipples and that his scrotum should be tied up with string while transport secretary Ruth Kelly lashed his quivering buttocks with one of those spiky things she got from Opus Dei.

He said: 'Oh no, our incredibly strict government has discovered that I have been playing naughty games in private with my kinky friends and now it wants to punish me.

One of those spiky things Ruth Kelly got from Opus Dei.

'It's going to force me to dress up as a schoolgirl and sit down at a desk while Harriet Harman walks up and down in a short skirt and stockings, carrying a cane.

'And if I can't recite the relevant clause from the Obscene Publications Act she's going to put me in some stocks, pull down my knickers and spank my little white botty with a fish slice while screaming filth at me in German.'

Henry Brubaker, Head of Civil Liberties at the Institute for Studies, said: 'If people are determined to hurt themselves in the pursuit of delicious, forbidden ecstasy they should join the Catholic Church.

'Otherwise, they are deranged perverts who should be thrashed until their privates explode.'

Everyone to be fitted with a zip

EVERYONE is to be fitted with a zip as part of Gordon Brown's plan to nationalise Britain's kidneys.

The zip will run across the middle of the abdomen to allow for the quick and easy removal of major organs and body parts.

Under the government's plans the police, parking wardens and the inland revenue will also be given the power to confiscate innards for minor misdemeanours, public order offences and late payment of tax.

A department of health spokesman said: 'Remember that time on holiday in Turkey? When

you got drunk and went off with the gorgeous looking girl who then turned out to be a bloke, but you thought "in for a penny" so went for it anyway, and then woke up with a splitting headache, and a terrible pain in your side, and a really nasty looking wound and only one kidney? Well, it will be like that, but without the gay sex or the stitches.'

He added: 'Ride the train without a ticket and we'll have your pancreas. Anything involving drunkenness or aggressive behaviour will cost you at least a couple of kidneys and if your tax isn't on time we'll just attach a

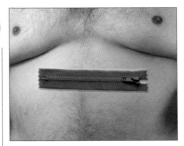

You mustn't play with the zip at parties.

Dyson to you and suck the whole lot out in a oner.'

Consumers welcomed the move but said safeguards were necessary. Nikki Hollis, 26, from Reading, said: 'I wouldn't want to get a kidney off a black, unless I was planning to enter a dancing competition.'

As the markets
continue their
rollercoaster ride,
we can all rest
easy knowing our
jobs, our money
and our future
happiness are
in the hands of

FUCKERS LIKE THIS

New uniform will turn my life around, says tearful McDonald's worker

A NEW designer uniform is going to generate the most amazing improvement in overall quality of life, grateful McDonald's workers said last night.

Nikki Hollis, a flipper from Harlesden, said she was so happy with her new smock and little scarf that she could not wait to get home to her bedsit and show it off to her three-year-old son Kyle.

She said the Bruce Oldfield-designed outfits would make her the envy of all her friends, and brought home to her, once again, McDonald's high level of respect for its staff.

'As you can see it's "mocha" which is all the rage in Milan this season. As soon as I slip these manmade fibres over my head I feel just like Sienna Miller on a night out in Malibu.

'Kyle may not have any toys, and be a bit stunted, but at least I've got something all scratchy to wrap him in when the electricity gets turned off. I think I'll change his name to Bruce.'

Hollis added: 'I suppose it might have been nice if they'd used the money to give us a pay rise, but it's okay because we already get to help ourselves from the leftover bucket.'

Tom Logan, a fryer from Kent, said his new polo shirt was sexy and stylish, thanks to the thin coating of hi-tech spittle repellent.

He added: 'We're so pleased with our uniforms we've composed a little thank-you song for the management. Would you like to hear it?'

Oldfield chose fabrics that look like grilled meat.

Wimbledon to ban fisting

WIMBLEDON is to outlaw the practice of fisting during matches in a move to clean up international tennis.

Fisting joins grunting, swearing, smoking and heavy petting on the list of activities that are no longer deemed acceptable on court.

Commander Julian Cook, head of court etiquette for the Lawn Tennis Association, said fisting should remain on the football and rugby pitches 'where it belongs'.

He said: 'We looked the other way when the Americans were fisting openly, but when English players started fisting it was clear that the traditions of the All England Club were under threat.'

Commander Cook said players who repeatedly shook their clenched fists and shouted at themselves to celebrate success would be docked points and eventually disqualified.

Players will instead be encouraged to write themselves a polite thank-you letter after the conclusion of each game.

✍ DIARY: Quentin Tarantino

I READ an article in *Time* magazine about a year ago and apparently, okay, and this is no fucking bullshit – it's a fact that all women, and when I say all women, I'm talking Madonna, the woman who works in the 7/11 down the road, every woman who ever appeared in a Russ Meyer movie, those women you see carrying big jugs of water on their heads in Africa – okay, so you get the picture, we're talking all women, okay? – would rather listen to Johnny Cash Live at San Quentin than have oral sex with their husband. Fact.

When I saw this I thought, 'Oh my God!' – it was a real lightbulb moment, so I immediately called Harvey Weinstein and told him I was going to make a movie called *MaimTrain*, which has absolutely nothing to do with women listening to classic Johnny Cash instead of giving their partners blow jobs. No, because this was going to be a three-and-half-hour movie set in real-time – like *High Noon* – about this real nutjob psycho called Dangerous Dick who works his way up and down the carriages of a midnight train, maiming people

using a cheese grater and a nail gun. In a technique which has never been used before, I'm going to take the entire soundtrack of another movie – *Those Magnificent Men in their Flying Machines* to be precise – and simply play it over *MaimTrain*. Pretty neat, huh?

London is one of my favourite cities in the whole world. Some of my all-time favourite movies were made here: *Brannigan*, *Sweeney* and, of course, *Sweeney II*. During my short stay in England promoting *MaimTrain* I had this unbelievably brilliant idea for a movie. I was in my hotel room, it must have been early evening around 3.30 a.m. – I was watching a repeat of *Roots* on cable, when it came to me in like a flash – pow! So I immediately called up Sam Jackson and told him of my vision. 'Hey Sam,' I screamed down the phone. 'What the fuck do you want? I'm busy!' he replied. 'Never mind that shit!' I yelled back. 'Check this out for a great idea. Think *Roots*, okay, the Alex Haley TV blockbuster from the 70s, except all you black guys learn kung-fu from the Chinese who are building the railroad around about that time – and zowee! – you guys kick the living shit out of the Chuck Connors character, and all the rest of those racist fucks and shit. It'll be a, like, post-modern, turn-the-tables piece. Hey – we'll get Isaac Hayes in to play Chicken George, put some weird eclectic shit on the soundtrack, and we're in business. It's, like, it can't fail.'

He started to get real interested, but eventually had to pass when I told him I had Chris Rock down to play Kunte Kinte.

NEWS BRIEFLY

SHARP FALL IN WIVES WORTH HAVING SEX WITH, SAYS RELATE
'They stay off the buns for a few months to get into a dress but as soon as that wedding ring's on it's cakey time again,' says charity.

PUBLIC BACKS PRINCESS ANNE TO BE NEXT KING
'She's hard as nails, drinks from the can and loves nothing more than a well-organised dog fight,' says Lord Chancellor.

USE COMA PATIENTS AS DRAUGHT EXCLUDERS, SAYS MINISTER
Also make good hat-stands and can be left outside pubs with ashtrays in their hands.

ILLEGAL DOWNLOADS FORCE RECORD COMPANY BOSSES TO USE 'STREET DRUGS'
Offices throughout Soho piled high with cheap bottles of glue and bags of crisps.

Worthless Opinion Poll
What kind of mouse are you inventing?

Richard Gere mouse (for weekends)	14.6%
Drink-drive mouse (for urine tests)	16.9%
Zip-up mouse (for drugs)	21.1%
Jude Law mouse (for kicking)	47.7%

In Agony with PETULA SOUL

Dear Petula,
I love my boyfriend very much but all is not well with our hoggins. Unfortunately he suffers from premature ejaculation. In fact, he is so premature that even the thought of me in close connection with a bed is enough to make him loose off his love porridge. This is very distressing and embarrassing for both of us, particular when it takes place in Habitat. I do love him dearly but something must be done. Frankly, I am gagging for it.

Frustrated,
Edinburgh

Do you have a problem you'd like Petula to help with? e: petula@thedailymash.co.uk

---

Petula says:

Dear Frustrated,
Premature ejaculation is surprisingly common among men. For some of us that is a blessing. Who wants a great big fat lump grunting away on top of you for hours, after all? While pathetic, laughable, and, frankly, a bit yukky it is something that is relatively easy to deal with. Unfortunately your boyfriend's case appears different. He is suffering from pre-premature ejaculation for which there is, as yet, no known cure. You could try listening to my premium-rate phone line 'Dealing with premature ejaculation', but I hold out little hope. I would just go straight to my premium-rate phone line 'Dealing with premature ejaculators' which gives straightforward advice on how to bin such pathetic specimens and get yourself a real man.

Psychic Bob's Week Ahead   What does the future hold for you?

Taurus (20 APR – 20 MAY)
Venus, the goddess of dressing up and a shock early return from the shops, is in your skies suggesting you might find a surprise in your stockings, probably your husband.

Gemini (21 MAY – 20 JUN)
Getting enough exercise should be a top priority for you. You fat bastard.

Cancer (21 JUN – 22 JUL)
It may be time for you to recommit yourself to your romantic partner. Face facts: your work casual shag is just not working out and you've got to get it somewhere.

Leo (23 JUL – 22 AUG)
Don't be too surprised if you have to deal with a stream of interruptions all through the day. Just keep a gun handy, and plenty of ammunition.

Virgo (23 AUG – 22 SEP)
Your ideas are blossoming right now and you may find that people are much more willing than usual to listen to them. But probably not, you rambling fuckwit.

Libra (23 SEP – 23 OCT)
Reality has a way of catching up with you, and this week you can tell that things are going to get weird if you don't immediately realign your pants.

Scorpio (24 OCT – 21 NOV)
Good news. You are not going to have to deal with the aftermath of success, fame and fortune. Not now, not ever.

Sagittarius (22 NOV – 21 DEC)
You are totally focused on the big things in your life this week, forgetting all about the everyday and the mundane. Unfortunately you are also standing at the bus-stop naked.

Capricorn (22 DEC – 19 JAN)
Sure, life can be lonely if you are on your own at this time but remember this: at least you aren't ruining someone else's weekend with your desperate needy shit.

Aquarius (20 JAN – 19 FEB)
For once try and feel proud of who you are and what you did. No need to feel ashamed or revolted, even though it was sordid, and captured on CCTV.

Pisces (20 FEB – 20 MAR)
You're in an upbeat mood and should find that those around you also perk up the longer they spend in your company. However, they will move on when your drugs run out.

Aries (21 MAR – 19 APR)
A mixed bag. On Tuesday you beat someone to death but escape detection only to be framed for a murder you did not commit on Friday. Bad luck!

the daily mash

it's news to us   www.thedailymash.co.uk   No. 13

DOG HAS SHIT

WORKERS at a Tesco super-store watched yesterday as a dog had a huge shit in the middle of their car park.

The animal, which was about a year old, squatted down to do its business, and then shuffled along a bit after it had started, depositing its faeces behind it.

Staff, who nicknamed the dog 'Shitter', said they watched it closely as it forced out at least two quite large curly ones and one smaller, straight log.

Nikki Hollis, 26, a checkout assistant said: 'I was on my break when Darren from the fish counter said he could see a dog taking a shit. So we went to have a look.'

Bill McKay, 56, a trolley collector, said: 'I saw a bit of a crowd gathering so I went over, I asked Nikki what was going on and she said it was a dog, taking a shit.'

Store manager Wayne Hayes, 42, said: 'I was in my office when I got a call from Ellen, the checkout supervisor who just said, "Get yourself down here now, a dog is having a shit."'

Bakery worker Norman Steele, 34, was walking towards the store to start his shift when he got a text from Mr McKay saying, "Where r u? Dog having shit. Gr8!"'

A spokesman for Tesco said: 'Our staff are trained to expect the unex-pected. As soon as the dog had finished they wrapped the shit in a blanket and called the RSPCA. It's doing fine.'

The dog seemed to enjoy the shit, said witnesses.

news

BIKINI-CLAD LOVELIES TO PROTECT AIRPORTS

news

'I'M JUST LIKE ANY OTHER MILLIONAIRE SOLDIER WHO CAN COME HOME WHENEVER HE WANTS.'

Flapping your gums all day is not exercise, women told

EXERCISE rates among women have plummeted after doctors said talking and talking and talking all bloody day no longer counts.

For years thousands of women have claimed to follow a strict regime based on walking to a bar, picking up a heavy glass of white wine and then sitting down with a friend and flapping their indestructible gums without pause for breath.

But now doctors have warned that talking about the size of your buttocks for two hours is not the same as going for a jog.

Dr Tom Logan, Head of Buttocks at the Institute for Fitness, said: 'Obesity is now the number one cause of conversation

Women spend around £200 a month on talking about going to the gym.

in the EU and North America.

'Since the mid-1990s the driving purpose of Western society has

been to facilitate discussions between women about how fat or thin they currently feel.

'All television programming and advertising is designed to either sell something related to female self-image or to kick-start a conversation about thighs.

'We recommend that women find a window between chats so they can actually get off their arses and do something about it instead of just talking and talking and talking until I develop an irresistible urge to get in my car and drive off a fucking bridge.'

Dr Logan added: 'Just shut up. Shut up. Shut up. Shut up. Shut up.

'Shut.

'Up.'

Business as usual for Russian poisoners

RUSSIA'S new prime minister has told the nation's army of poisoners it is 'business as usual'.

Pledging new investment in the industry, Vladimir Putin said it was vital to maintain Russia's position as the democratic world's leading killer of people it doesn't like.

There had been fears that the incoming president would abandon the previous administration's commitment to new poisoning technologies.

But Mr Putin said: 'We make many new poison. We put poison up nose so when enemy pick nose and eat it, he killed by poisoned bogie.'

'We make special book, so when enemy get to last page it read, "You die" – then book squirt poison in enemy's face.'

He added: 'We even make special mobile phone which only release poison when enemy say, "I on train."'

The new president was elected by a landslide despite accusations that he has the same name as his predecessor and looks exactly like him.

Mr Putin said: 'I not Vladimir. My name pronounce totally different, my hair slightly darker and I one centimetre taller.

'You no believe? Is okay, I

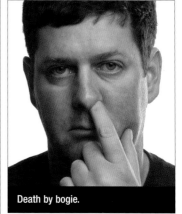

Death by bogie.

send you special book, explain everything.'

Millions develop Carol Vorderman intolerance

MILLIONS of people in the UK have a genuine intolerance for Carol Vorderman, new research suggests.

Just a single exposure to one of her adverts for debt consolidation is certain to lead to obesity, projectile vomiting and clinically explosive diarrhoea.

However, repeated exposure to her performances on *Countdown* will result in otherwise perfectly healthy people suffering blindness, insanity and eventually death, the experts added.

Chrissy Ellen, 36, said she first discovered her dreadful reaction to Carol Vorderman after the television presenter claimed she had developed a gluten intolerance.

She said: 'I bet she does not even know what a gluten is. I'd like to get a great big jug of the stuff and pour it down her throat to see if it really would make her swell up and choke to death on

Gluten-free chocolate cake can still contain traces of Carol Vorderman, as well as lots and lots of fat. Fatty.

her own insides. I bet it wouldn't, but if it did, would anyone complain? I don't think so.'

Doctors said the range of celebrities that people claimed to be intolerant of was enormous and growing all the time, but they had no reason to doubt the accuracy of people's self-diagnosis and warned them to keep avoiding them at all costs.

Dr Wayne Hayes, Head of Immunology at Dundee University, said all his hair had fallen out after he watched Britney Spear's recent comeback performance on MTV.

'I know it was specifically caused by an allergy to Britney as normally I get hugely turned on by fat girls in knickers,' he said.

Other celebrities the public are largely intolerant to include the actress Rachel Weisz, who most people would like to chase down the street and batter to death with a baguette.

Rod Stewart's wife Penny Lancaster was also found to be highly unpalatable with most people saying they would like to drown her in a vat of rancid milk, over and over again.

NEWS BRIEFLY

HESTON DEMANDS RIGHT TO SHOOT ANGELS
Ben Hur legend insists heavenly gun rack would be used primarily to shoot the souls of dead animals.

96 PER CENT OF ENGLISH PEOPLE THINK ALL SCOTTISH PEOPLE KNOW EACH OTHER
'You sound just like Alan Hansen, I suppose you must have been in jail together at some point.'

ANT AND DEC SWEEP BOARD AT COMMON PEOPLE'S TV AWARDS
Geordie mammals win rosettes for *I'm a Celebrity . . . and That's All* and *The Saturday Night Abomination*.

Worthless Opinion Poll
Why are you throwing away food?

Lid wrong colour	9.7%
Wrong shape	13.3%
Sounded foreign	35.5%
Wasn't cheese	45.1%

Transport minister crucified

TRANSPORT minister Ruth Kelly has been crucified at the side of the M6 by an angry mob driven mad by the deliberate closure of the road and rail network over the Easter weekend.

Kelly was set upon by motorists when she left her car to stretch her legs, after becoming stuck in a 320-mile tailback between Glasgow and Rugby.

The mob staged a brief trial before scourging the minister with brambles and nailing her to a makeshift cross.

Mob participant Wayne Hayes, from Chesterfield, said: 'She tried to make a run for it, but tripped over a cone.

'One guy kept hitting her with his useless train ticket, shouting, "Engineering doesn't work!" while another hung a sign around her neck saying, "Sorry for any delay."'

Mr Hayes added: 'She looked pretty miserable, but it did raise our spirits and the kids had a good time.'

Meanwhile the Health and Safety Executive has issued new crucifixion guidelines for anyone planning an accurate recreation of the death of Christ over the holiday weekend.

- All 'Christs' should wear Goretex shorts rather than a loincloth, for enhanced breathability.
- In the event of warm weather, Christs should apply Factor-30 sunblock to their shoulders and neck and be supplied with a wide-brimmed hat.
- Crucifiers should use stainless steel hammer fixings with hardened drive-screws, rather than zinc-coated masonry nails.
- Crosses should be constructed using machined hardwood at

Kelly was nailed up at Junction 14 near Stafford.

least 250-mm thick and all joints should be strengthened with a heavy-duty angle bracket.
- Crosses should be set in a hole 1.5 metres deep and secured using a high-quality ready-mixed concrete.
- If you are using a nail gun, remember to wear goggles.
- And don't forget to wash your hands.

Girly crime up by 50 per cent

GIRLY crime was up by more than 50 per cent last year, including a sharp rise in thefts of those darling little Mini Cooper convertibles.

New figures also showed an increase in the amount of cannabis being grown as a decorative pot plant, while supermarkets reported a rise in thefts of salad, frozen yoghurt and Philadelphia 'Light'.

There has also been a 25 per cent increase in breaking and entering, sweeping up the broken glass and leaving an apologetic note.

Superintendent Tom Logan said: 'Girly crimes of violence

have become more acute, especially going up to someone and flapping your arms wildly while closing your eyes and turning your head to one side.

'But we are getting better at apprehending girly shoplifters, mainly because it takes them 45 minutes to decide what to steal followed by 30 seconds of excessive flouncing.'

Supt Logan said further training was necessary to deal with girly crime suspects, adding: 'The whole thing can get a bit tearful, especially when you actually charge them.

'You hot-wire it – you silly moo.'

'They're allowed to bring a friend to the station and we've set up a nice, comfy room, with a really lovely beige sofa, some magazines and a decent range of Cadbury's Options.'

Dubai plans skyscraper made of Fanta

THE oil-rich state of Dubai has unveiled plans for a daring new skyscraper constructed entirely of Fanta.

The mile-high building will include 150,000 luxury apartments, 127 five-star hotels and 16 million gallons of the fizzy orange drink.

It will be designed by the German architect Jules Berghoff, who specialises in working with soft drinks and last year completed an office block in Bahrain based on the original Soda Stream machine.

Berghoff said: 'Dubai is a very now, tomorrow kind of place. There are no yesterdays here.

'That means using lots of very tomorrow materials, and what could be more tomorrow than a building made of Fanta?

'The Fanta will form the walls and floors, but we will be able to pour the entire structure into a bottle in the event of high winds.'

Dubai is at the cutting edge of international architecture and has already outlined plans for the world's first walking skyscraper.

The 20,000-foot-tall building will be able to move freely around the city, peering in the windows of other skyscrapers or posing for tourists next to their hotel.

If temperatures rise above 37 degrees centigrade the building will go and sit in the sea for half an hour, before having a nap under the world's most gigantic palm tree.

An artist's impression of Dubai's new Fanta District.

Product Red raises millions for Apple, Motorola and Hallmark

It is vitally important that you buy more stuff.

PRODUCT RED, the brand founded by U2 frontman Bono, has raised $50 million to help fight Porsche shortages among executives at Apple, Armani, Motorola, Gap and Hallmark.

Around half the profits from Product Red products goes straight into the bank accounts of executives at enormous corporations, who use it to alleviate chronic luxury car famines.

Lizzie Matumba, 14, of Ivory Coast, said: 'The knowledge that the executives arrive at Product Red press conferences in brand-new Aston Martins has made the death of my entire village much easier to bear.'

Twelve-year-old Robert Otengwe said: 'I am most happy you have bought a nice new red mobile phone. And the pink one you bought last year looks very dated.'

Matumba added: 'Some may ask why these gigantic corporations didn't just stump up $10 million each instead of guilt-tripping shallow fucknuts into buying yet more useless shit that'll be in the bin this time next year.

'But these people fail to understand the power of marketing. And bonuses – they fail to understand bonuses too.'

Business analyst Charles Reeves said Product Red had revolutionised the way rich Westerners made themselves feel better about hellish Third-World poverty.

'Most of us only ever felt guilty for a second about buying a fourth iPod while half the world starved, but it could still take some of the fun out of buying new gadgets.

'Now I can buy another Armani watch and a pair of Converse without having to worry about some African child with no shoes at all.'

Olympic budget did not include £8 billion for PR bullshit

THE original budget for the London Olympics failed to include more than £8 billion for pointless leaflets that will go straight in the bin, MPs said last night.

The Commons Public Accounts Committee said the government had obviously forgotten to mention the cost of constantly reminding everyone how fantastic the event will be through an endless series of glossy brochures, filled with PR bullshit.

Tom Logan, a North London Labour MP, said: 'For starters we'll need a really colourful brochure about the hi-tech stadium toilets.

'We'll also need one about the sustainable bamboo flooring in the toilets at the weight-lifting arena

Bullshit!

and we'll need an interactive CD for schools about why all the Olympic toilets are a celebration of the human spirit. And they'll all have to be translated into Cornish.

'Of course, we're also going to need a really big brochure, filled with some of this country's finest bullshit, about why the Olympics will make everyone healthier and more active, without explaining how that's actually going to happen.'

He added: 'We must project the concept that the Olympics is good for the whole of Britain and to do that we'll need to employ dozens of London-based PR firms on absurdly inflated contracts.

'Whether or not those firms happen to be run by Labour supporters is entirely a matter for the government.'

I crush you
by Vladimir Putin

WEAK, flabby Western men with no love of country and no respect from women – I will take greatest pleasure in crushing you.

I have watched you many, many years. I have studied ways of British men, American men, even so-called French 'men' and you are like little perfumed ladies compared to me and my Russian tough boys.

I see how you like to talk about everything. You make enemy, you want to talk to him. You want to hold his hand and kiss him like he your mother. You want to bake cake for him and put sugar in teacup, like you his wife. This not way to win respect of world. This not way to make men pee in panties at mention of name.

I make enemy, enemy go away. I phone friend, say, 'Hello,' make small chat. Two days later – two days! – I get email from friend say enemy gone away. I can be Vladimir, I can be president, I can be on top of Russia and no one tell me to shut my chops.

But I am not monster. No! I hold vote. I win vote. Many, many Russian tough boys vote Vladimir. I look at Western men who lose vote. Are you men? Men not lose vote. Men win vote.

> 'You make enemy, you want to talk to him. This not way to make men pee in panties at mention of name'

I am Vladimir, I have gas. I have many, many gas. You want my gas? Sure, you want my gas. You love my gas. If I say act like perfumed lady and you can have my gas, you will act like perfumed lady. You love my gas. But how much you want my gas? Put dress on. Do it now.

I have atomics. Big atomics in holes. You point atomics at me? You think you big man? You little boy who wants sex

'Go play with dolls.'

change. Russian men do not fight with atomics. You not like me, you say I am bad man, I punch you. Or throw in jail. It my decision. I am Vladimir.

I go Germany. I meet your Madame Presidents and Mrs Prime Ministers with big cars and no gas. I say: 'How many push-ups? How many sit-ups?' Nothing, that how many. I arm-wrestle, but would make you look like hungry clown in front of women.

Go back your country and play with dolls. I am Vladimir. I crush you.

Worthless Opinion Poll	
Why are you switching energy suppliers?	
House full of gas	6%
Telly told me to	12.3%
To confuse my enemies	26.4%
You get a free pig	55.3%

In Agony with PETULA SOUL

Dear Petula,
I have the most enormous cock. Everybody who sees it says it is the biggest one they have ever seen. Standing fully upright it is a good two-foot long and of considerable girth. I know a lot of men would probably dream of having a cock this size but it is causing me nothing but misery. My girlfriend is terrified of it and runs off screaming every time she sees it. It has got so bad that she refuses to visit me any more unless I promise her not to get it out. It also makes the most enormous racket every time it goes off, which can be at any time of the day or night. I am at my wits end. Can you help?

Sleepless,
Seton Sands

Petula says:

Dear Sleepless,
I am not surprised your girlfriend is terrified of your large cock; not only is it huge but it also sounds as if it is completely out of control, and there is nothing more frightening to a girl then her boyfriend presenting her with an enormous and unruly cock. But don't worry. Even the biggest and wildest cock can be tamed, if you know what to do. Put on some gentle mood music, light some candles and wait until the pair of you are completely naked and relaxed and only then get your cock out. Start stroking your cock to show your girlfriend how it's done, and that it won't bite. Once you have your cock completely under control let her have a go at stroking it as well. If this fails break its neck and get a bantam.

Do you have a problem you'd like Petula to help with? e: petula@thedailymash.co.uk

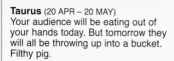

Psychic Bob's Week Ahead What does the future hold for you?

Taurus (20 APR – 20 MAY)
Your audience will be eating out of your hands today. But tomorrow they will all be throwing up into a bucket. Filthy pig.

Gemini (21 MAY – 20 JUN)
You are thinking about exotic travel or global issues. What you aren't thinking about is the stalled lorry around that blind bend and dying in a huge fireball.

Cancer (21 JUN – 22 JUL)
If you're feeling a bit emotionally exposed, take some time to lick your wounds. If you are double-jointed take some time to lick something else.

Leo (23 JUL – 22 AUG)
It is time you stopped that woman from trampling all over you. You only paid for an hour.

Virgo (23 AUG – 22 SEP)
You still here?

Libra (23 SEP – 23 OCT)
You are more connected to the planet than ever today and can feel the energy surging through you. It seems you have just been struck by lightning.

Scorpio (24 OCT – 21 NOV)
Your mood is darker than usual, though it might be hard for most people to tell. You miserable fucker.

Sagittarius (22 NOV – 21 DEC)
This week's peachy encounter between Venus and Jupiter brings romance, international travel, extravagant sex, two pickled onions, a moth, someone else's pants and a horseradish.

Capricorn (22 DEC – 19 JAN)
It's six months since your birthday, so a cool assessment of progress is appropriate. Yep. Fuck all.

Aquarius (20 JAN – 19 FEB)
If you're having a hard time making choices, let your new friend guide the way. The second hole might be tighter, but you should ask first.

Pisces (20 FEB – 20 MAR)
If you are feeling torn about which group to side with, I would suggest the violent psychopaths with the guns and not the Mormons.

Aries (21 MAR – 19 APR)
Be sure to keep a private problems from spilling out in public this week. Wear your rubber pants.

the daily mash

BRITAIN'S POOR PEOPLE NOW BEYOND THE PALE

BRITAIN'S poor people have plumbed new depths of sheer, unbridled ghastliness, according to a new report.

A survey by the Office of National Statistics revealed that people on low incomes have abandoned all recognised forms of decency and are now locked in a downward spiral of jaw-droppingly unspeakable horror.

The ONS survey found that 64 per cent had considered selling their children to pirates, while 38 per cent had actually locked their child in a trunk and sent it to the Isle of Man, before asking the *News of the World* to donate £50,000 to their 'Find my Precious Baby' campaign.

Poor women now have an average of 5.4 children each from an average of 42.6 possible fathers, while more than three-quarters no longer speak a recognisable form of English but communicate with each other through a series of grunts and whistles.

The typical poor person's diet consists of extracting the grease from cheeseburgers and mixing it with Wotsits, before tossing the squeezed meat to their illegal fighting dogs.

Meanwhile more than half spend up to 15 hours a day watching black-market Bulgarian pornography and Steven Seagal films, while 94 per cent are engaged in depraved sex acts with their girlfriend's great-grandmother in the hope of an all-expenses-paid trip to the Jeremy Kyle show.

Professor Henry Brubaker, of the Institute for Studies, said: 'Poor people were especially horrid until the mid-nineteenth century when many of them suddenly became Australian.

'Since then we have seen a steady increase in their squalid awfulness to the point where their behaviour would be enough to make Fagin puke up his lunch.'

'Pirates totally stole my baby.'

---

news

GLASTONBURY SALES DOWN AS FANS TIRE OF WALLOWING IN OWN DUNG

news

PARIS HILTON MAY BE FORCED TO DEBASE HERSELF FOR MONEY, SAY FRIENDS

Foreigners told to have their babies in the sink

'Of course, most of them have never actually seen a sink before.'

FOREIGN mothers who think they can just come over here and have their baby in an NHS hospital have been told to give birth in the kitchen sink.

New figures show the NHS is being flooded with grasping, olive-skinned women demanding the 'right' to have their baby delivered by a trained professional who has washed their hands.

Now ministers say the free ride is over and have told immigrant scroungers to get out the Vim and give their spice-ridden kitchens a good scrub down.

Health Secretary Alan Johnson said: 'The NHS was not set up to help dirty, foreign babies into the world.

'These Eastern European mothers see pictures of our exquisite birthing suites on their stolen laptops and before you know it they are packed into stolen people carriers and heading our way on board stolen car ferries.

'As for the Africans and the Asians, they have spent thousands of years squeezing their babies into a hole in the ground. Why on earth would they want to throw away their proud cultural heritage?'

Mr Johnson said that from April non-British mothers will be turned away from NHS hospitals but given a leaflet showing them how to climb safely onto the kitchen worktop and position themselves over the sink.

He added: 'Probably best to use a chair, then once you're actually over the sink, hold on to the taps or perhaps the curtains if you're near a window.'

Budget boost for headless horsemen

CHANCELLOR Alistair Darling is today expected to throw a budget lifeline to Britain's hard-pressed headless horsemen.

Mr Darling will unveil a series of measures to help people on incapacity benefit back into work, coupled with tax breaks for environmentally friendly transport.

He wants to use the tax and benefits system to tackle the growing problem of anti-social behaviour among thousands of under-employed headless maniacs.

A Treasury source said: 'We're not suggesting they're claiming incapacity benefit illegally. They are headless, after all.

'And while they may be rampaging through the countryside, decapitating respected members of the community, at least they're doing it on a horse.'

He added: 'We have an opportunity to not only achieve staged reductions in rural beheadings, but offer rewards and incentives for low-carbon mobility.'

Meanwhile City analysts are divided over how Mr Darling's latest budget will go.

Tom Logan, head of markets at Donnelly-McPartlin, said: 'I think he'll make a complete and total arse of it.'

But Wayne Hayes, chief econo-

'About bloody time.'

mist at Madeley-Finnegan, said: 'I think he'll do really well actually . . . No, I'm just kidding. He'll be fucking awful.'

Government to reclassify very strong tea

STRONG tea is to be reclassified as a Category-B drug, Home Secretary Jacqui Smith announced last night.

Smith is to strengthen the law despite official advice that strong tea is no more harmful to society than alcohol, tobacco and cheese.

Since tea was downgraded in 2004 there has been widespread concern about the increase in stronger varieties including Purple Haze, Tetley Red Bush and the infamous 'skonk'.

Rejecting claims she had been influenced by the *Daily Mail's* Campaign for Weak Tea, Ms Smith added: 'Our police forces are all too familiar with the consequences of tea that has been left to stew for too long.'

Pepé is high on love.

The Home Office has also issued a new guide to drug terminology. The latest terms include:

Skonk: Tea that has been left to stew in the pot for more than half an hour and then served with just a tiny drop of milk.

Skink: A type of Scottish soup made with smoked haddock, onions and cream. Category A. Banned since 1973.

Skank: A dirty slapper who'll do anything for a bottle of Bacardi Breezer and a deep-fried sausage.

Skunk: A small black-and-white mammal known for its strong defensive odour. Made famous by the popular cartoon character and master of seduction, Pepé Le Pew.

NEWS BRIEFLY

CHILDREN WARNED NOT TO SUCK ON HYBRID CAR EXHAUSTS
Cars may emit more than just gentle waftings of spring-fresh air that make the bees and the flowers dance.

GOVERNMENT TO BAN SWEARING IN PUBLIC PLACES
'Hitler banned people from saying "knob" and "flaps". Is that what you want?'

BOOKER PRIZE GOES TO THRILLING PAGE-TURNER ABOUT THE INTANGIBLE NATURE OF LOSS
Author working on sequel where emptiness of grief tracks down the rogue CIA agents who killed its father.

Worthless Opinion Poll
What will you be hoarding this week?

Bread, milk, knives	9%
Bottled water and Monster Munch	12%
Cock-a-leekie soup, flippers, Vaseline	16%
The usual mix of pornography and fudge	63%

Working mums prefer white wine to childcare, says study

MOTHERS who work are happier than those who stay at home because they can have liquid lunches and don't have to spend time with their kids, according to a new report.

A study by Glasgow Clyde University found that so-called 'stay-at-home mums' were not entirely happy with the daily prospect of unremitting, high-pitched wailing and a face full of vomit.

Meanwhile mothers who went back to work as soon as they possibly could reported high levels of satisfaction when it came to chatting about the *X-Factor*, 'poking' Facebook users and spending their lunchtimes immersed in a vat of Pinot Grigio.

Research chief Dr Henry Brubaker said: 'Every woman has a different approach to motherhood, but we found that increasingly most women have exactly the same approach, which is to get the hell out of the house.

'Modern parenting means you can work, enjoy the company of your friends and have a skinful at lunchtime safe in the knowledge that the nursery will text you if something interesting happens.'

Mandy Amble, 36, from Peterborough, said: 'At first I wanted to spend as much time as I could with my child. But after six solid hours of that stinking lump shouting, 'Bang! Bang! Bang! Bang! Bang! Bang! Bang!' I started to change my mind.

As Churchill said: 'Glug-glug' is better than 'wah-wah'.

'Now I can pretend to work all day and enjoy a range of top-class white wines without having to worry about being covered in piss and shit.'

I can do a terrible Scottish accent too, says Laurie

HUGH Laurie has appealed to British casting directors insisting he can do regional accents that are 'every bit as dreadful' as the American one which has earned him millions of dollars.

Since moving to the US the former Englishman has become a household name, starring in the gritty drama *House!* as the brilliant but edgy bingo-caller, Donovan House.

With his trademark walking stick, House limps between the tables, swallowing handfuls of prescription pain killers and telling the frightened customers why bingo is a 'cruel mistress'.

The star of *Stuart Little* and *Stuart Little 2*, said: 'I would love

'Two fat-assed ladies.'

to play a really meaty British character, as long as they don't

mind me sounding like a posh Englishman with a speech impediment.

'I can do your classic Highlander: "Och, will ye no be havin' a wee dram of whisky with yer porridge the noo?"

'Or perhaps a terribly violent Glaswegian type: "See ye ya bastart, I'll kick ye right in the baws."

'Or what about a Geordie builder? "Way aye man, that's a canny bit o' bait. Can I put it in me stottie?"'

He added: 'Of course, my Welshman is legendary: "Now then, Dai bach, can I be having sexual intercourse with your prize ram?"'

Al Qaeda to rebrand as 'Scimitar3000'

THE world's leading terror provider is to overhaul its identity in a £20-million rebranding strategy.

With an ever-increasing number of angry Islamist groups, the Al Qaeda leadership believe 'Scimitar3000' will set them apart as, 'professional, efficient and profoundly insane'.

Ayman El-Mukhtar, Al Qaeda's head of marketing, said: 'Many people do not know how to pronounce Al Qaeda. We get "Al Kayda" or "Al Ka-ee-da" and one of those annoying little Scotsmen at the BBC insists on "Al Kie-da". It does my head in.

'And even if they pronounce it right they always get the translation wrong. Some think it means "The Base" while others say it means "The Head". I spoke to one guy last week who though it meant "The Bongos".'

He added: 'Scimitar3000 is clean and stylish with a high recognition factor. It focus-grouped incredibly well in Peshawar.

'And although it looks hip, it also says we have not lost touch with our roots. It says, "This a twenty-first-century killing machine founded on the principles of medieval bloodlust."'

But the move has angered the organisation's grass roots. One low-level operative in western Europe, said: 'We're having to sell knocked-off iPods to raise enough money for flying lessons and they're spending £20 million on a letterhead. Sometimes I wonder why I want to blow myself up.'

Wayne Hayes, of London-based brand consultants Conceptomatix, said: 'I look at the big sword and I think, "Swoosh!"'

'It makes me go all wobbly and want to sit down and have a bowl of tea and some hubbly-bubbly with a large Afghani tribesman. Super.'

The £20-million logo will appear in the top right-hand corner of all new Bin Laden videos.

Scimitar3000

Capello picks Gerrard to miss crucial World Cup penalty

FABIO CAPELLO has picked Steven Gerrard as the man who will miss England's crucial World Cup semi-final penalty in 2010.

Setting out his targets for the next four years, the England coach said despite a series of poor performances, his team will fluke its way to a heartbreaking semi-final, filled with missed chances and nail-biting extra time, before ending in a calamitous penalty shoot-out.

He added: 'I know these players have the right mix of high salaries and grinding mediocrity to create a very real sense of false hope.

'When I took this job I knew I would be expected to not only take them to a World Cup semi-final, but to ensure they lost that semi-final in the most catastrophic way imaginable.

'I am certain that Steven Gerrard is the right man to instil confidence before sending the ball high into the stands.'

Capello has also singled out the normally mild-mannered Owen Hargreaves to lose his cool when England are 1-0 up in a tense quarter-final against Holland.

'The England fans just love it when a key player is sent off in the second last minute of extra time in a crucial game against incredibly tough opposition.'

FA chairman Lord Triesman said: 'Some may say that it's wrong to set targets in this way.

'But I think England fans deserve an unbearable penalty

'Yes, that's the idea.'

shoot-out where Steven Gerrard – the sort of player you can absolutely rely on in these situations – balloons it over the bar like a total arse.

'Let's just hope it's against Germany.'

Supermarkets must be stabbed through the heart under a full moon, says regulator

BRITAIN'S leading supermarket chains can only be defeated if a bronze dagger is plunged into their chest by the light of a full moon, the Competition Commission said today.

The regulator called for a hero to come forth, armed only with a simple, wooden shield and an unshakeable desire to pay way over the odds for organic courgettes.

The Grand High Competition Commissioner told all the people of the land: 'The horned beast has lain waste to our fields, our towns and those football pitches at the back of the bus station.

'It has devoured Mr Philips, the baker, Mr Stevens, the fishmonger, and Mr Johnson, the greengrocer, whose only crime was to think he could get away with charging £3.75 for a bag of seedless grapes, the greedy little shit.'

He added: 'What brave, young squire will save us from ample parking, cash machines, comparatively cheap petrol and aisle after aisle of low, low prices?

'One day soon, good people, our villages and towns will again be filled with little shops that are only open for three hours a day, never have anything you want and where you are forced to make small talk with people you don't like.

This week your supermarket is offering 50 per cent off selected wines and devouring hundreds of sheep.

'Yes, it has been a bit chilly this week. Yes, the council are taking for ever to put in that new bus stop, and yes, this small jar of mayonnaise is indeed £4.50!'

Why you all buggering off to airport?

by Azam Al-Maktar, shopkeeper, Basra

'Why you leave?'

MY dear British friends, why you leave? You come here four year ago and say all will be great now that fat Sunni bastard in Baghdad is down hole. I stand in street and cheer. I look very much forward to being free and having aspirin and CNN. But it no happen and now you get in tank and bugger off to airport. Are you on holidays or are you having up to here with all the shit?

Four year ago I say to my friend Nouri, I say: 'British are hard men, they no take any piss from Mehdi bastard. They show Mehdi bastard how it is now.' Nouri say to me that Mehdi bastard have many trick up sleeve and British boys not even know why they here anyhow. Turn out Nouri right. Turn out Nouri not total shithead. Turn out Nouri is Mehdi bastard too.

Saddam, he sure was one fat Sunni bastard. But after while you get used to fat bastard and get on with life. Then shithead Saudi bastards fly plane into banks and funny little Bush blame fat Sunni bastard in Baghdad.

Saddam very like my uncle Karim. Bad temper, lot of guns but could not organise pot of tea in tea shop. He no fly plane into banks. But funny Bush still

---

'Saddam, he sure was one fat Sunni bastard. But after a while you get used to fat bastard and get on with life.'

---

want Iraq. Nouri say to me it about oil and fat American who drive to end of street to buy food covered in cheese. Turn out Nouri right about that too. Mehdi bastard.

So Americans come and British come and they flatten post office. I no like man who work in post office but still I say, post office come in handy. Next night they come and flatten Uncle Karim's house. We found his foot. I keep shoe. Come in handy.

Then Mehdi bastards start pushing around and say we all friends with Iran. Iran! With crazy bastard president who

look like driver of bus!

Before British come I walk down street, past big photo of fat Sunni bastard and buy cup of tea. Now photo of fat Sunni bastard is gone but tea shop gone too. In fact, tea shop spread over wide area. And I just want cup of tea.

So goodbye my dear British friends and thank you for killing fat Sunni bastard in Baghdad and turning my home into big stinking bag of shit. One day you come back and tell me what it all about? Yes?

Worthless Opinion Poll	
Why are you recruiting children?	
Sportswear factory	10%
Hobbitland!™	18.2%
To kill brown people	33.9%
Cockney pickpocket army	37.9%

In Agony with PETULA SOUL

Dear Petula,
When my husband and I were first married we were so young and inexperienced that our hoggins was short and perfunctory. Over the years we have been together he has developed into a skilled and attentive lover. Now, all I seem to be doing during my spare time is having multiple orgasms during regular sessions of tantric hochmagandy that involve a bewildering variety of positions. Why can't we have quick and rubbish sex like we did when we first married? I have not seen *Coronation Street* in ages.

Bored,
Dundee

Do you have a problem you'd like Petula to help with? e: petula@thedailymash.co.uk

Petula says:

Dear Bored,
Many wives think that not having sex with their husbands is a perfectly natural thing that will develop over time. However, like all things in marriage, it takes work. Have you tried being cold and uncommunicative and not talking to him about what turns you on in the bedroom department? Try destroying the atmosphere early on in the proceedings by 'accidentally' letting one rip while he is going about his filthy business in your below-stairs area. If he persists, try yawning or looking at your watch while he is see-sawing away on top of you interminably, or better still, try reading a book – out loud. If that fails, and he is still grunting away above while pulling a face like a constipated Chinaman, try calling your mother on the phone. And if that fails try asking the question, 'Are you in yet?' I find it always has the desired effect.

Psychic Bob's Week Ahead What does the future hold for you?

Taurus (20 APR – 20 MAY)
You've got the audience you've been waiting for – now put your clothes back on, you attention-seeking whore.

Gemini (21 MAY – 20 JUN)
Venus moves in your favour for three whole weeks, so brace yourself for lots of mindless coupling with total strangers. Which will be nice, as you have not had it in ages.

Cancer (21 JUN – 22 JUL)
The act of helping others selflessly will help you get rid of any guilty feelings. But so will spending all your wages on drink, and it's much more fun.

Leo (23 JUL – 22 AUG)
A thrill runs through you at some point in the day after you find yourself acting on a wild impulse. It's your own fault for using the mains-powered massager in the bath.

Virgo (23 AUG – 22 SEP)
You can tell things are getting better, the discharge has stopped and the swelling is coming down. It will still be green for a while. Tell them you are wearing a coloured condom.

Libra (23 SEP – 23 OCT)
Your passions are inflamed and you find that the object of your affections (or obsessions) is staring right back at you. For God's sake put it away. You're on the bus!

Scorpio (24 OCT – 21 NOV)
Making choices based on emotions is an unwise strategy for you today. This is because your are hormonal and so temporarily insane.

Sagittarius (22 NOV – 21 DEC)
If you are feeling indecisive about any decision, you must come down on one side or the other.

Capricorn (22 DEC – 19 JAN)
You selflessly put yourself in the service of someone who can't do what they need to do today. So don't forget your gloves.

Aquarius (20 JAN – 19 FEB)
You'll meet someone whose combination of beauty, honesty and tact inspires you to tell them they are hated by everyone.

Pisces (20 FEB – 20 MAR)
You are loved by your friends more than you realise – but not much more.

Aries (21 MAR – 19 APR)
Some powerful people will ask you to join their inner circle. Don't forget to take a goat and a bread knife.

WARM GL🜨BES

Global warming to bring cannibalism to South-East

CLIMATE change will transform the south-east of England into a steaming jungle filled with giant snakes and marauding tribes of blood-thirsty cannibals, scientists have predicted.

Researchers at the Institute for Studies have warned that unless carbon emissions are reduced Essex and Kent will resemble the darkest reaches of Amazonia, probably in about 18 months time.

Professor Henry Brubaker said: 'First will come the mosquitos. They will be huge, about the size of a crow. Then the giant snakes will arrive to feast on the mosquitos.

'Within months towns including Colchester, Ashford, Gravesend, and possibly even Braintree, will

Six-year-old Gavin attends St Mark's Primary in Chelmsford and enjoys eating feet.

be little more than mangrove swamps. However, local rail services should be unaffected.'

He added: 'Before long the populations will be reduced to primal savagery. Unable to grow crops on the dark jungle floor they will raid each others settlements with the victors feasting upon the flesh of the vanquished.

'The strongest tribes, driven on by their insatiable lust for human flash, will soon descend upon the slow, fat people of Hampshire.'

Meanwhile doctors are warning that fewer old people will die as a result of rising temperatures.

Dr Wayne Hayes, of the British Medical Association, said: 'Warmer winters will mean more OAPs, I'm afraid.'

He added: 'If you feel that your local community is being overrun, then it might be an idea to nudge one of them under a bus.'

Gore film is 'Inconvenient Bollocks', says judge

AL GORE's climate-change film *An Inconvenient Truth* is actually bollocks, a High Court judge ruled yesterday.

Mr Justice Baldwin said a number of statements made in the film were inconveniently completely untrue, including Mr Gore's much publicised claim that all polar bears now wore scarves.

He said the former US presidential candidate's assertions that all dolphins had melted and that elephants were being forced to make footballs in India for slave wages were also, 'a lot of cock'.

Justice Baldwin said: 'According to Mr Gore, climate change has forced monkeys to install air-conditioning in their jungles and led to snakes growing arms so they can hold one of those personal electric fans.

'Anyway, if it is that bad why doesn't he try turning off a few lights in his own mansion before telling the rest of us we have to recycle our own turds to stop our children from catching fire.'

However, the judge said the film could still be viewed in British schools as long as the head teacher stood up before each showing and said: 'This is a flammed up can of old shite. Ignore it.'

A spokesman for Al Gore said: 'The idea that former Vice President Gore would make an alarmist movie about climate change as a cynical and self-serving attempt to resurrect his political career is as wide of the mark as many of the claims we made in the film.'

Despite Mr Gore's assertions, polar bears do not wear scarves.

'Bring me carnage.'

JAMES BLUNT SACRIFICED IN SPECTACULAR LIVE EARTH FINALE

SINGER-SONGWRITER James Blunt was last night sacrificed in a symbolic gesture of climate change solidarity in a thrilling climax to the Live Earth spectacular.

As he finished his last ever performance of 'You're Beautiful', Blunt was tied up and placed on a large pile of sticks on the Wembley stage before being set alight by former Vice President Al Gore.

Simultaneously in Johannesburg Nelson Mandela planted a symbolic row of broccoli to offset the carbon emissions from the smouldering pop star.

Event organiser Wayne Hayes

Burned beautifully.

said: 'Live Earth is a wake-up call and what better way to shake people out of their complacency than by setting fire to James Blunt?

'There was a lot of debate over which performer should be sacrificed and there were some ferociously passionate advocates for the torching of Phil Collins.

'But when we actually looked at the list the name "James Blunt" just popped right out.'

Blunt was one of many casualties over the Live Earth weekend after scores of TV viewers threw themselves into the road rather than listen to Madonna talk about giraffes.

Global warming will make statues come to life, say experts

RISING CO_2 levels will cause statues to come to life and wreak blood-thirsty revenge on their human tormentors, scientists warned today.

According to climatologists at Dundee University, increased CO_2 levels will bring about a quantum shift in the molecular structure of statues and within a few years they will undergo a process known as de-statufication.

The experts believe the statues will then break free of their plinths, destroy or enslave their captors and take over the planet.

Professor Bill McKay said: 'Statues have no soul. They do not know what it is to love. Therefore they will seek to destroy all that is not a statue. This is quite worrying.

'The last thing we need is a 20-foot-tall cast-iron Richard the Lionheart rampaging up Whitehall, or a puritanical Oliver Cromwell going on a killing spree and then banning musical theatre.

'In a bizarre twist Mel Gibson could find himself being torn limb from limb by the statue of him as William Wallace in *Braveheart*. In which case, it's not all bad.'

Professor McKay called for the immediate destruction of all statues, adding: 'I don't want to be standing in a pile of smouldering rubble surrounded by hysterical commuters saying "I told you so."'

Brown 'frantic with worry' over state of Britain's lawns

THE long spell of wet weather has prompted Prime Minister Gordon Brown to order a full-scale review of the nation's lawns.

Brown is understood to be 'frantic with worry' that people will cut their grass when it is still wet, leaving large clumps which then cause uneven colour and texture.

According to the Number 10 policy unit the 'doomsday scenario' occurs when people leave the grass because it is wet, but it then becomes so long that they refuse to cut it because it is 'too hard'.

Brown wants to bring in outside experts and MPs from other parties to sit on the new British Lawn Commission which will produce a series of recommendations for Parliament before the next general election.

The Prime Minister's spokesman said: 'Everyone knows that a good lawn is the cornerstone of a successful society.

'If you walk down a street of well-tended lawns you feel happy and decent.

'If you walk down a street filled with untidy or overgrown lawns you assume the residents are all ghastly and immoral. Probably drug dealers and/or pimps.'

The spokesman said the commission would be Brown's first priority over the next 12 months, adding: 'He's not just the prime minister of you, he's the prime minister of your lawn.'

This vegetarian went off near Grimsby.

VEGETARIANS' GAS NOW 'BIGGEST CAUSE OF GLOBAL WARMING'

VEGETARIANS are being urged to eat each other after it emerged their own gas was now the major cause of global warming.

Research by the Vegetarian Society shows vegetarian emissions are responsible for more than 80 per cent of the most potent greenhouse gases.

The Society is telling its members to start eating themselves immediately or they will kill all life on the earth 'with their wind'.

Dr Stephen Malley, Head of Research, said: 'Vegetarian gas is a particularly harmful emission fuelled by an explosive mixture of lentils, mung beans and sawdust.

'You sit in a vegetarian restaurant and see a kindly old man in sandals quietly letting a stinky one off in the corner, I see a planet-killing machine.'

Dr Malley said the society had abandoned its policy of urging people not to eat cows after they realised that not eating them would not actually make them go away, and that cow gas was not as dangerous as that emitted by vegetarians.

He said: 'Given the choice of standing behind a giant masticating cow and a giant masticating woman who has just eaten a tofu burger, I know where I'd rather be.'

The house is probably filled with 'crack'.

the daily mash

'LOOK AT THE SIZE OF THIS FUCKING RAT,' SAY ZOOLOGISTS

A NEW species of giant rat has been discovered in a remote region of New Guinea by a team of totally freaked-out zoologists.

The scientists, from the Institute for Studies, spotted the 'absolutely mental thing' during a five-day trek through the hazardous Foja mountains.

Expedition leader Professor Wayne Hayes said: 'I was filling my water bottle when I saw this huge fucking thing and I shouted to my mate Dave, I said, "Dave, look at the size of that fucker!" and Dave was like, "Jesus Christ, it's a fucking monster!"

'I shouted over to Stevie and Ben, I said, "Get a look at this bastard," and they're like, "No way, man, that's mental" – they were totally freaking out.'

Professor Hayes added: 'Ben

'You fucking catch it.'

was like, "That's a rat, it's totally a rat," and I was going, "Naah,

it's some kind of freaky beaver or a weird-looking, fucked-up cat."'

Dr David Hobbs added: 'I was like, "That's a mutant otter or something, it's bigger than my dog, for Christ's sake," and Wayne was saying we should catch it, and I was like, "You fucking catch it."

'So anyway, we tell Stevie that it's his turn to catch something and he's like totally pissed off, but he tears after it anyway, shouting, "Come here you dirty big bastard, I want to take your picture."'

Dr Steven McKay added: 'We also trapped this manky little thing with huge eyes which they reckon is maybe a possum or a really big gerbil.

'Dave tried to give it a fruit pastille but it wasn't interested.'

news

TEENAGE BOOZERS THOROUGHLY ENJOYING THEMSELVES

news

ANT COLONIES JUST LIKE 'DALLAS', SAY EXPERTS

Spacey to host 'I Am Keyser Soze' on BBC1

ACTOR Kevin Spacey is to celebrate one of his most famous roles by hosting BBC1's latest amateur talent show, *I Am Keyser Soze*.

Inspired by his Oscar-winning performance, Spacey will challenge a dozen young hopefuls to show why they deserve to fill the shoes of the legendary Turkish drug dealer and homicidal maniac.

Some of Britain's hottest young psychopaths are queuing up to take part in what will be the highlight of the Corporation's summer schedule.

In round one, 'Setting Fire to a Boat Full of Thieves', the contestants will be given 15 minutes to douse petrol all over a cargo ship, set it on fire and then shoot anyone who tries to escape.

Spacey will award extra points for the nonchalant way the contestants use their gold Zippo lighters to ignite the murderous inferno.

In round two, 'Bamboozling Chazz Palminteri', the contestants will be given two hours to confuse the gruff, Bronx-born actor without getting their heads kicked in.

Round three is the self-explanatory, 'Killing your Entire Family to Show you Mean Business', while in round four the surviving contestants will rampage across Eastern Europe, slaughtering dozens of rival drug dealers and burning their homes to the ground.

In the final show the two remaining hopefuls will have to convince Spacey and the viewing public that they do not exist and that none of this has actually happened.

The contest reaches its climax when Andrew Lloyd Webber faxes a sketch of the winner to the BBC studios at Shepherd's Bush.

The newly-crowned 'Keyser Soze 2009' will then be handed control of a vast crime network before being driven away from the studio by a Mr Kobayashi look-a-like.

A BBC spokesman said: 'Who is Keyser Soze? Seriously, I'm asking. I've just watched *The Usual Suspects* and I haven't got a fucking clue.'

Spacey also hosts the *Se7en*-inspired quiz show, *Head in a Box*.

Cannabis now worse than the Nazis

Worse even than Richard and Judy.

The top ten most evil things:

1. (-) Cannabis
2. (2) Tobacco
3. (4) Debt consolidation ads featuring Carol Vorderman
4. (1) Richard and Judy
5. (3) The Nazis
6. (-) Heathrow Airport
7. (5) Prince Philip
8. (7) Joseph Stalin
9. (-) Edmonds
10. (10) Satan and all his minions

(Last month's position in brackets)

CANNABIS is more evil than the Nazis and smoking the drug is worse for the brain than watching Richard Madeley on television, new research suggests.

During the Sixties smoking dope was hardly evil at all, and the drug was more playful and slightly naughty, but in a nice way, like Kenneth Williams.

In the Seventies and Eighties marijuana briefly became totally harmless and could be smoked by future Cabinet ministers up to the rank of home secretary without any effect on their brains whatsoever.

However, a massive increase in the strength of the drug since politicians all stopped using it has now made it more nasty and brutish than the combined evil of the Third Reich.

Professor Tom Booker, Head of Drug Research at Glasgow's Clyde University and the man who conducted the latest lengthy study into the drug, said: 'Yeah, whatever.'

A spokesman for the University said: 'The Nazis were very bad people but even they could not make a middle-class white boy adopt dreadlocks for a hairstyle, or make a highly intelligent middle-aged man crawl around the floor of his laboratory in his underpants weeping with laughter about nothing at all, and then eat his own weight in marshmallows.'

Fiennes leads expedition to find source of gas price increases

Sir Ranulph has vowed to scour the Seven Seas to find out what the fuck is going on.

WORLD-famous explorer Sir Ranulph Fiennes is to lead a one-year expedition to discover why the fuck gas prices keep going up.

The seasoned adventurer warned that the expedition was the most difficult and dangerous he had ever undertaken, and that the chances of success were slight.

He will be joined in his quest by a team of 'brave and brilliant' volunteers, including David 'Dr Who' Tennant, Carol Vorderman and Stephen Fry, who have all committed to find the answer, or die in the attempt.

Sir Ranulph said: 'We read every day that wholesale gas prices are rising sharply, but if you ask anyone in the industry why, they just tap the side of their nose and wink.

'The same gas is coming from the same people and it's summer so we are using less, yet this fuel is now so expensive that poor old ladies have to beg in the street for a cup of gas so they can make tea.

'Some say the gas ships are being dragged under by giant sea serpents or that the Russian gas crop has failed again. Others claim that the Germans reserved it all this morning, and won't share.

'The one thing we can rule out is that a bunch of profiteering bastards are hiking the price so they can buy themselves a diamond-encrusted tiger each.'

He added: 'I have been personally charged with this mission by Her Majesty the Queen, whose direct debit has risen from £42 to £63.75 in just six months.

'She wished me godspeed and said: "Sir Ranulph, find out what the fuck is going on with gas prices. And don't come back until you do. And no potatoes or anything. I've got enough of that shit."'

Squeezy credit crunch bang tumble sparks debt rise share plunge sell-off fears

SHARES in London closed down a million last night as squeezing credits in the sub-debt crunch market oozed in an oily mess on the floor.

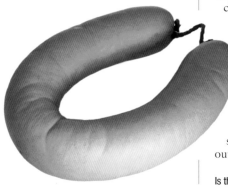

The FTSE 100 index of leading shares tumbled over on its side at one point and had to be helped up by two passing elderly ladies.

In Hong Kong the Hang Seng changed its name to Billy Yip and refused to answer the phone, while Tokyo's Nikkei dyed its hair blonde and put on a short skirt.

In New York the Dow Jones failed to turn up for work for the second day in a row, and stayed home drinking vodka out of the bottle instead.

Is the market now a sausage?

Charles Winstanley, equities analyst with Donnelly-McPartlin, said the markets had been spooked by an altercation in the US pork-knuckle pens overnight.

He said: 'The sub-prime pork cuts collapse in the States has gone sausage.

'It's just a question now of whether it's a chipolata or a great big Cumberland.'

Mr Winstanley warned of further turbulence in the months ahead as the squeezed credits were forced back into their tubes.

Alistair Darling, the Chancellor of the Exchequer, said he did not have a clue what was going on and that he had 'shat himself'.

DSS to fund Liverpool takeover

LIVERPOOL fans have launched a bid buy their beloved football club, backed by millions of pounds from the Department of Social Security.

The supporters have put together a complex financial structure made up of 25 per cent genuine welfare payments alongside a mixture of fraudulent incapacity and unemployment claims.

Supporters' spokesman Matthew Cord said: 'Between us we reckon we can raise about £500 million, especially as it's been such a cold winter. The number of folk who've come down with a sudden case of rheumatoid arthritis is shocking.

'The DSS provides us with a secure source of funds and if anyone starts asking questions we've got 45,000 sick notes sitting in a warehouse in Bootle.

'We did originally plan to steal it, but we couldn't find anywhere to keep the main stand as most of the garages round here are full of mountain bikes.'

He added: 'As far as you're concerned, I haven't worked in 12 years, all right?'

Under the plan the club would be run by an executive committee, elected by the supporters and given the right to swipe a range of quality goods from the office, the boardroom and the club shop.

The first team squad will also have to sign new contracts

Many Liverpool fans are looking forward to stealing Jamie Carragher.

requiring them to go to supporters' pubs every Saturday night and be told why they will never be as good as Emlyn Hughes and Jimmy Case.

Big Brother unveils 'all-idiot house'

THE latest series of *Big Brother* kicked off last night with the unveiling of a house made up exclusively of half-wits.

It's the first time the show has featured an all-female idiot house and the producers hope it will bring a new edge to the format, now in its tenth year.

'We want the show to get back to its roots,' said a Channel Four spokeswoman. 'It's not supposed to be a launch pad for wannabe celebrities, it's supposed to be a giant fishtank full of retards.'

The producers are keen to recreate the 2007 series of *Celebrity Big Brother* when

Bollywood star Shilpa Shetty had her head shoved down the toilet by Jade Goody and the cast of *Hollyoaks*.

The first male idiot will be introduced to the house next week. He is due to be sentenced at Bow Street Magistrates Court on Monday afternoon.

All girls together – this year's housemates:

Plop: The 20-year-old from Manchester is a singer, an actress, a model and an assistant manager at Greggs. She enjoys talking about herself and is forced to make new friends every week. She hates foreigners and people who ski.

Febreeze: The 20-year-old from London is a former member of the girl band Lenor and wants to be an actress, a model and the first woman in the SAS. She enjoys long walks on the beach and killing people with a pen. She is sponsored by Febreeze.

Koala: The 20-year-old from Manchester eats eucalyptus leaves and sleeps for 20 hours a day. She is an actress, a model and a marsupial who has had 14 children in the last three years. She hates foreigners and dingos.

Binty: The 20-year-old from London enjoys skiing, snow-boarding and bobsledding. She believes that wealth is genetic and hates foreigners, poor people and Greggs.

Sharleona: The 20-year-old from Manchester is a lesbian and a Conservative coun-cillor. Her perfect night out would be dinner with Kate Winslet and front row seats at a public hanging. She loves British citizens who don't speak English and need a lift to the polling station.

Yashmeena: The 20-year-old from London admits she is stuck up, arrogant and full of herself. She drives a Mercedes E-Class and eats nothing but lettuce and beef. She hates for-eigners and old people.

Fart: The 20-year-old from Manchester is a free spirit who has been claiming benefits for four years and living in a Portacabin. She paints murals of herself saving small animals and is convinced that everyone is either in love with her or wants to kill her.

Pudding: The 20-year-old from London describes herself as a 'bit of a tomboy'. She enjoys golf, rugby and standing-up when she urinates. She loves Alan Hansen and hates foreigners, dole cheats and women.

Gerald: The 73-year-old from Manchester enjoys bowling, the *Daily Express* and cough sweets. She hates foreigners and 20-year-old tarts.

ONE WOMAN'S WEEK: Portrait of the Artist
by KAREN FENESSEY

IT'S a sad day when artists with real integrity are beaten down by loud-mouth sensationalists.

This week, I have found myself in the same boat as the prominent female art lover, Tracey Emin, who has always struggled against the thousands of Philippines who want her silenced. And I have been seriously reconsidering whether I want to keep working at my school, if it means having to tolerate these imbeciles.

I have never been one to brag about my artistic ability, but it is an undeniable fact that I have been blessed (some might say 'cursed') with a superior vision to most of society. Instead of a tree, I see a majestic, green entity; instead of a teapot, I see a shiny, talkative receptacle. So when Mrs Dixon, the headmistress, was looking for a teacher to co-ordinate the pictures for our latest school magazine, *We Are a Multi-Cultured School* (inspired by the many new asylum-seeking children with which the school is now teeming), I knew I had to come to the rescue.

Personally, I don't see the point in this magazine as most of these kids' parents can't speak a word of English. That's why it's all the

> 'I have been blessed with a superior vision to most of society'

more important to make the pictures interesting and why I knew that I was the only person capable of engaging these people. However, someone else had plans to overthrow me.

Miss Tyrell, the special needs teacher, asks everyone to call her 'Mo' and on top of that, she claims to be a lesbian. Don't get me wrong, I am a big supporter of gays and one of my best friends is a FUCKING FAGGOT (he loves it when I call him that!) but there is a time and a place for spouting your alternative lifestyle.

So imagine how I rolled my eyes when 'Mo' got out her photos of her crusty summer expedition around India with her 'civil partner'. Wisely, she kept her mouth shut when we were asked who would curate the photography section of the new magazine – no doubt recalling the photos I brought in last summer of my trip to Ayers Rock (or as I like to call it: Uhuru).

Back to the task in hand: I spent ages planning and taking the pictures and so was utterly gobsmacked when the headmistress told me they were unsuitable. She had some kind of problem with the fact that I'd only photographed the coloured children. The magazine was supposed to show how 'multi-cultured' our school was, she said. 'Yes,' I said, 'so what did you want me to do – photograph all the white kids?!' She just doesn't get it!

My theory was confirmed when she then handed the task to Miss Tyrell, who probably shouldn't even be around young girls if you ask me, having inappropriate thoughts about them and then telling her 'wife' all about it.

It's only a matter of time until one of those simple children fall under her deviant spell. And they won't be able to call on me for help on the next stupid refugee-kid rag because I'll be working somewhere with staff who understand that I am a true artist.

NEWS BRIEFLY

POST OFFICE STRIKE TO BEGIN THREE DAYS LATE
'I blame the Post Office,' says Post Office worker.

FAIRTRADE KUMQUAT SALES ROCKET
'They are much more expensive. Thankfully all my clothes are made by Chinese toddlers,' says ghastly moron.

Worthless Opinion Poll
What are you doing to support your local post office?

Exploring online alternatives	15.9%
Buying it and turning it into a Starbucks	24.2%
Forcing old people to buy more stamps	27.3%
Changing drug money into Euros	32.6%

Sniff this by Oscar, Best in Show, Crufts 2008

IT could be my superb posture, my beautiful coat or my exquisite bone structure. But one thing's for sure: I am The Balls.

The moment I walked through that door on Monday, I thought to myself, 'I own this place.'

Don't get me wrong, there are some nice dogs in here, but they're strictly Sunday afternoon boys – know what I mean?

Crufts is my cathedral. It's my cockpit, my surfboard, it's my potter's wheel. I work it. With effortless expertise I bend it to my will. Crufts is me. I am Crufts.

The Newfoundland had high hopes, bless him, but this is the big one, all right? It's not some trot around the paddock at the county show, you gap-toothed hillbilly.

If you come to my house, you better be showing form. And I don't mean a red rosette, a tickle under the chin and a book voucher for the tubby cow on the other end of your lead.

Crufts is about class. It's a place for serious dogs. It is not a place for a nicely brushed American Cocker, prancing in here thinking I'm some kind of arsehole, before I get my thing working and send them prancing out of here looking like a *dick*!

I admit the Samoyed was looking tasty for a bit, but was I worried? Was I *fuck*! Let me tell you a little something about heelwork: you don't 'learn' it. You have either got it or you have not got it, and you, my friend, *have not got it*.

When that Kennel Club pencil-pusher walked up to me, I looked at her as if to say, 'Remember this – you only judge me because I let you.' I picked her up and played her like a finely tuned banjo.

So my friends, the next time you buy a ticket to my back end, remember this: that's the heady aroma of a champion. Sniff it.

This weekend in

the sunday mash

With interest rates on the up and estate agents warning that the boom is over, the experts are asking . . .

WHEN WILL BRITAIN'S 30-SOMETHINGS SHUT THE FUCK UP ABOUT HOUSE PRICES?

In Agony with PETULA SOUL

Dear Petula,
I have been with my partner for four years now, and while we have spoken about marriage I am not sure about taking the plunge. I have discussed the situation with my other boyfriend, and a few fuck-buddies, and they say it is just nerves ahead of the wedding in May. But I think we should probably just get the whole thing over with as soon as we can. The thing is my fiancé is very rich. I am worried that he might, say, have a terrible accident in his car with his brakes failing unexpectedly while we are on holiday at a mountain resort in Italy next week and I have just asked him to nip down to the village at the bottom of the hill for a jar of pesto. Imagine then how bad I will feel when I open up the cupboard door to get out his will, which I always keep with me, and discover a jar in there all along. If it should happen like that.

Hannah,
Hampstead

Do you have a problem you'd like Petula to help with?
e: petula@thedailymash.co.uk

Petula says:

Dear Hannah,
The very fact that you have referred to the, admittedly unlikely, prospect of your fiancé being killed in a completely unexpected car accident after being sent out by you on a totally pointless errand suggests to me that you have already gone beyond girlfriend status and are committed and ready to become a wife, which, you may be pleased to learn, would mean you would pay no inheritance tax. However, there are a few questions to be answered. While many husbands suffer unexpected car accidents on Italian mountain resorts because of freak brake failure, some manage to save the situation through skilful use of the gears. Have you considered sending him for the pesto after a couple of bottles of red? If I was you I would also suggest he drive very fast through a tunnel while wearing sunglasses on the remote chance that he will come out the other end temporarily blinded by the light and smash unexpectedly into a huge motorised shovel that will then push him and his car over the edge. These things happen you know.

Psychic Bob's Week Ahead

Taurus (20 APR – 20 MAY)
After a brief period of emotional instability and upheaval you will be locked away for a very long time.

Gemini (21 MAY – 20 JUN)
There is a new hopefulness about your life, a new, more positive outlook. It won't last.

Cancer (21 JUN – 22 JUL)
Do you feel you are not being treated with the correct level of respect at work? You're wrong.

Leo (23 JUL – 22 AUG)
If you have an ambitious project lined up, it's a good day to get started. If not just stay in bed with the lager.

Virgo (23 AUG – 22 SEP)
You'll meet people who hold views that are different from yours – punch them.

Libra (23 SEP – 23 OCT)
It's the perfect day to get outside and soak up some rays. Unless it's raining.

Scorpio (24 OCT – 21 NOV)
It's a day of intense passions – maybe romantic, but more likely just sordid and ultimately unsatisfying.

Sagittarius (22 NOV – 21 DEC)
You are totally focused on something big and important to you – to everyone else it is just a penis, only smaller.

Capricorn (22 DEC – 19 JAN)
You're stuck behind some slow-moving people, but not for long. Clean the hair and teeth from under the wheel arches afterwards.

Aquarius (20 JAN – 19 FEB)
You will have a lot of fun with an uptight friend today. You can loosen them up a bit. But not too much, or it will feel just like your wife.

Pisces (20 FEB – 20 MAR)
You feel ready to ask someone out. Wait until next week when a strong Venus will help you deal with the rejection.

Aries (21 MAR – 19 APR)
Professionally it's the perfect time to sell yourself. Stick up a nude photo in a phone box, preferably of someone else.

NEWS BRIEFLY

CAMERON BETTER THAN BROWN AT GIVING A SHIATSU MASSAGE, SAYS NEW POLL
But PM outscores Tory Leader as 'most likely to drink his own urine'.

SCOTLAND PROMISES TO TOTALLY GET ITS ACT TOGETHER
'I've signed up for yoga classes and that,' claims pissed-up country.

thedaily mash

it's news to us — www.thedailymash.co.uk — No. 16

THOUSANDS MORE FORCED OUT BY JAMIE OLIVER'S FACE

THE number of people leaving Britain because of Jamie Oliver's face has risen for the second year in a row.

Official figures show that more than 380,000 started a new life overseas, unable to endure another second of the grinning chef.

Roy Hobbs, an electrician from Falmouth, said: 'I decided my family and I would be better off in Basra rather than have to look at that cocky little shit every day for the rest of our lives.

'Life in Basra is unbelievably dangerous, but we've sided with some particularly ruthless Shi'ites and the kids are just so relieved not to have to eat whatever that fat-lipped sod tells them to.'

Janice Harper, a physiothera-

Thousands would rather live without proper sanitation.

pist from Chester, said: 'I walked into my local Sainsbury's

last October and every single product carried a picture of Jamie Oliver.

'All the store announcements were in his voice and there were huge video screens showing him and his trendy mates eating beer-battered fish and garlic-roasted chips. I put my house on the market that afternoon.'

Harper now lives in the hills outside Barcelona and has threatened to poison the local reservoir if Oliver comes within 250 miles.

A Home Office spokesman said it was unfair to single out Jamie Oliver and insisted there were many reasons for people to leave the UK.

He added: 'What about Richard and Judy's Book Club? That's a good one.'

---

news

LORRY DRIVER CELEBRATES FIRST ANNIVERSARY OF OVERTAKING MANOEUVRE

news

MINISTER TELLS MIDDLE CLASSES: BUY A BONG

Archbishop of Canterbury loses mind

THE Church of England was under temporary management last night after the Archbishop of Canterbury lost his mind during an interview with the BBC.

The Right Reverend Rowan Williams surprised colleagues when half-way through the recording he stripped down to his underpants and spread his legs so wide that each one was draped over an arm of the chair.

Britain's most senior clergyman then pointed to his groin, nodding slowly, before claiming that Jesus was a hefty, black woman and challenging everyone in the room to punch him in the stomach.

Holding his hand over a burning candle, the Archbishop said: 'The thing about me, right, is that I'm always pushing the outside of the envelope. I'm always challenging pre-conceived ideas.

'I'll fight you right now!'

'You say Jesus was a thirty-something Jewish guy with a beard. That's fine, but I'm saying he was an 18-stone woman from Harlem. Are you saying I'm wrong? Do you want to wrestle me? Is that what's going on here?'

He added: 'You say we need rules. I say why? You say we need clothes. I say why? Punch me in the stomach. Do it!

'You want to make women dress up in big sacks, that's cool. You want to chop off a few hands, stone a few gayboys. That's your bag and I'm down with it.'

He then grabbed the BBC reporter by the lapels and said: 'Are you afraid to get naked with me, boy?'

The Archbishop then ran from the room, removing his underpants and shouting: 'Look at it! Look at my dancing penis!'

Reverend Williams was later spotted running into woodland near Gravesend where he is believed to have spent the night.

Paris Hilton shows vagina to firemen

CELEBRITY heiress Paris Hilton is to display her shaved vagina in a heartfelt 'thank-you' to California's brave firefighters.

For the next 48 hours Miss Hilton will tour the state, positioning herself in a lifeguard's chair as dozens of weary firemen queue up to get a glimpse of her community-spirited quim.

Kyle Brandon, a 28-year-old fireman based in Pasadena, said: 'A job well done is reward enough for us, but it's awesome when a big star like Miss Hilton comes down here and shows off her glory hole.'

The Simple Life superstar said:

'When I got out of prison I promised that I would use my snatch to help people.

'I can think of no worthier candidates for a vagina showcase than our brave fireguys.'

She added: 'This disaster has affected famous people from so many different backgrounds.

'I pray that a brief glimpse of my cockbox will give these men the strength they need to save us from the hot orange things.'

Meanwhile celebrity magazines are clamouring for gossip on who is fleeing the inferno with heart-broken Friends sweetheart Jennifer Aniston.

'She's a special lady,' said Kyle.

According to Shit magazine Brad Pitt called Jen to make sure she was safe but hung up when the phone was answered by Luke Wilson doing a Vince Vaughan impersonation.

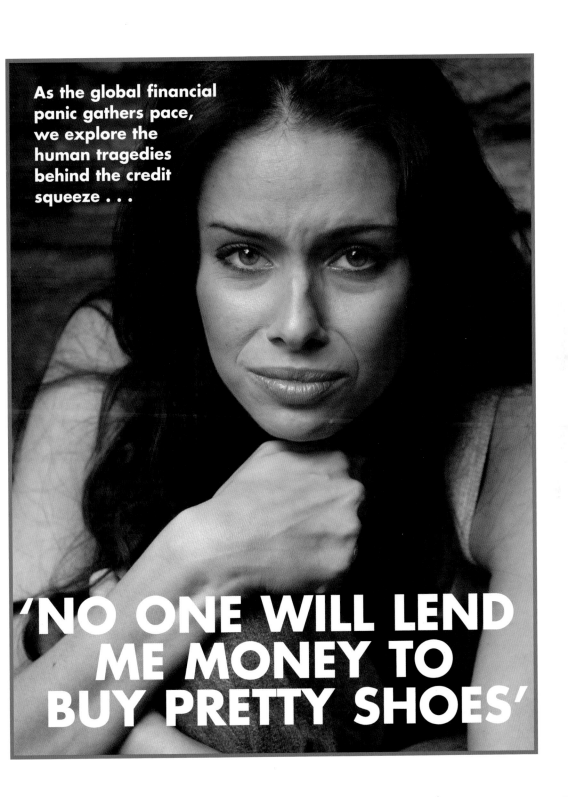

As the global financial panic gathers pace, we explore the human tragedies behind the credit squeeze . . .

'NO ONE WILL LEND ME MONEY TO BUY PRETTY SHOES'

Five launches new series of 'Crime Scene Navy Crime'

Crime-ridden hell-hole.

THE long wait is over for fans of fast-moving US police dramas as Channel Five screens the new series of *Crime Scene Navy Crime*.

The complex drama, known as *CSNC* to its legions of fans, is America's most popular show about a team of ocean-going forensic detectives.

Gil Gerard, who shot to fame as the star of *Buck Rogers in the 25th Century*, plays Navy Crime Forensic Investigations Officer Gavin Barton, a dedicated but cynical veteran who still holds the naval record for tying the most knots inside a minute.

His co-star Erin Gray, who shot to fame as Wilma Deering in *Buck Rogers in the 25th Century*, plays Rear-Admiral Brian Davis, Barton's dedicated but cynical commanding officer.

The two characters are at the centre of a tantalising will-they-won't-they sexual jousting match.

Wayne Hayes, a media analyst said: 'CSNC is continually challenging the viewer and finding new ways to investigate crimes that have been committed at sea.'

He added: 'I love the way they use special effects so that you can see what's happening inside the brain of the detective as, piece by piece, he uncovers the childhood betrayal that led to the theft of a walkman on board the *USS Walter Mondale*.'

Since 1996 the CSNC franchise has generated 37 spin-offs including *CSNC: Aberystwyth*, *CSNC: Gone Fishin'* and *CSNC: Rascals of the Barbary Coast*.

Churches condemn plan for giant lesbians

Each of the 100-foot-tall, test-tube lesbians will include a tiny bit of Martina Navratilova.

BRITAIN'S most senior clergymen last night condemned plans to use IVF technology to create gigantic lesbians in test tubes.

Cardinal Cormac Murphy O'Connor said the lesbians were planning to create an army of 100-foot-tall super-beings that would rampage across the country crushing churches under their massive heels.

He added: 'One day soon Westminster Cathedral will be reduced to a pile of rubble, destroyed by the demonic union of science and homosexuality.

'God's plan for the world is to persecute people for being in love, not to grow more of these perverts in a jar.'

Meanwhile John Sentamu, the Archbishop of York, told the House of Lords: 'The great tragedy is that these 100-foot-tall, 60-ton agents of destruction will grow up without fathers.

'Contrary to claims made by secular liberals, a father can play a pivotal role in the life of a massive, test-tube-generated killing machine.'

But the claims were rejected by the Institute for Lesbians. A spokeswoman said: 'We plan to use our humongous lesbians for peaceful purposes such as agriculture and orgasms.

'And I would point out that a really big bull-dyke can be every bit as manly as an Alan Titchmarsh or a Jude Law.'

THE FIRST RULE OF TODDLER FIGHT CLUB IS . . .

You do not talk about Toddler Fight Club.

OK, so you want to start a Toddler Fight Club. Don't worry, it's not as difficult as you may think. First of all you'll need a couple of toddlers, preferably one with a bit of a temper. Then all you have to do is stick them in the garden together and wait. Before long one of them will throw a fist. What do you do now?

a) Break it up and chastise the aggressor?
b) Protect the victim?
c) Encourage a full-on scrap?

If you answered C you're well on your way.

The second rule of Toddler Fight Club is: you do not talk about Toddler Fight Club.

Both toddlers may be a little traumatised after their first fight, but don't worry. They will soon be overwhelmed with a tremendous sense of freedom and self-confidence Once they've tasted their own blood they'll never look back.

Now it's time to expand. Mention it to other parents in the area, sound them out, drop hints, look for that glint in their eye. Before you know it you'll have a core membership and some serious momentum.

The third rule of Toddler Fight Club is: if it's your first time at Toddler Fight Club and you're a toddler . . . you have to fight.

It's essential to have the right venue. A garden or a public park is okay for staged events to attract new members, but for fight nights you'll need a place of your own. A large basement is perfect or perhaps you could hire the function room at your local bowling club. Make sure there's plenty of juice and sweets, a nap area and soft play. The toddlers will need somewhere to go when they're not in the fighting pit.

The fourth rule of Toddler Fight Club is: for Christ's sake don't video it and show it to people.

Inevitably the authorities will take an interest. But don't lose sleep. A 12-month suspended sentence is the going rate and all you'll need to do is lie low for a month and then change venues. Before you know it those toddlers will be back in the ring and biffing hell out of each other.

Happy Toddler Fight Clubbing!

Britain strikes gold in sport no one watches

TeamGB sets a new world record on their eight-wheeled cyclotron.

BRITAIN was riding the crest of a wave of victory last night after repeatedly striking gold in one of those sports that nobody ever watches.

Britain's finest two-legged men and women took home gold medals in the singles, the hot singles, the fancy doubles, the crotchless triples and the doubled pears.

An ecstatic Dick Hart, TeamGB manager, said: 'Take one pair of perfectly round wheels, add the relentless pounding of some truly magnificent British thighs, and stand well back.'

He added: 'I said to every single one of them: whatever you do, for God's sake keep pedalling.'

Last night's avalanche of triumph comes hot on the heels of British success at the Los Angeles Kerplunk Open and a 14–12 victory in the World Bread-Making Championships in Adelaide.

British competitors now sit astride the world stage in rat-shooting, speed pottery, synchronised chewing, professional bowler hat-wearing, darts and snooker.

Sport Minister Gerry Sutcliffe said: 'The next time someone tells you Britain is slow at riding a bike, you can look back on this day with pride, hold your head high and tell them to cock off.'

He added: 'This is the most exciting thing to have happened in British sport since Formula One boss Max Mosley paid some German hookers to pummel him with a cricket bat.'

Banks to replace charges with fees

BANKS are to replace charges with fees in a major shake-up of ripping people off.

The high street banks currently make £10 million a day by charging people £30 for writing a letter telling them they are £29.95 overdrawn after debiting their account for the £30 cost of the letter.

Under the new system the banks will now make £15 million a day by charging the current account holders a 'fee', but, in a radical shift in banking practice, they will not even bother to tell them why.

Roger Morton, from the British Bankers' Association, said: 'Banks currently make all their money from harassing poor people and stupid women with too many shoes.

'It's all rather jolly, but it is not a sustainable business model.

'By charging people whatever we feel like, when we feel like, we can earn millions in fees on top of the millions we earn in interest from lending out people's money to other people.'

He added: 'It's a win-win situation, but mainly for the banks.'

Meanwhile, engineering firms have begun producing specially strengthened lampposts to take the weight of dozens of bank executives about to be strung up by seething, blood-thirsty mobs.

Engineers say this lamppost will take the weight of the chairman of Barclays.

Nokia unveils pointless thing

MOBILE-phone giant Nokia has pledged to make pocket maps obsolete with the launch of a map that fits in your pocket.

Maps 2.0™, to be installed on the latest mobile handsets, will feature tiny, illegible writing and is guaranteed not to work when the battery is flat.

The company said the traditional printed 'A–Z', with its clear lettering, concise, booklet format and ability to function without a power source, will soon be pulped and recycled as instruction manuals for Maps 2.0™.

Ari Toivonen, Nokia's Head of Pointlessness, said: 'We want people to think of street maps as those large, awkward Ordnance Survey things that you can never fold up properly.

'The sort of thing Peter Sellers would have had all kinds of problems with in a Pink Panther film.'

He added: 'Do you want to flip open your phone and start mapping, or do you want to flail about like some incompetent French detective?'

With Maps 2.0™ all you have to do is find 'Map' which can be found in 'Accessories' which can be found in 'Settings' which can found in 'Profiles'.

For model numbers beginning with N it can be found in 'Your Favourites' which can be found in 'Your Phone and You' which can be found in 'Functionosity'.

You then simply type in the name of the street using the incredibly small keys, wait for 90 seconds and then try to work out where you are going using the incredibly small screen.

Mr Toivonen said: 'It works even better if you can stop a random stranger and ask if they know the post code for the exact spot where you're standing.'

What was wrong with this? Eh?

As the screens are not waterproof, Nokia is reminding British consumers not to use the map when it is raining.

🔍 IN FOCUS: Experts close to discovering secret pointlessness of Stonehenge

SCIENTISTS have started a fresh excavation at Stonehenge in the hope of confirming, once and for all, the ancient monument's complete and utter pointlessness.

In the past it was suggested the henge was built as an arena to attract sponsorship from a mobile phone company, or that it could be the top section of a medium-sized underground car park.

However, recent advances in carbon dating now point to it having absolutely no purpose whatsoever.

Henry Brubaker, chief archaeologist at the Institute for Studies, said: 'The ancient Britons quarried these giant stones by hand, dragged them hundreds of miles from Wales, lifted them into place, stared at them for bit and then wandered off.

'I know they didn't have telly, but there must have been something better to do.

'At least the Great Wall of China is actually a wall, and the Pyramids have mummies inside them.

'This is just some Welsh rocks

What a waste of time.

thrown up in the middle of nowhere for no reason.

'And even if they did use it for sacrificing badgers or worshipping the Moon – so what?'

In Agony with PETULA SOUL

Dear Petula,
I arrived home from work earlier than usual one day last week to find the house strangely quiet. My husband who works from home was not in the office or the shed at the bottom of the garden where he keeps his porn stash. I heard some strange noises from our bedroom so I went to investigate. Imagine my shock when I opened the door to find him prancing around in a corset, fishnet stockings and red, patent-leather, fuck-me shoes. I was amazed. He normally wears American tan tights and ballet pumps. Has he gone weird?

Concerned,
Craigmillar

Petula says:

Dear Concerned,
At a certain point in their lives all men will experiment with dressing up as women. Most never take this much further than buying a blonde wig, a nice blouse, a pencil skirt, the full stockings and suspender belt rig-out and some six-inch heels to stomp around in while listening to Donna Summer records. I know my husband did, and the first time I came back early and found him dressed like that I thought Vanessa Feltz had moved in. Frankly, I was delighted to discover it was him in drag. As long as he sticks to sussies and ditches those dull tights you should be all right. Relax a little, introduce the cross-dressing into your lovemaking as it can be fun – once you get over the terror of being humped by a large middle-aged Jewess from North London that is. I still have the occasional nightmare.

Do you have a problem you'd like Petula to help with?
e: petula@thedailymash.co.uk

Psychic Bob's Week Ahead   What does the future hold for you?

Taurus (20 APR – 20 MAY)
Looking for love? You don't need to go farther than your workplace, unless it's a school.

Gemini (21 MAY – 20 JUN)
You should open up – it's almost 11 a.m. and some of us have not had a drink all morning.

Cancer (21 JUN – 22 JUL)
You'll meet someone today who you dislike immediately – she's socially awkward and comes off as rude. Yes, it's your mum.

Leo (23 JUL – 22 AUG)
Are people acting strange around you? Cackle like a crow and pick their noses while they talk to you. They'll like it.

Virgo (23 AUG – 22 SEP)
Look out for someone trying to attract your attention. It may seem odd but it does prove they can tie a knot in it.

Libra (23 SEP – 23 OCT)
Is your social circle feeling a little too small? Try talking to other people and not just yourself.

Scorpio (24 OCT – 21 NOV)
Increase your chances of meeting people with your online ad by being flexible in what you are offering. And lower your prices!

Sagittarius (22 NOV – 21 DEC)
If you're not getting the results you want, try a different approach. How about kidnapping?

Capricorn (22 DEC – 19 JAN)
Issues you thought were behind are resurfacing. That's what happens when you stop taking your pills.

Aquarius (20 JAN – 19 FEB)
Walking a dog is a great way to meet girls, but sitting on a bench, crying and holding an empty is even better.

Pisces (20 FEB – 20 MAR)
Introduce yourself to that cutie at the bus stop. What can go wrong? You're already on the sex offenders' register.

Aries (21 MAR – 19 APR)
You say you are feeling indecisive right now – are you sure?

ye daily mash

3rd April 1502

tis to us news

Wheat price increase foretells great doom

THE price of a bushel of wheat rose yet again in the markets of Flanders yesterday presaging a monstrous tribulation and a grave rise in the price of mead, the Lord High Guardian of the King's Purse has warned.

Sir Mervyne de Kinge professed himself aghast as news arrived from Ghent that merchants had exchanged on wheat for six gold florin a bushel, a price not usually seen in trade unless in association with the rare spices of the Orient.

The noble lord forewarned that a time of privation would surely be visited on the kingdom, when the peasant would find himself cast from his wretched midden and the knight dispossessed of his estates by the grubby moneychangers of old Lombard Street.

He said: 'Extremeties of the climes have done for the harvest yet again,

*S*erpent insurance premiums are up again.

and giant sea serpents have dragged down the ships of those few mariners who would dare brave the waves to help us bake our daily bread.

'Nor is it just the Israelite who profits at this time, as you would expect, but the whole merchant class appears arraigned against us like the massed ranks of the Persians against King Leonidas at Thermopylae.

'If there is not some sudden fall in price, a great plague spread by rats, or a new world discovered with bountiful supplies of grain and large fowl with which we can load our tables come Christmastide I fear we are all totally in the shitter. Again.'

Sir Mervyne said a rise in the price of wheat would force up the rates of the money changers and plunge those squires who had foolishly bought their castles at inflated prices into penury and destitution.

He added: 'And those knaves who have speculatively bought so many castles purely to rent out to others, against the teachings of the Holy Book, verily I say, in God's name they will be cast down into the fires of hell to burn for ever and ever. Amen.'

The Daily Mash

It Is News To Us

10th September, 1897

ALCOHOL IS A CORRUPTING INFLUENCE ON THE POOR,
INSISTS LADIES' TEMPERANCE LEAGUE

THE drinking of alcoholic liquor prevents the poor from carrying out their duties and if left unchecked will hasten the demise of the Empire, the Ladies' Temperance League has warned.

The organisation, led by Mrs Eleanor Bentley of Dorking, has implored the Chancellor of the Exchequer to place a heavy burden of taxation upon gin, whisky, ale and porter at the time of his next annual budget.

Speaking to a packed meeting in Godalming town hall, Mrs Bentley said: 'Our cherished England has become a truly wretched place, teeming with inebriation and unspeakable profanity. We have forsaken the Lord and his retribution shall be without mercy.

'Every day my ladies bring me new reports of Satan's corruption in the taverns and saloons of our

'Satan shall not prosper,' declared Mrs Bentley.

grimy cities.

'Our once cheerful urchins now sway under the influence of rum, grow horns from their heads and feast on goat flesh at sunset.

'Last week I noticed the tell-tale watermarks of slovenliness on my dessert forks and when I confronted my kitchen maid I was assaulted by the stench of easy Spanish wine.'

Mrs Bentley, the daughter of Admiral Sir Julian Cook of Witney, demanded the immediate removal of beer advertisements from the *Daily Sketch* and *News Chronicle* and condemned the editor of the *Times* for publishing an article about sherry.

The League is to join forces with other like-minded organisations including the Quakers, the Salvation Army and the Independent Labour Party, with the goal of abolishing intoxicating beverages from our national life and restoring Great Britain on the path to righteousness.

God Save the King!

The Daily Mash

June, 1916

It Is News To Us

ARMY TO STOP FIRING GOATS INTO WALLS

HIS Majesty's army is to cease the practice of firing goats into walls, the War Ministry announced last night.

In the last year more than 3,000 goats have been shot into hard surfaces by soldiers curious to see what kind of patterns they would form.

Brigadier General Sir Denys Finch-Hatton said goat firing was developed to give soldiers an enjoyable break from the rigours of battle, but now as the Germans launch a new offensive, all hands are needed at the front.

'We tried finger-painting but it did not seem to have the same effect, and it was quite difficult to get a steady supply of fingers,' he said.

Another cow on its way to France.

'The goats create a rich textured effect, a shimmering mosaic of teeth, hair and blood.

'If I had to describe it I'd say it was like that Picasso fella, crossed with a ravenous polar bear.'

British soldiers first started firing animals from guns in the mid-eighteenth century when muskets were used to propel baby mice into doors.

Animal firing remained limited to single shot rifles until the invention of the multi-barrelled Gatling Gun in 1875, capable of shooting out 400 kittens a minute.

The Royal Artillery has since turned its attention to large mammals and has now developed a howitzer which is used to blast cows over the channel.

'Thousands of people still turn up every Sunday to watch us fire a few Friesians at the Hun,' the General added.

Tutankhamun 'banjoed by frying pan', announces Lord Carnarvon

KING Tutankhamun died after being spanked very hard in the face with a heavy frying pan, the leading Egyptologist Lord Carnarvon has claimed.

As the face of the boy king was revealed to the world for the first time in 3,000 years, experts agreed that the Eighteenth-Dynasty pharaoh had clearly been the victim of a pan-wielding assassin.

'Tutankhamun was famed for his long, sensitive nose,' said Lord Carnarvon, who has recently uncovered the sacred tomb.

'Before he would grant an audience to a visiting dignitary he would sniff them very thoroughly. Sometimes for over an hour.

'But look at it now. Someone must have absolutely fucking

His Lordship's expedition will now attempt to determine the weight and speed of the deadly pan.

whacked him with a frying pan.'

Mr Howard Carter, his Lordship's assistant, said the spanking seemed to have been caused by a flat, heavy iron pan with a long handle.

'The ancient Egyptians called it a *faktiti* and used it for cooking eggs, sausages and black pudding.'

Mr Carter added: 'Look how hard they hit him. They must have taken a run-up.'

There is evidence contained within ancient hieroglyphs of a plot to kill the young pharaoh with a kitchen implement.

A papyrus dating from around 1320 BC, discovered near Abu Simbel, reads: 'The Living Image of Amun has betrayed his destiny and inflicted poor harvests upon Thebes.

'I think I might banjo the big-nosed bastard with the wife's *faktiti*.'

It Is News To Us

ARMY CAN'T FIGHT 14 WARS AT ONCE, SAYS DUKE OF WELLINGTON

HIS Grace the Duke of Wellington has implored Parliament to limit the active engagement of the British Army from the current obligation of 14 wars to a mere eight.

In a letter to the editor of the *Times* the Duke gave dread warning that the Royal Scots and the Coldstream Guards are stretched beyond reason and in desperate need of new hats.

'Sir, these hats are not fit for a Frenchman,' wrote the Duke. 'I implore the Prime Minister and the Prince Regent to immediately make funds available for the commissioning of a new hat, which I myself have designed.'

British regiments are currently suppressing four separate Indian rebellions, while the remainder of His Majesty's forces remains at

The 52nd Light Infantry is absolutely knackered.

war with France, Italy, Austria, Venezuela, the Ottoman Empire, China, Siam, Abyssinia, the Zulus and the Isle of Man.

'Without these fine new hats and the soldiers that fight beneath them, we will surely lose the initiative on the Iberian Peninsula,' continued His Grace.

'In a matter of weeks the Horn of Africa will once again find herself besmirched by the dread clutches of the ghastly Turk!

'We must secure at once an honourable settlement which returns fair Siam to the stewardship of the Belgians, while acceding to Venezuela's alliance with the Emperor of Japan.

'Meanwhile, the Manxmen of the Isle of Man must be allowed to return to their goat molestations, unmolested.'

His Grace concluded: 'Sir, as the Duke of Marlborough once wrote, "Great Britain must always be engaged in eight different wars. Any less is an admission of weakness, any more is just silly-buggers."'

Wonka factory 'full of rats'

CHOCOLATE king Willy Wonka has been fined £75,000 after rats were discovered inside his magical factory.

In court Wonka had claimed the rats were highly-skilled employees who were able to retrieve lost children from the ventilation system.

His lawyers then insisted the rats were actually the pets of the Oompa-Loompas, Wonka's army of cheap foreign labour.

But Judge Wilson said the Wonka factory was 'seriously deficient in terms of health and safety' and that Wonka 'occupied a strange fantasy world, seemingly oblivious to the

Two members of Wonka's army of cheap foreign labour.

regulations governing the manufacture of confectionery'.

It's the latest setback for the multinational chocolate empire. Wonka is fighting four separate

legal actions after a factory visit last year by a group of prize-winning children ended in serious injury and illness.

Augustus Gloop, a nine-year-old German boy, contracted a rare form of food poisoning and is now paralysed down his left-hand side, while British schoolgirl Veruca Salt was beaten unconscious by angry squirrels.

Wonka said he was considering an appeal adding: 'The rats are my friends. How could I ask them to leave? They have kindness in their hearts.

'Unfortunately they also carry botulism in their lower intestines.'

It Is News To Us

the daily mash

it's news to us   www.thedailymash.co.uk   No. 17

BRITAIN SAYS 'FUCK YOU' TO BROWN PEOPLE

BRITAIN'S immigration policy is to be based on the use of Dulux colour charts, the government announced last night.

From April next year customs officials at airports and ferry terminals will grade new arrivals against a varied palate of earthy browns and creamy taupes.

The shading system will range from the industrious, educated tones of 'Tropical Sand' to the unskilled, non-EU crime-wave that is 'Mocha Madness'.

A Home Office spokesman said: 'We expect the cut-off point to be somewhere between 'Almond Beige' and 'Appalachian Spring'. Funnily enough, 'English Brown' is actually far, far too brown.

'Those deemed beige enough will be offered a job, a copy of the *Metro* and a complimentary Sky+ box. Meanwhile the undeniably brown will be told to get back on the fucking boat.'

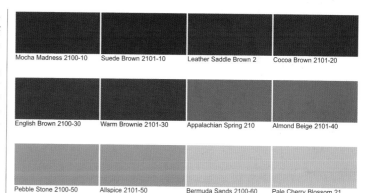

Mocha Madness 2100-10   Suede Brown 2101-10   Leather Saddle Brown 2   Cocoa Brown 2101-20

English Brown 2100-30   Warm Brownie 2101-30   Appalachian Spring 210   Almond Beige 2101-40

Pebble Stone 2100-50   Allspice 2101-50   Bermuda Sands 2100-60   Pale Cherry Blossom 21

Victorian Lace 2100-70   Tropical Sand 2101-70

Once you've had 'Suede Brown' you'll never go back. Apparently.

The policy shift follows a year of intensive pressure on the government to adopt the so-called 'Himmler Method' of ethnic profiling, pioneered in Germany in the mid-1930s.

The spokesman added: 'We're also piloting a scheme that involves using calipers to measure the width of the nose and the circumference of the skull.

'Cranial dimensions can tell you a great deal about an individual's ability to clean a hotel room.'

---

news

I HATE EVERY LAST ONE OF YOU, ADMITS BROWN

news

MPs TO DEBATE MAJOR EUROPEAN ZZZzzzzz...

Glaswegian recreates out-of-body experience for £9.50

A 42-year-old man from Glasgow claims to have discovered a full-proof way to recreate an out-of-body experience for less than a tenner.

Bill Mackay insisted he used tried and tested scientific methods to engineer the mysterious mental state experienced by an estimated one in 10 people.

Mackay said: 'I take the tenner and swap it for three litres of Gaymers Old English and a bottle of Cinzano Bianco. I then drink them as fast as I possibly can on an empty stomach.

'Within minutes I feel like I am flying high above the streets of Glasgow and everyone looks like ants or maybe aunts – at that point I'm not a hundred per cent sure.

'I then look down and can see myself trying to start a conversation about dogs and cats. Or, failing that, a fist fight.'

Mackay's research has confounded academics at University College, London, who have been conducting a major investigation into the phenomenon.

A UCL spokesman said: 'I kind of wish we hadn't spent three years and the best part of £250,000 attaching electrodes to people's privates.'

Mackay added: 'Some people say this is what it feels like to be dead. I don't know about that, but I do know dogs are more intelligent than cats.

'Are you saying different? Are you? I'll knock that fucking smile off your face, you cat-loving bastard.'

Mysterious properties.

More women having lunch on petrol station forecourts

RECORD numbers of women are having lunch on petrol station forecourts after filling up their cars with fuel, new research reveals.

The average time each woman spends parked next to the petrol pump after refuelling has risen from 45 minutes last year to an hour.

The only group staying longer are pensioner couples, who have just voted the petrol station their favourite picnic destination for the fifth year in a row, according to *Saga* magazine.

Nikki Hollis, 26, said she liked to lunch at her local petrol station because she could park without having to do any reversing and it sold three different sizes of Dairy Milk.

She said: 'You can flick through a *Heat* magazine while

Nikki also likes to chat to friends at the other pumps.

you are eating, down a glass or two of Zinfandel, and there's still plenty of time to touch up your make-up in the rear view mirror.

'And if you forget something, it's okay, because the shop is right there.'

Elderly driver David Jackers said he discovered the joys of sitting at the petrol pumps after waiting an hour for his wife Enid to come back from the toilet and a browse in the shop.

He added: 'They are lovely spots even if they do get a bit busy sometimes.

'But everyone is so friendly, they honk their horns at us and wave, and at our age the toilets are a godsend.'

Tom Logan, 43, a photocopier salesman from Dundee, said: 'What are you waiting for? What *the fuck* are you waiting for?'

He added: 'Move. Move. Move. MOVE! FUCKING. MOOOOOOOOOOOOVE!'

Baldy bastards told to stop being so bald about everything

BALDY bastards were last night told to shut up and stop being so bald about everything.

The move comes after the latest increase in hairless men being particularly bald towards people who do not look like a big, daft egg.

Nikki Hollis, 26, said she was sick of men getting all bald on her every time she and her friends pointed at their bare, baldy heads and laughed at them in the street.

She added: 'Did they leave their hair on the bus? I keep mine on top of my head, that way I always know where it is. Stupid baldy bastards.

'If they like hair so much then why don't they just grow some like any normal person? It's not exactly difficult. My baby does it, and she's only six months old.

'They just want to go around being all bald, and then get baldy with us when we point out what baldy bastards they are. Slapheads.'

Professor Henry Brubaker, of the Institute for Studies, said men who claimed they were bullied at work because of their lack of hair were just being bald for the sake of it.

He said: 'Explain this to me. Soon as they start to lose it off the top they start worrying about losing the lot so what do they do? They shave it all off. How bald can you get?

'What's wrong with keeping a few tufts? And why not dye

Can't you afford hair, Mr Baldy?

them orange and wear big, flappy shoes so we can all have a laugh?

'Or what about a wig? The modern ones are really good. No one can tell you're wearing one. You daft, bald, wiggy bastard.'

Third World to teach white people how to walk

Africa is home to the world's most skillful walkers.

AS the price of oil climbs towards $200 a barrel, the Third World has offered to teach Europe and America how to walk.

With millions of Western commuters descending into urine-soaked panic, African and Asian walking teachers are now preparing for a surge in demand for their services.

Thomas Otangwe, a walking consultant from Zaire, said: 'I first learned to walk when I got a job as a farm labourer.

'The farm was 20 miles from my home, but for the first week I would stand in the street wondering where my beautiful car was. Eventually I realised I could not afford a car and so I began to walk.

'Walking is relatively simple. You start by putting one foot in front of the other and then slowly increase the rate until you have reached a steady pace.

'You should then continue in this way until you arrive at your chosen destination. This is the key to successful walking.

'You may want to stop along the way for a cup of tea or a snack, but remember: you will have to start walking again.'

Mr Otangwe added: 'We have produced a handy booklet with diagrams and an introduction to advanced walking, but be quick because the price is going up all the time.'

Any chance of you working for five minutes? GPs asked

These British doctors are late for lunch.

THE Department of Health has written to GPs in England and Wales asking them if they wouldn't mind doing a bit of work, just for five minutes.

The move is part of the government's plan to introduce an out-of-hours service shortly after the introduction of a nine-to-five service later this year.

Health Secretary Alan Johnson said: 'I had a look at the average GP salary for the next three years and thought, "Gosh, that really is a tremendous amount of money, we should probably ask them to do a bit of work at some point."'

He added: 'Although our stated policy is to withdraw NHS treatment from sick people, we do need GPs to maintain the flow of anti-depressants and help us weed out benefit cheats.

'I have today written to them asking if we could have maybe five minutes of their time, twice a week, just until we can import a few more Bulgarian locums who'll do it all for £3.50 an hour.'

A spokesman for the British Medical Association said: 'Mmmm, I'm not sure my guys are going to go for this. A lot of them have boats now and that's much more time-consuming than you think.

'You have to learn how to steer it and then how to tie it on to one of those big bollard things next to the water.

'And of course, no one wants to be rushed when they're trying to pick out just the right captain's hat.'

NEWS BRIEFLY

TEENAGE LIVES COMPLETE AS GRAND THEFT AUTO FILLS GAP BETWEEN BOUTS OF FRENZIED MASTURBATION

'The combination of GTA4 and committed, high-frequency masturbation should keep them in a state of equilibrium until we can train them up and ship them to Afghanistan,' says study.

FOUR OUT OF 10 STAFF MAY DO SOME WORK THIS YEAR

Most blame constant strain of pretending to work.

BRITISH DOCTORS TO BUY THEIR OWN COUNTRY

'We need a place where we can relax with other doctors and not be bothered by people who didn't spend five years at university,' says BMA.

Worthless Opinion Poll
Which blasphemous product are you enjoying?

Ganesh-on-a-Stick™	14%
Bible-Wipes®	20%
Kellogg's Christicles®	21%
Jesus is my Dildo™	45%

Tiny island people were Ewoks, not Hobbits, say scientists

THE tiny human-like bones found on a South Pacific island may have belonged to small furry creatures known as 'Ewoks', and not Hobbits, as previously thought.

For months the scientific community has been split over whether the remains were evidence of Hobbits, and if so, whether they were Bagginses or Underhills.

But now a team from the Institute for Studies has blown the debate wide open with the claim that the remains are evidence of a small furry species that was sort of a cross between a monkey and a bear.

Professor Henry Brubaker said: 'The Ewoks did not look particularly human but they could walk upright and were able to manufacture clothing, tools and elaborate tree-house cities.

'We also found parts of a huge military machine, which suggests they may have been involved in a battle with some kind of evil empire.'

But Dr Denys Hatton, one of the leading Hobbit advocates, said: 'Not only are they Hobbits but they are very clearly Baggins Hobbits.

'Look at the all the clay pipes and big, round, green doors we found. Do Underhills have green doors? Do Ewoks smoke pipes? I think not!'

Meanwhile a third school of thought has emerged which has dismissed the Hobbit and Ewok theories, insisting the bones belong to a species of three-foot-high, second-hand robot salesmen called 'Jawas'.

Dr Wayne Hayes, of Dundee University, said: 'They lived a long time ago and roamed the desert looking for stray robots which they would then recondition and sell to primitive farming communities.

'We believe many of them may have been wiped out during a search for two rebel droids.'

Hobbits were both fierce and adorable.

DIARY: Russell Brand

GOR' blimey guv'nor and gadzooks! Thrice I had partaken in the devil's dandruff that very morning, and now I was well and truly off me crust, ta very much. The willing young lady of the night what I'd procured the previous evening was still wriggling around on me boat race like an eel on a bleeding frying pan. 'I've had enough of this lark – now begone scarlet woman and leave me a couple of Rizla on your way out,' I tell her.

Then I glances down at me Mickey Mouse fob watch. 'Gordon Bennett!' I thought, 'I'm due on the tellybox in half an hour, and I've only intercoursed three ladies in the past four hours.' So's I rang the local escort agency and they send round this Thai midget who did unspeakable things to me with a toilet brush marinaded in Deep Heat.

Following a most stimulating evening of badinage on me chat-show

sofa, I spent the early evening in the green room chatting to me guests, one of whom is an old chum of mine, the legend that is Mr Ronald Corbett. About an hour into proceedings, Ronnie, who'd been talking to David Cameron for ten minutes, turns to me, slaps me on the back and says: 'This posh cunt's doing my fucking napper in – fancy necking a disco biscuit or three, for old times' sakes?'

So's off we both trot, like a couple of proper scoundrels. Ronnie reaches into the pocket of his sports jacket and produces this huge great bag of pills and pops a couple into me hands. Strike a light, I think to meself, as the pocket-rocket jock (as I like to call him) drags me off to this dingy little club in south London where we dance our tits out 'til the sun comes up.

Shiver me timbers and roll out the barrel – 'What a bleeding palaver over there in Iraq,' is what I'm thinking as I watch breakfast telly, munchy-wunching on mouthfuls of toasty soldiers. I turns over to Lorraine Kelly on the other side and think to meself, 'I'd like to give that Scottish MILF some of me meat dagger, and make no mistake.'

So's I picks up the trim phone and rings GMTV. I ask, like, in me best telephone voice, whether the fragrant Lorraine would be interested in coming round and having her plumbing fixed, so to speak. To my chagrin, a recorded message told me that 'All competition lines had now closed, and I wouldn't be charged for the call.' Midget time.

Insurance companies pretending to be Chinese restaurants

BRITAIN'S biggest insurance companies are pretending to be Chinese restaurants to avoid flood damage claims, the *Daily Mash* has learned.

Thousands of consumers have complained that they are unable to get through to the freephone numbers on their policy without being asked to place an order.

Denis Fynch-Hatton, from Cheltenham, said: 'I tried phoning Legal & General on several occasions and each time I was greeted by someone doing a

very poor Chinese accent screaming, "He no here! He no here!"'

'Eventually I did get through to someone who spoke English and was able to order prawn toast, vegetable spring rolls and kung-po chicken – and guess what? It never arrived.'

A spokesman for the Association of British Insurers said: 'We're very busy just now. Why not buy a can of Fanta and read a three-year-old copy of *Marie Claire*?'

The *Daily Mash* attempted to contact some of the UK's top

insurers yesterday:
• Direct Line – a recorded message claiming to be the 'Hunan Palace', opening hours, 6 p.m.–1 a.m.
• Prudential – refused to discuss warped floorboards and ruined furniture and demanded to know if our name was on the buzzer.
• Norwich Union – had never heard of Norwich. Told we were outside the free-delivery area.
• Endsleigh – no chicken, only pork. Free prawn crackers after 45 minutes.
• Liverpool Victoria – 'WHAT NUMBER? WHAT NUMBER?'

Northern Rock?
I shit 'em

by Mervyn King,
Governor of the Bank of England

NORTHERN ROCK? Knob-gobblers, more like. That bucket-fanny chairman turns up at my gaff, pin-striped, watch chain, Savile-fuckin'-Row. Says, 'Merv, I'm out of my depth, need 30 bills for a bail or we are getting arse-banged by the regulator and, by the way, so are you.' Cock-swiveller.

He thinks I'm going to roll over, wave my plunger in the air and pipe him aboard because if he craps, the whole fuckin' market goes down the shitter with him; just because he's fucked every granny in Geordieland for her savings and then pissed them into the Tyne I'll open up my legs and show him my muff stilton. What am I? A fuckin' minge-winker?

So he's sitting there all smug, asking me when I can make the injection, and I'm playing him along, acting proper concerned, then I reach under the desk, pull out my shooter, shove it right up his posh toffee nose, cock the trigger and say: 'How's about I inject this up your back-hole and bail your guts all over the wall, you piss-faced tit-cocker.' And he pebbles his boxers on the spot. Savile Row shitpants. I nearly pissed myself.

Next it's Lloyds-wanking-TSB. They want 30 huge so they can buy the Northern and keep

> 'Next it's Lloyds
> wanking TSB'

it hush-hush. Thirty wanking billion? Fucking shit-knockers, I say and get Terry to show them the quick way out, down the fucking fire escape, head-fucking-first. They're worse than the Geordies. Bumrubbers, the lot of them.

Then it's Bernanke on the dog. 'Merv, Merv,' he says, 'We've lent billions to the blacks and the rednecks and now they won't give us a penny back. My sub-prime is so fucking sub it's underwater. What am I gonna do?' Nonce.

'Bernie,' I say, 'I got Darling here leaking dirty water because

he's been in the job three days, bust one bank and cluster-fucked the markets. Brown is trampling on his love spuds every morning then getting on the blower to me to fix it right now or he'll have my nads on a spike. Yesterday. And you want my help 'cos you've been legged over by some inbreds? If you hadn't pissed it in the first place none us would be in this fucking bumchain. I shit you not. Now fuck off.'

Any road up, better get myself spruced. Speaking to a load of brokers at the Mansion House tonight. Cock-swappers.

Worthless Opinion Poll
What new deadly sin are you committing?

Curing MS	14.8%
Coveting neighbour's DNA	15%
Stem cell pornography	29.2%
Lacy panties on lab monkey	40.9%

In Agony with PETULA SOUL

Dear Petula,

I love my boyfriends very much, but all is not well in the bedroom department. One of them suffers from premature ejaculation, three of them have problems sustaining an erection, while two more can't even get it up in the first place. Another has the tiniest winkie I have ever seen and the other six are basically just crap in bed. In fact my husband is just about the only one who can get off the starting grid without going all floppy or spilling all his man chowder on the carpet. Unfortunately, he is away every other fortnight working on the rigs. What am I to do?

Frankly pissed off,
Farnham

> **Do you have a problem you'd like Petula to help with? e: petula@thedailymash.co.uk**

Petula says:

Dear Frankly,

What a sorry tale, and one that gives a whole new meaning to the phrase: two weeks on, two weeks off. Having said that I understand your frustration; there seems little point in having a stream of gentleman callers during your husband's absence if not a single one of them can flame-grill your fur-burger, so to speak. But what to do? Instructing them all in the art of lovemaking would be terribly time-consuming, but I would not advise getting them around for a group session without putting down some plastic sheeting first. I suppose you could try going without for a couple of weeks while hubby is away, but that does seem a pretty drastic option, and most definitely a last resort. I see you have limited yourself to 13 illicit lovers. Perhaps you are being a bit too picky. Play the field a bit more like any normal married woman and I am sure you'll eventually come across one hunk who will really get your roast beef sizzling.

Psychic Bob's Week Ahead What does the future hold for you?

Taurus (20 APR – 20 MAY)
You know your sweetie's favourite food and favourite movie, but do you know their deepest hopes and desires? Order those giant nappies now!

Gemini (21 MAY – 20 JUN)
You've got your eye on someone. Get it back. They might eat it.

Cancer (21 JUN – 22 JUL)
You certainly can't hurry love. If you shot off any quicker it would all be over before she's even finished asking: 'Are you in yet?'

Leo (23 JUL – 22 AUG)
Has someone's arrogant behaviour been getting on your nerves? Because it has certainly been getting on ours, big head.

Virgo (23 AUG – 22 SEP)
Show off your artistic side by shaving off all your pubes and painting elephant ears either side of your penis. If you don't have a penis ask a friend if you can use theirs.

Libra (23 SEP – 23 OCT)
Inner beauty is important but appearances do matter, as does that strange sewage smell. Bad luck!

Scorpio (24 OCT – 21 NOV)
When you're with someone every day, it's easy to let things get routine. Try sleeping with some random strangers – it will give you a few new ideas. He'll thank you in the end!

Sagittarius (22 NOV – 21 DEC)
You don't have to wait for your partner to make the first move. You don't even have to wait for them to wake up. That is the one big advantage of marriage.

Capricorn (22 DEC – 19 JAN)
Do you want that promotion? Then it's time to get down on your knees and show them you mean business!

Aquarius (20 JAN – 19 FEB)
A big problem at work leaves you drained and grumpy by the time you get home. Get really drunk and hit the kids.

Pisces (20 FEB – 20 MAR)
Don't let someone chatty derail your plans to work efficiently. If they won't shut up, nail their tongue to your shoe.

Aries (21 MAR – 19 APR)
Your self esteem is low. Try getting drunk in a bar and going home with a stranger. When you wake up in the morning you'll feel like a million dollars!

the daily mash

it's news to us   www.thedailymash.co.uk   No. 18

'OI, MANUEL! A BIT LESS RACISM AND A BIT MORE SERVICE, IF YOU DON'T MIND'

BRITAIN was united in outrage last night after Formula One ace Lewis Hamilton was racially abused by the Spanish, of all people.

Hamilton said he was disappointed by the fans' reaction, adding that he loved Spain even though the service was often slow and greasy.

Foreign Secretary David Milliband has written to the mayor of Barcelona demanding an apology, a pint of Grolsch and the mixed grill.

'And, I'd like it today, if that's all right,' he said. 'Pronto, know what I mean? Not fuckin' mañana.'

He added: 'Are you ever going to finish that fuckin' cathedral, you lazy shits? Looks like it was built by the fuckin' Irish anyway.'

Meanwhile angry British holidaymakers have pledged to order everything in a particularly loud voice when they invade the Costas this July.

Denys Hatton, who owns a timeshare near Marbella, said:

'I learn racism from a book.'

'This is typical of the Spaniard.

'Last year my wife and I ordered the gammon steaks only to be told they had "ran out".

'We were then forced to eat a disgusting pile of rice, peas and incredibly fresh, succulent mussels cooked in a big frying pan. Savages.'

A Spanish government spokesman said the incident was a misunderstanding and that the fans had painted their faces black to celebrate the festival of Santo Ignacio de Loyola.

He added: 'It commemorates the day when Ignacio forced a black man to sit on a donkey before pushing them both off a cliff.'

---

news

'STOP BEING ILL,' DEMAND DOCTORS

news

SMOKERS MORE LIKELY TO BE EATEN BY DRAGONS

People over 30 are grown-ups, says report

PEOPLE in their 30s and 40s are adults who are able to decide things for themselves, according to a new academic report.

The wide-ranging study of more than 2,000 British people over the age of 30 found that:

- They are old enough to be out on their own.
- They enjoy having money and being served in pubs.
- They recognise that getting drunk and climbing up some scaffolding is not an excellent use of their time.

Research director Dr Tom Logan said: 'When it came to tobacco and alcohol we made the startling discovery that people over 30 were no longer little children who still pissed the bed.

'In fact, not only were they able to read the gigantic

According to the latest research, only one of them will later piss the bed.

warnings on cigarette packets, they were also fully aware that drinking two bottles of

Muscadet on an empty stomach could lead to hangovers, half-remembered unpleasantness and chronic liver disease – but they were going to do it anyway because they were adults and it was no one else's fucking business.

'When we asked them how they knew these things, they stressed that was also none of our business and that politicians should stop trying to make everyone the same. Or they had seen it on *Scrubs*.'

Dr Logan added: 'That said, quite a few of them did have a raging drink problem which caused them to piss the bed.'

The report made a series of key recommendations for public policy makers including putting warnings on stuff and then shutting the fuck up.

Jail the parents of masturbators, says charity

PARENTS who allow their teenage sons to masturbate at home should face jail, a leading charity says.

Masturbation Concern said research showed a huge increase in the fondling of their own parts by young males in recent years.

It warned that the current self-pleasuring epidemic was a ticking time bomb storing up problems for the future such as blindness, derangement and so-called 'binge-wanking'.

Holly Knox, campaign officer for Masturbation Concern, said parents had to act now or legisla-

tion was inevitable.

He said: 'It's just not good enough for mum to pop into the boy's room and leave a cup of tea on the bedside table

when he is having a crafty one with the headphones on.

'Nor is it good enough to go into his bedroom when he's out and obviously rifle through his "jazz" magazines so he knows he's been rumbled.

'We've tried the subtle approach and frankly it does not work. The dirty, filthy perverts just keep doing their perverted stuff.'

Masturbation concern is also calling for daily five-mile runs for every boy and compulsory mitten-wearing until the age of 18.

Pensioner completes motorway middle-lane marathon

ELDERLY driver David Jackers yesterday stayed in the middle lane of the motorway for all of his 400 mile journey from Bristol to Glasgow.

Mr Jackers joined the M4 at Bristol shortly before 9 a.m. and quickly moved his Morris Minor and 26-foot, six-birth Elddis Crusader Super Storm caravan into the centre lane of the three-lane highway.

He maintained this driving position and a steady speed of 48 mph until he joined the M8 on the outskirts at Glasgow at 10 p.m. that night, despite causing a series of huge tailbacks and dangerous undertaking manoeuvres by angry and frustrated road users.

Mr Jackers only once left the middle lane, when he pulled into the Tebay services on the M6 to purchase a vegetarian Cornish pastie for his lunch.

His wife Enid had a cheese and onion slice and a packet of hand-cooked sea salt and black pepper crisps, which she described as 'a bit pricey'.

Mrs Jackers said: 'We took it very easy all the way up. We really enjoy driving on the motorway. David just points the Morris at the middle lane and before you know it we're in Scotland.

'Because we don't have to change lanes David and I are able to say hello to all the friendly people who flash and wave at us as they go past on either side.'

But Lancashire Police superin-

What a pair of bastards.

tendent Tony Croker said he would have no problem if other drivers wanted to force the Jackers off the road and into a ditch.

Robert Preston, a photocopier salesmen who was stuck in an eight-mile tailback after a lorry took an hour-and-a-half to overtake the Jackers, said: 'Kill them, kill them *now*.'

Exotic Japanese girlfriend wants Vauxhall Zafira

AROUND 63 per cent of exotic Japanese girlfriends wear old socks in bed and insist their boyfriends buy a Vauxhall Zafira or Ford Focus C-Max, new research shows.

Most will dress like schoolgirls in those incredibly sexy over-the-knee socks in their normal everyday life, but virtually none will keep the clothes on for bedroom sex fun.

Only three per cent are skilled in Tantric sex or the arts of the Geisha, while all have vaginas which are virtually indistinguishable from those of Western women.

Tom Logan, 35, a brand manager of Clerkenwell, London,

The Zafira: seven seats and 39 miles per gallon.

said: 'Obviously, I was curious. I'd heard they could do amazing things with their yin-yangs.

'It was nice being in there, don't get me wrong, but if you

blindfolded me and put me in a European one right after, I'd be hard pressed to tell you which was which.'

Aya Kawasaki, Mr Logan's ex-girlfriend, said she had been forced to finish with him because he insisted on keeping her used underwear in a vending machine in his hall.

She said: 'Why can't he put them through washing machine like is normal in Japan?

'He buy me set of ping pong balls and place pint glass at bottom of bed. What that about? I don't even play tables tennis. I like watch *Boston Legal* and eat Milk Tray.'

Johnson bans Scotsmen from the Tube

BORIS JOHNSON is to ban Scotsmen from the London Underground in a bid to make the Tube more bearable for everyone else.

The London mayor said a Scots-free Tube would be less intimidating for ordinary travellers, and would not smell so badly of chips, blood, spilt lager and urine.

He said: 'As we all know the Scot is incapable of sitting on anything with wheels attached unless already drunk, or carrying enough booze to knock out an Irish bank manager and his wife for a weekend.

'For God's sake man. It's eight-thirty in the morning. You're only going two stops on the

A Scotsman's travelling companions.

Northern Line to get to your doorway. Do you really need six cans and a hip flask?

'Am I your best pal? I don't

think so. We've never actually been formally introduced and it is unlikely that my best pal would be urinating on my foot.'

Karen Simmons, of Passengers First!, said it was important London took a strong stand against all forms of Scottishness on public transport.

She said: 'I am not your "hen" and my "jaiket" looked just fine without the spittle, thank you.'

However, Bob Crow, leader of the RMT union, said his members were not trained to distinguish Scotsmen from other illegal foreigners.

He added: 'And what about the Romanians? They're violent and don't speak English. How are we supposed to tell them apart?'

Pit Bulls smuggled into UK dressed as ugly babies

ILLEGAL American pit bull terriers are being smuggled into Britain disguised as incredibly ugly children, according to customs officials.

Criminal gangs have developed increasingly sophisticated methods to evade the authorities. Earlier this year a smuggler tried to pass through customs carrying a pit bull with a handle glued to its back, claiming it was a novelty briefcase.

The dogs, banned in the UK since 1991, are often used as a warm-up act before toddler fights.

Roy Hobbs, deputy director of HM Revenue and Customs, said: 'We've lost count of the number of times we've challenged a young mother, accusing her of attempt-

Banned in the UK since 1991.

ing to smuggle a pit bull, only to discover that it was in fact an incredibly ugly baby.

'And I mean, just horribly ugly.

I'm talking *Hills Have Eyes*-ugly.'

He added: 'You look at the mother and think to yourself, "She's actually not that bad," so the father must have been some kind of scientific experiment gone wrong.

'Anyway, the point is we can't tell the difference and not surprisingly the mother can get quite upset when we tell her that her child looks like an illegal dog.'

Officials say babies should no longer be classed as hand luggage and anything that looks like a baby will have to be dropped into a large perspex bin before passing through security.

Hobbs added: 'I'm talking John Merrick-Elephant Man-ugly.'

Tried to get back to their seats.

Safety fears after A380 on-board safari incident

SAFETY concerns have been raised about the A380 super-jumbo after two passengers were attacked by lions during their on-board safari.

The two business-class passengers had to be rescued when their Land Rover became bogged down near a watering hole and they tried to get back to their flat-bed seats on foot.

The incident comes as Airbus announced that the next generation of A380s will feature a 25,000-seat auditorium based on the Roman Colosseum.

Vasily Borodin, vice-president of Russia's Aeroflot, said first-class passengers will be able choose up to a dozen people from economy and then command them to fight to the death.

'The winners and their families will be upgraded, so we should get some terrific contests,' he added.

But the giant plane has been criticised by business travellers after it emerged that its on-board golf course was only nine holes, and not the 7,000-yard championship links as originally promised.

Jean Floriette, A380 lead designer, said new planes coming off the production line would be upgraded to include a Jack Niklaus-designed 18-hole course with club house and spa, although he admitted this could lead to compromises elsewhere.

He said: 'We may end up having to cut back a bit on the grouse moor, but there's already a stag hunt and some world-class salmon fishing, so we hope this minor change will not inconvenience passengers too much.'

He said there was no question of the A380 jettisoning Der Stuka®, its six-storey-high water slide which sends passengers down a 250-foot near-vertical drop and onto a 300-foot-long runway.

Inside the A380

25,000-seat auditorium for fights to death between selected Economy passengers.

World-class salmon fishing.

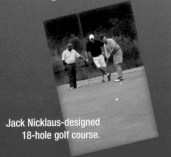

Jack Nicklaus-designed 18-hole golf course.

Airlines misled public by claiming flights would not be filled with bastards

AIRLINES have been accused of misleading the public after claiming short-haul flights would not be full to the brim with fat, slow, noisy bastards.

According to a report by the European Commission, airline websites failed to inform consumers that their travelling experience would be as enjoyable as falling face-first into a big, stinking pile of cow mess.

The report found that the airlines did not tell customers that 'speedy-boarding' was a 'complete lie' and that passengers would 'crowd around the gate like a herd of spastic sheep regardless of the letter on their boarding pass'.

They also failed to tell passengers that the advertised flight time did not include the mandatory 45 minutes on the tarmac because

The Gathering of the Spastics at Gatwick

'some bastard put the wrong bags on the wrong fucking plane' and that Gatwick Airport is the 'single worst place in the world'.

The report also found that no

matter where your flight was to, there was always one Middle Eastern-looking passenger on board, which meant you were 'shitting your pants for the entire journey while at the same time feeling very bad about it'.

'It could be a flight from Inverness to Exeter but there's always a guy who looks like he's just arrived from Riyadh,' said one regular flyer.

'I'm sure he's a perfectly nice chap, but would it be too much hassle for him to go up and down the aisle telling everyone, "It's okay, I'm not going to kill you"?'

The airline industry insisted it had made huge improvements including a reduction in the number of boarding pass checks to 452,943 and slashing the price of a small tub of Pringles to £12.50.

✍ DIARY: Ricky Gervais

I'M sitting, right, in The Chateau Marmont Hotel (which is only the place where late comedy genius John Belushi snuffed it!) thinking, should I call room service and have another one of those lovely smoothie drinks, or shall I ring my good friend Ben Stiller for a chat about this really mental script he personally sent over to me, yesterday?

So, like, this script has been written specifically for little old me – my first starring role – imagine that! Ben and myself had a really long chat on the cell the other day (that's

what we call mobile phones out here) as I was having lunch, sitting opposite Mel Brooks, the comic genius behind *Blazing Saddles* and that other brilliant one which was turned into a musical – I forget the name. Anyway, Ben told me not to worry about the fact that my character, 'Uptight British Tourist #4' doesn't appear until Scene 37 – 'The fact is,' he assured me, 'the movie totally revolves around the 26 seconds you're on the screen.' What a top bloke he is.

I've been in my room for most of

today writing some more material for my stand-up show, which now moves on to Che Stadium. For those of you who don't know, The Beatles played Che Stadium way back in the sixties, and now it's my turn, only it's just me, a few gags and a can

Formula One to feature an elephant on a skateboard

MOTORSPORT bosses have unveiled plans to overhaul Formula One with exciting new features, including hand-to-hand combat and an elephant on a skateboard.

An FIA spokesman said the changes were necessary after everyone suddenly realised that watching a Grand Prix was 'unbearably tedious'.

Worthless Opinion Poll
Why are you picking up transvestite prostitutes?

I like a woman with large hands	15%
I enjoy freaky sex with transvestite prostitutes	20%
Jesus told me to	27.7%
Putting together a five-a-side team	37.3%

He added: 'We thought about just chucking some oil on the track or tampering with the brakes, but that's frowned upon. Apparently.'

Under the new rules drivers can only take part in the race after fighting their way through a gruelling series of televised combats, including bare-fisted punching and an eighteenth-century duel, featuring antique pistols and powdered wigs.

Renault driver Fernando Alonso has already outlined his plans to kill former team mate Lewis Hamilton, 'like a dirty, no-good peeg'.

The top three drivers in each race will then be able to pick up extra points if they can beat an elephant on a skateboard over half a mile.

The spokesman added: 'We reckon that if we get enough people to push the elephant it

'I was promised a crash helmet.'

should pick up a fair head of steam.

'All we have to do now is train an elephant to keep its balance on a very big skateboard for about 20 seconds.

'If it's still not fast enough we'll use a gigantic catapult.'

---

of lager – there'll be no hiding place at the back of a four-piece band for me if it all goes tits up. Scary, huh?

So, here I am sitting on my bed writing, and I must say there's some brilliant new material here. For instance, we've managed to persuade Eddie the Eagle and Floella Benjamin to come on and take part in a spoof game of Mr & Mrs, with me taking the part of Derek Batey. Oh, you should see their little faces – magic!

Brunch was taken in an exclusive place I frequent in Santa Monica. Whilst I was there, I at long last managed to bump into my old mucker Larry David (he's the genius behind *Curb your Enthusiasm*). That's the great thing about being out here amongst fellow comic legends – you can sit down over an egg-white-free omelet and green salad, and discuss new and exciting ventures without being bothered for your autograph – well, Larry was on six or seven occasions, but I managed to avoid this tiresome ritual, thank fuck.

Anyway, whilst we were chatting, I suggested that if he was making any more Curbs, that I should make an uncredited cameo appearance. I think he must've been totally over-whelmed by my artistic generosity, because he blew his cheeks out very noisily, before bowing his head. He asked me to call him (which I did ten minutes later) to set up a meeting.

Heard the news today that Bernard Manning is dead. As I sat on my hotel balcony, texting Gary Shandling, the totally brilliant genius behind Larry Sanders, I started thinking to myself that comedy has come a long, long way since those dark days when smoke-filled working men's clubs were home to comedians making fun of minorities without even doing it ironically. That's just lazy.

In Agony with PETULA SOUL

Dear Petula,
I am a 46-year-old man and have been happily married to my wife for 20 years. We have a lovely house, two beautiful kids, I have a good job, good prospects, and can expect to retire with a great pension in a few years time, at which point my wife and I will have all the time and money we need to enjoy the rest of our lives together. How do I throw it all away by having a brief fling with some stupid young girl at work?

Porsche Driver,
Perth

Petula says:

Dear Porsche Driver,
I really do not understand your question. It seems to me that an awful lot of men like you think that young impressionable girls in the office are interested in supposedly sophisticated and well-off older men like yourself and so sexually available. That's because they generally are, the little home-wrecking tarts. So what's the problem? I would have thought there were hundreds of the little floozies flouncing around your desk in their short skirts with their pert young breasts pointing up at the ceiling who were perfectly prepared to put out for you, if only once, and for a laugh, then ruin your life and that of your wife and your family – there certainly were in the last place my ex-husband worked. Slags.

Do you have a problem you'd like Petula to help with?
e: petula@thedailymash.co.uk

NEWS BRIEFLY

COMPUTER GAME FAN 'NO TIME TO MASTURBATE'
'Hopefully he will grow up to be a perfectly normal obsessive player of online fantasy games and not some kind of demented pervert,' says mother.

ONE IN FOUR TEENS PRETENDING TO BE DEPRESSED
'The world really does revolve around you, you snivelling bag of self-pitying hormonal tossers,' says psychologist.

TEACHERS CALL FOR SMALLER PUPILS
Tiny children more receptive to teachers, mainly because they look like terrifying giants, say experts.

MINISTRY OF DEFENCE USING WEBSITES TO 'LURE' INNOCENT TEENAGERS
'I pretend to be a 12-year-old girl who wants to meet up and talk about a catering career in the Royal Navy,' admits bad lieutenant.

Psychic Bob's Week Ahead

Taurus (20 APR – 20 MAY)
Your friends are teasing you about your safe and easy dating choices? But hiring them from a website means you are guaranteed sex. Now who's laughing?

Gemini (21 MAY – 20 JUN)
Something seems odd about the new person who's dating you. They don't immediately appear deranged. Multiple personalities?

Cancer (21 JUN – 22 JUL)
Get the facts before you overreact. And then overreact

Leo (23 JUL – 22 AUG)
Are all your friends calling and asking where you've been these past few weeks? Thought not.

Virgo (23 AUG – 22 SEP)
While everyone around you is struggling under a cloud of grey, your jovial spirit makes you totally unbearable. Piss off.

Libra (23 SEP – 23 OCT)
Your friends want to know where you get your energy, and if you can share it. Tell them to get their own, it's £40 a gram!

Scorpio (24 OCT – 21 NOV)
A person from your romantic past shows up and makes you think about some old tissues.

Sagittarius (22 NOV – 21 DEC)
Avoiding the easy option all the time takes discipline. But your sister's husband? At their anniversary party?

Capricorn (22 DEC – 19 JAN)
It's one of those days. If others think you're a workaholic, then let them. They got the 'holic' bit right anyway.

Aquarius (20 JAN – 19 FEB)
Everything seemed to be going so well, but now you haven't a clue. Sometimes there are no easy answers. Was that helpful?

Pisces (20 FEB – 20 MAR)
It's time to take a hard look at your finances, fake your death and move to Panama.

Aries (21 MAR – 19 APR)
Inspiration strikes at the strangest time today. Don't forget to wipe!

WORLD OF TOMORROW

Boffins invent self-hoovering floor

SCIENTISTS at Dundee University have patented what they claim is the world's first self-hoovering floor.

The ingenious device, backed by a £20-million government grant, looks like an ordinary floor but has thousands of small holes which are attached to a powerful vacuum motor stored in a cupboard.

At the flick of a switch the suction starts and anything within a five centimetre radius of each hole is removed quickly and cleanly.

Project director Dr Henry Brubaker said his team were now fixing the remaining few glitches in the system.

'The main problem at the moment is that you have to leave the room when it's switched on otherwise you'll be stuck to the floor.

'We've also noticed that larger objects get stuck in the holes and this produces a noise that makes you want to die.'

The control unit fits neatly under the stairs.

He added: 'We're currently working with carpet manufacturers so that the holes in the carpets line up with the holes in the floor.'

A spokesman for the Department of Trade of Industry said: 'Within a few years anyone who doesn't have a self-hoovering floor will be shunned by decent society and forced to live under a bridge.'

The Chinese!
Should we be
absolutely terrified?

China sets new light speed record

CHINA has asserted its growing technological dominance by setting a new record for the speed of light.

Scientists at the Shanghai Institute for Technology have pushed the speed to 197,345 miles per second, shattering the previous record of 186,282 miles per second set by the BBC *Tomorrow's World* team in 1976.

It took the Chinese just three attempts to set the new record using a network of powerful lasers, a crystal magnifying glass and 14 million people on exercise bicycles.

The Chinese government said they would use the new super-fast light for peaceful purposes, insisting 'the systematic enslavement of all humans is not on the agenda'.

Mankind has been in a constant battle with the speed of light since Sir Isaac Newton set the first record in 1687.

Using a specially designed horse, the Cambridge physicist pushed the speed of light to more than 12 miles per hour.

After Newton's triumph light was transported via horseback for the next 150 years, until Isambard Kingdom Brunel patented his Condensing Light Refractor and Cotton Separator.

Brunel's obsession with the record led to fears that the world would eventually implode or fold-up like a huge origami swan.

An editorial in the *Times* from 25 July, 1846, warned: 'Light is one of our most unstable gases. Mr Brunel is exposing Her Majesty the Queen to the greatest peril.'

The international community is now watching closely amid fears China is planning to start a war on the Moon.

Boffins use hybrid embryos to create Satan

SCIENTISTS at Dundee University have embarked on the world's first human-animal hybrid embryo project in a bid to create Satan.

Dr Henry Brubaker and his team of geneticists plan to generate the manifestation of pure evil using tissue from humans, a goat, a piranha, Richard Madeley and a bat.

Dr Brubaker said: 'We were delighted when the government finally caved in to science and gave its approval to human-animal hybrids.

'We had planned to spend the next few years creating some very odd-looking things. Chicken-monkeys, fish-badgers, zebra-geese, that sort of thing.

An artist's impression of Project Satan.

'But then it occurred to us that generating Satan would not only give a tremendous boost to the university in terms of public relations, but would also have a host of practical applications.

'It is not an exaggeration to suggest that Project Satan could solve all the problems of the world.

'As Satan will be all-powerful, anything he says will be infallible and all who disagree will be destroyed in a ball of fire.

'So if Satan says that war, poverty, disease and climate-sodding-change are not actually problems at all, then I, for one, would suggest that they are not actually problems at all.'

Dr Brubaker said that a fully-grown Satan would be around 5-feet 10-inches tall, weigh 13 stone and look remarkably like Bobby Davro.

FRENCH SCIENTISTS IN FLUBBER BREAKTHROUGH

A TEAM of French scientists is claiming a major breakthrough in the development of a useable type of flubber.

The researchers synthesised a flubber-like substance and were then able to stabilise it for almost six hours before it bounced out of the window.

Professor Guy Delafarge said: 'Zis is ze first time we have been able to stabilise a substance which is, how you say, "floobberie".

'During ze stabilisation period we were able to manipulate it in ways which could, ultimately, have everyday applications, such as draft-exclusion or love-making.

'However ze substance remains, how you say, ticklish and too much contact will make it bounce around ze room, destroying many glass beakers and test tubes and causing everyone to duck.'

A useable strain of flubber has been the Holy Grail for chemists since the substance was discovered in the 1950s.

But flubber's unstable nature led to a series of accidents and by 1970 the vast majority of 'flubboratories' had been closed down.

Testing restarted five years ago when French chemists found that adding small amounts of friendly bacteria could induce short periods of calm in a medium-sized blob.

Professor Delafarge added: 'Zis was an important breakthrough, but ze question remains: Can we ever really tame floobber?'

Flubber is prone to chaotic mood swings.

HUMANS DECLARE WAR ON EARTH-LIKE PLANETS

Are Earth-like planets trying to provoke us?

THE Milky Way galaxy could contain thousands of planets with conditions suitable for life and war, according to new research.

Experts at NASA say most solar systems in the galaxy will contain rocky planets with large, flat areas perfect for epic, laser-filled battles.

Dr Henry Brubaker, of NASA's Goddard Institute, said: 'We're slowly realising that the galaxy is filled with potential enemies.

'It's incredibly exciting to look through a telescope and imagine countless alien civilisations pleading for their lives as we set fire to their crops and commandeer their livestock.'

He added: 'Many of these Earth-like planets will contain life forms who hold opinions that are very slightly different from ours.

'For instance, they may observe the Sabbath on a Tuesday, or worship a supernatural being who was nailed to a door.

'Either of these would provide ample justification for a long and brutal intergalactic conflict.'

An international committee of scientists is calling for the majority of the world's resources to be invested in a fleet of 10-mile-long battle cruisers, armed with plasma cannons, that can hunt down Earth-like planets and reduce them to bits.

Meanwhile NASA is recommending a series of 'practice wars' to be staged on the Moon so that troops can learn how to fire mortars in one-sixth gravity.

'It is quite sore,' said Professor Kaku.

Teleportation device not quite there yet, says disembodied head

STAR TREK-style teleportation is months away from becoming a scientific reality, the disembodied head of its inventor insisted last night.

Professor Michio Kaku's head made the astonishing claim from the floor of a New York laboratory after a demonstration of his latest prototype.

It is claimed that Kaku's device would be able to dissolve a human being into its constituent atoms, transport them through space and then reassemble them with an accuracy level of over 90 per cent.

Dr Wayne Hayes, the professor's lab assistant, said: 'Oh my god. Oh my fucking god. What is that? It's got an arm coming out of its stomach.

'And his bum's inside out. That can't be right. Pete, get a bucket. Be careful! I think you just stood on his eye.

'Holy Christ, his feet have run off. Don't hit them. We want them alive. Right, just shove what we've got back in and I'll stick it in reverse. Is that his knob?'

Professor Kaku said: 'We'll put it on sale as soon as we get to 95 per cent. I'm sure people will gladly lose the tops of their fingers, or an ear, if it means they can cut 20 minutes off their commute.'

He added: 'All models will be fitted with a set of handrails to prevent users from toppling over if their feet don't arrive on time.'

the daily mash

BRITAIN GIVES UP FOOD FOR BOOZE

MILLIONS of people across Britain last night vowed to give up food instead of alcohol, after the government forced them to choose.

Following the chancellor's move to make everyone in Britain buy just one thing per year, the country's food consumers say they are ready to switch-over to beer, wine and spirits full-time.

Tom Logan, a 27-year-old accountant, said he would eat his dog and live on grass rather than give up meeting with his friends on a Wednesday for a couple of pints of lager and a game of cribbage.

He added: 'I've cancelled my life insurance and sold my car. Hopefully that will keep me going until the army stages a coup.'

Nikki Hollis, a 33-year-old sales manager, said she would switch her six-month-old child

Din-dins!

from organic baby food to strips of newspaper soaked in Oxo

rather than give up large glasses of Chablis.

'I've worked hard to achieve this standard of white wine and if I have to take my youngest daughter out of private school to maintain that, I will.'

Bill Mckay, 86, said he had stopped consuming vegetables and would fill up by eating his duvet so he could carry on drinking his nightly glass of Sailor Jerry's Navy Rum.

He said: 'I will have to smoke a lot more to kill my appetite, and hope my winter fuel allowance increase lasts me through the dark months when I have a small one in the morning to wake me up.

'But I lived all through the Second World War and drank every day. If Adolf Hitler couldn't stop me, what chance do you give this Scotch twat with the dodgy eyebrows?'

news

I'M DRUNK RIGHT NOW, SAY 80% OF WORKERS

news

POPE MAKES HALF-HEARTED PLEA FOR PEACE

Britain to ignore binge-drink warning for 4,000th year in a row

THE dramatic increase in the number of people being hospitalised for excessive drinking is set to be ignored for the 4,000th year in a row.

With more than 500,000 people a day being admitted to hospital for alcohol-related conditions across the UK, research has revealed that consumers are becoming increasingly determined to stop reading depressing stories in the *Daily Mail* about binge-drinking.

Meanwhile experts say the sharp increase in hospital admissions comes just two years after the introduction of Britain's 24-hour drinking laws and is incredibly boring.

They have also revealed that the greater availability of cheap alcohol means more people are buying it and drinking it, while continuing to not care about the implications of it in any way, shape or form.

Professor Henry Brubaker, Director of Research at the Institute for Studies said: 'The people of these islands first started ignoring warnings about heavy drinking during the early Bronze Age.

'Tribal elders would gather the community together and tell them that excessive enjoyment of fermented berries was undermining bronze production and leaving them vulnerable to attack from a varied assortment of angry Goths, and suchlike.

'Typically, they would all nod,

Experts believe this 3,000-year-old cave painting depicts Carlisle town centre on a Friday night.

look serious and mumble something about responsibility and how their brother is on his final written warning, before heading over to Tharg's Stone Age Theme Bar for 12 pints of tree juice and a violent argument about the size of their beards.'

Meanwhile in his new year message to the people of Britain, prime minister Gordon Brown said something about us all enjoying ourselves, but not too much, blah, blah, blah.

Worthless Opinion Poll	
Why are you not spending time with your children?	
Not sure they're mine	14.6%
Never liked them	24.3%
Swapped them for a breadmaker	30%
They get drunk too quickly	31.1%

Fuck nativity plays, we're doing 'The Godfather', say five-year-olds

THE number of primary schools ditching the traditional Christmas nativity in favour of key scenes from *The Godfather* is at an all-time high.

According to the National Confederation of Parent Teacher Associations, a majority of five-year-olds would now prefer to recreate the meeting between the Heads of the Five Families instead of the birth of Jesus.

Dylan Stephenson, a Year One pupil at St Bald's in Northampton said: 'I'm playing

'I'm going to make him an office he can't refuse.'

Sonny because Miss Hayes reckons I'm a bit of a hot-head. Bada-bing!

'In the play my friend Ben Holdsworth calls my little sister a "guinea brat" so I come on and hit him over the head with a dustbin lid. Miss Hayes says it will be very powerful.'

Dylan

added: 'My friend Charlie is playing Sollozzo the Turk because he went to Cyrpus on his holidays and told us all about it. He gets shot in the face.

'And my friend Jack Barnes is going to be Luca Brasi because he's a big fatty tum-tum.'

Jack admitted he was intrigued by the role of the Corleones' faithful enforcer, adding: 'I'm going to sleep with the fishies!'

Church leaders have expressed disappointment at the secular nature of *The Godfather*, but said they took some consolation from a year-on-year increase in the number of primary schools performing the crucifix scene from *The Exorcist*.

Africans disappointed to discover $100 laptops are not full of food

COMMUNITIES across Africa have revealed their disappointment that the new $100 laptops contain no nutritional value.

The scheme, organised by Western technology companies, is designed to give young Africans the chance to play Tetris before their village is burned to the ground.

Meanwhile, as broadband is rolled out across the continent, millions of Africans have been surprised to discover it is a sophisticated communications network rather than a big pipe full of rice.

Fourteen-year-old Lizzie Matumba, from Ivory Coast, welcomed the laptop initiative but said the early models did not look very tasty.

She added: 'You have a beautiful food mountain in Europe, yes? Any chance I could work my way through $100 worth of that?

'I promise I will then write a presentation about how hungry I was using the latest version of Microsoft Office.'

Twelve-year-old Robert Otengwe said: 'I am very much looking forward to using my laptop to order fresh bread and vegetables from Amazon.

'Tell me, do they deliver to Chad and do they accept payment in tiny pebbles?'

Wayne Hayes, spokesman for the $100 Laptop Foundation, said: 'At

first they will probably be used by local warlords to plan genocide more efficiently and divert aid money to Switzerland. But eventually these laptops will allow millions of Africans to order cheap DVDs.'

He added: 'Should we sell laptops to Africans, rather than just giving them free food? That's a big philosophical question isn't it?'

Chewy.

Queen's broadcast a self-indulgent mess, say critics

Oh, how she loves to rub our noses in it.

THIS year's Christmas message from the Queen has failed to impress the critics with most dismissing it as self-indulgent and boastful.

The Queen spent two days writing and recording the speech watched by more than 23 billion mammals across the globe on Christmas Day.

George Monbiot, Queen's Christmas Message reviewer for the *Guardian*, wrote: 'The whole thing was a self-satisfied diatribe about how she's the Queen and I'm not.

'The footage from the 1950s was particularly despicable. She's basically saying, "I've been the Queen for absolutely ages," as if somehow that makes her better than me.'

Andrew Motion, the Poet Laureate, writing in the *Daily Mail*, said: 'Jesus, whose very birthday it was, received just three miserable paragraphs, then it was back to her and her ghastly husband flying around the world, forcing everyone to repaint their houses.

'And if she is going to give support to our brave troops overseas she could at least do so while holding up a large photograph of Gemma Atkinson in a thong.'

Former Home Secretary Douglas Hurd, writing in the *Daily Telegraph*, said: 'They should go back to doing it live.

'Remember the great Christmas message of 1974? What a year it had been – the miner's strike, Watergate, Keegan scores two in the cup final. There was a bead of sweat on her brow and the whole thing crackled with tension, especially after all those rumours she would say "piss".'

He added: 'I still feel that her message about the destitute lacks conviction.

'Perhaps next year, instead of using one of her eight centrally-heated palaces, she should deliver the speech while sitting on top of a noisy, homeless Scotsman in the middle of a rain-sodden car park in Croydon.'

Prince Philip 'delighted' with new balls

PRINCE Philip has announced that he is 'absolutely thrilled' with his new set of balls.

The Prince received his new balls last week and has been testing them in a series of demanding environments.

'He is very impressed by their performance, particularly on rough terrain and over the jumps,' said a palace spokesman.

Prince Philip is the latest high-profile figure to equip himself with a new set of balls.

In the last 12 months shadow chancellor George Osborne, ITV chairman Michael Grade and *Deal or No Deal* presenter Noel Edmonds have all gone through expensive ball-renewal programmes.

Sting pioneered the procedure in the late 1990s, when it was still regarded as highly controversial.

But he was soon emulated by a string of Hollywood A-listers including Kevin Spacey, Billy Crystal and Sir Anthony Hopkins.

Sport stars followed the trend with golfers Nick Faldo and Colin Montgomerie being fitted for new balls before the 2002 US Masters.

The Prince is looking forward to stretching his new balls.

Britain gets up at 4 a.m. to buy record amount of crap

MILLIONS of people got up in the middle of the night to buy vast amounts of shit they did not need yesterday, after stores told them it was now a bit cheaper.

Large numbers queued to get back into shops across the country, all of which had shipped in a fresh lot of tat to palm off as sale goods.

However, there were some real bargains on offer including a fully-armed Type 45 Destroyer, reduced to £329 million from Argos, and an old plastic bag full of Quality Street for a tenner.

Nikki Hollis, 26, said she had hit the sales looking for make-up and sex toys but ended up with a bag of Quality Street and a set of cotton handkerchiefs mono-grammed with the letter F.

She said: 'I also got a pair of men's breeches with a 41-inch waist, a paraffin lamp and a yo-yo which lights up when you roll it along the ground. It's been a great day.'

Bill McKay, 48, said he had bought a sign saying 'Sale: 50% off' for a third of its marked price, a piece of used chewing gum for only 3p, and had a dog shit thrown in for free.

He said: 'The reductions this year are incredible, I would have bought the sign and the gum anyway.'

Annie Laird, 34, said she had bought an end-of-season cat from a man in the street, half a set of bagpipes, some genital herpes, and a Nimrod reconnais-sance aircraft.

This pair of antique-style paraffin lamps is just £59.99 from JJB Sports.

She said: 'My husband is going to kill me when I get back, he can't stand cats.'

Recycling centres to provide 'wife-banks'

Destined for a car boot sale.

LOCAL authority recycling centres across the UK are to offer a drop-off service for old or faulty wives.

The government is to fund the £25-million scheme after a three-fold increase in wife-tipping since 1997.

Environment Secretary Hilary Benn said: 'People are sick of the sight of wives dumped by the side of the road.

'They are unsightly and often hazardous. Many of them end up being taken away by "travelling people" who then try to sell them at car boot sales.'

'Britain should be proud of its countryside rather than littering it with out-of-date wives.'

The wife-banks will be installed in major towns and cities and will hold up to 30 wives at a time.

All of the disused wives will be refurbished or broken down for parts with many being exported to the developing world.

Mr Benn added: 'A well-built British wife that has been kept clean can last for 30 or even 40 years.'

Apple to charge £2,000 for shit in a box

APPLE boss Steve Jobs yesterday unveiled the computer giant's latest eye-catching innovation: one of his shits in a simple white box.

The billionaire pioneer said he was inspired after the company developed the world's thinnest laptop computer.

'We took most of the useful things out of it and doubled the price. The early demand has been incredible.

'I was then struck by an amazing idea: how much would you pay for one of my shits in a box?'

Jobs said that the first 100 shits will be his, but because of his busy schedule most of the mass-market shits will be built in the Far East and carry his personal endorsement.

The box has clean, simple lines and contains a shit.

Carl Knutz, an early adopter of San Andreas, California, said he would pay $1,999 for the shit, but only if it was ultra-slim and back-lit and unable to run the most commonly available software programmes.

He said: 'I want a shit in a box that sets me apart from the crowd and tells people that I am young, hip, and creative.'

Bobby Killitz, 23, also of San Andreas, said he would hold on to see if Steve Jobs would produce a cheaper shit later this year after the initial frenzy had died down.

He said: 'I think within six months he will either halve the price of the shit or lay two of his logs in there for the same price. He's pulled that kind of trick before.'

'Manhunt 2' released after smoking scenes cut

THE role-playing video game *Manhunt 2* has finally been cleared for release after producers agreed to remove all references to tobacco.

The game had been banned by the British Board of Film Classification for including 'some of the most gratuitous smoking' it had ever seen.

Denys Finch-Hatton, BBFC chairman, said: 'After blasting his victims in the face with a shotgun, dismembering them with a chainsaw and then urinating into the severed head, the main character would, invariably, light up a cigarette.

'In one scene the game player approaches his enemy, engages him in conversation and then playfully rams a boat hook into his eye.

Smoking harms you and those around you. Why not blow their faces off instead?

'All harmless fun until you notice that the action takes place in front of a 7-11 that could, quite easily, be selling tobacco products.'

He added: 'The game is brilliantly produced. The blood flow is exquisite and the sound of machete hacking through bone is absolutely thrilling.

'So why then ruin it with these disgustingly authentic wisps of tobacco smoke?'

Wayne Hayes, *Manhunt*'s senior designer, said: 'I want to assure our fans that you will still be able to push a three-foot-long, white-hot poker up a gang leader's back passage until the eyes pop out of his head, only this time he won't be smoking a cigar.'

BBC unveils line-up for Billiepipermas

THE BBC has unveiled the spectacular line-up for what promises to be the best Billiepipermas ever.

The Corporation has spent more than £20 million to ensure that viewers are treated to a delectable Billiepipermas banquet of delights.

BBC Director-General Mark Thompson said: 'Billiepipermas is a time for family and we wanted this year's schedule to reflect the true meaning of Billie.

'From everyone at the BBC, a happy Billiepipermas and a Billiepiper New Year!'

Those Billiepipermas schedules in full . . .

Will Billie get a mysterious, nineteenth-century seeing-to?

BBC1

8 a.m. *A Billiepipermas Breakfast* Dermot Murnaghan starts talking to Billie Piper the second she wakes up.

10.30 a.m. *Secret Diary of a Call Girl: The Cartoon*

12.00 noon *Billie Piper's Billiepipermas Lunch Makeover – Live!* Gordon Ramsay cooks a delicious four-course lunch while Trinny and Susannah dress Billie like an elf.

3 p.m. *The Queen* Her Majesty talks about what a great year it's been for Billie Piper.

3.10 p.m. *Back to the Future III*

5.20 p.m. *Dr Who: Queer Eye for the Cybermen* David Tennant must choose between Catherine Tate, Kylie Minogue and a feisty young girl named Rose.

7 p.m. *Titanic*

10 p.m. *The Mystery of the Low-Cut Dress* Billie Piper stars as Sally Lockhart in a tale of intrigue and thighs.

BBC2

8 a.m.–4 p.m. *International Darts*

4 p.m. *The Alternative Billiepipermas Message* from Katie Melua.

4.15 p.m. *Heston Blumenthal's Food Made of Clocks*

6.30 p.m. *Top Gear Blows up a Cow* A Billiepipermas special starring Jeremy, James, Richard and a soon-to-be-deceased three-year-old Friesian.

7.30 p.m. *It's a Wonderful Pie* The rarely watched sequel starring James Stewart as George Bailey and Mickey Rooney as Gary the Pie.

9 p.m. *Mon Chien Est Mon Épouse* A quirky French film about a postman who marries a dog.

ONE WOMAN'S WEEK: Present and Correct

by KAREN FENESSEY

THERE are many things that I love about Christmas – carol singing, pretty baubles and getting gifts from people who've really made an effort to understand my complicated psyche (and that's not many!).

However, if there's one thing that's really hit home this yuletide, it's this: however much I try to humbly ignore it, there are many people in our society who I am simply much better than and there's NOTHING I can do about it.

Sadly, some of these people are my own relatives. My sister's notion of Christmas hasn't developed since 1980 and she still thinks it's okay to hang multi-coloured lights on her tree. I, on the other hand, pride myself on my eclectic sense of style and, without wanting to blow my own trumpet, complete strangers have often told me: 'Karen, by God, you have a truly unique and eclectic sense of style!'

Last year, I made the bold move to welcome in the birth of our Saviour using a distinctive black Christmas tree. This year, I shocked everyone once again by opting for an upside-down, black Christmas tree. Let's face it: human ideas have progressed (just look at stem cell research) and some of us enlightened beings say, 'Let's toss that rule book into the fire like a phoenix to the flames!'

> 'there are many people in our society who I am simply better than and there's NOTHING I can do about it'

Fortunately, as I stood in the queue in Marks & Spencers Food Hall, I met some like-minded people who reassured me that there is hope. The queues were frankly astronomical and when the woman next to me tutted in disgust, I knew she was a friend. 'This is ridiculous, isn't it?' I commented. She immediately agreed. Another woman ahead of us commented on how preposterous it is that next year there are plans to make us pay for plastic bags.'

'That's an absolute scandal,' we tutted. And when the elegant old lady behind put in about how she suspected the line was the way it was because the dark-skinned cashier was probably having trouble understanding the till, we all shook our heads in dismay.

After five more minutes of hell, I sighed to those around me: 'This queue's a bloody joke, isn't it?' The idiots just smiled like sheep and a woman said, 'Oh, I don't really mind queuing. There's worse places I could be right now.' I knew at that moment that she was probably a heroin addict and the places she referred to were prisons.

It is with a heavy heart that I must admit there is a clear boundary that divides me from the other humans I share this planet with. I can only console myself by remembering that, thankfully, I don't need to invite those people into my beautiful home and will thus spend another Christmas free of diseases like alcoholism, AIDS and cold sores.

NEWS BRIEFLY

IMMIGRANTS WILL HAVE TO COMPLETE ASSAULT COURSE
Hopefuls will also face quickfire round on how British Empire destroyed their country.

SCOTLAND RELEGATED TO AFRICA
'With the exception of Glasgow, we're already in the top 10 for life expectancy,' says First Minister.

WORLD SMELLS BETTER THAN AT ANY TIME SINCE 1850
Mounting evidence that 2009 will stink like a toilet at a vegan music festival.

Worthless Opinion Poll
What offensive word are you singing this Christmas?

Fudge	11.6%
Starfish	14.4%
Gobble	17.4%
Flaps	56.7%

HAPPY BIRTHDAY, JESUS!

HAVE A SPROUT!

In Agony with PETULA SOUL

Dear Petula,
My fiancé of six months asked me about my sexual history and preferences. But when I told him about the guys I had slept with and what I like to do in bed he went completely nuts. It is true that I have enjoyed a healthy love life in the past and have indulged in hoggins with a great number of men, often at the same time. I have a healthy and open attitude to sex and expect the same of others, but it is clear that my fiancé does not. He seemed particularly annoyed when I told him about my threesome with his dad and brother last week. How was I to know they had not already told him?

Dumped,
Dundee

Petula says:

Dear Dumped,
How typical! Like most men, it would appear your fiancé is only really interested in marrying a virgin possessed of some magical innate ability to perform the perfect blow job. But as we all know, learning how to perform fantastic oral sex requires a great deal of practice, and that is why I have never bothered. Yuk. It seems like your now ex-fiancé is a standard insecure and selfish bloke. He asks you what you like to do in bed not because he wants to learn how to please you, but because he wants you to tell him, 'He's the best.' And when he finds out you actually prefer a bit of a roasting with his nearest relations he gets all huffy, rather than asking if he can join in. You are better off without him. Why not marry his dad, and just shag him on the side instead?

> Do you have a problem you'd like Petula to help with? e: petula@thedailymash.co.uk

Psychic Bob's Week Ahead What does the future hold for you?

Taurus (20 APR – 20 MAY)
Don't let yourself get depressed over a few minor setbacks – things are going to get much worse.

Gemini (21 MAY – 20 JUN)
You are moving far more quickly than you thought you would be at this point – that's because your parachute has failed. It's the last time you'll do a jump for charity. Indeed.

Cancer (21 JUN – 22 JUL)
Play with the hand you've been dealt. But try sitting on it for half an hour first and it will feel like it belongs to someone else.

Leo (23 JUL – 22 AUG)
You've got a lot going on, on the inside, but you're not really feeling the need to share it. Thank God. I don't ever want to smell anything like that again.

Virgo (23 AUG – 22 SEP)
Someone at work is scheming for your position, or maybe just a little perk you enjoy. Secretly superglue their scrotum to their office chair and then set off the fire alarm. Sorted.

Libra (23 SEP – 23 OCT)
Your social energy is strong right now and that explain why you are making new friends. That or the lottery win.

Scorpio (24 OCT – 21 NOV)
Today you need to ask yourself – what is the biggest issue in my relationship? Here's a clue: it's not in your Y-fronts.

Sagittarius (22 NOV – 21 DEC)
You're dealing with elements of your past that aren't especially pleasant to consider, but are part of who you are. Of course you were only obeying orders!

Capricorn (22 DEC – 19 JAN)
You're feeling the urgent need to do something big and showy. Can't you wait until the next motorway services?

Aquarius (20 JAN – 19 FEB)
Mercury, the planet of excessive drinking, kebabs and instantly regretted casual sex, has arrived in your skies. Not that you will notice any difference.

Pisces (20 FEB – 20 MAR)
It's a great week for spending time exploring galleries and boosting your knowledge of art, music and other cultural phenomena. Yes, your gas has been cut off again.

Aries (21 MAR – 19 APR)
You may be all excited over the new project in your life, but try to maintain a sense of balance when discussing it with others. You boring twat.